In
YOUR
POCKET

Following
—*The*—
Fairways

GW00497577

Editor Nick Edmond

KENSINGTON WEST PRODUCTIONS LTD

HEXHAM ENGLAND

Following

— The —

Fairways

Acknowledgements

Kensington West Productions Ltd
5 Cattle Market, Hexham,
Northumberland NE46 1NJ
Tel: (0434) 609933 Fax: (0434) 600066

Front Cover : Paul Gribble The Putting Green *Courtesy of Rosenstiel's*
Back Cover : Craig Cambell An Eagle Putt *Courtesy of Montfort Fine Art*

Print Catalogue available Tel: 0434 609933 Fax: 0434 600066

Editor Nick Edmund

Design Kensington West Productions Ltd

Cartography Camilla Charnock, Craig Semple

Typesetting Tradespools Ltd, Frome

Origination Trinity Graphics Hong Kong

Printing Emrierre

Contents

Introduction

The primary aim of *Following The Fairways* is to guide the golf enthusiast and beginner alike around the many delightful courses of Great Britain and Ireland. The first edition of this pocket guide is in fact, a condensed version of the coffee table guide of the same name. That 'par 5' edition spans an impressive 360 pages of colour and gives a vast amount of detail together with fine illustrations. This more humble 'par 3' version contains all the information needed for the nomadic follower of the fairways.

We hope the book will give equal pleasure to the beginner and weather beaten linksman alike. We also hope that even the most devoted club member will be lured from his favourite fairways to sample the delights of others. Equally, we anticipate those who are not members of other clubs will find many a warm welcome at a whole host of courses included within these pages. However, while our information is up to date at the time of going to press we can not guarantee that individual clubs have not changed their green fees or procedure of play in the meantime.

In closing, we very much hope that in conjunction with the hotels recommended at the back of the book, you will have any number of memorable rounds of golf. Please let us know of any information that would improve future editions. It is only with this type of help that a book of this type can be effectively updated and improved.

Cornwall

'Brandy for the Parson, Baccy for the Clerk'

Cornwall is the land of the smuggler's cove. It is also the land of King Arthur and the Knights of the Round Table—a land of legends. To cross the Tamar is to enter foreign soil: for centuries the Cornish Celts had more in common with the Welsh and the French Bretons than the ever-invading Anglo Saxons. Well, the Anglo-Saxons still invade but nowadays in a more peaceful manner: 'grockles' they are called in Cornwall and they come in search of sun, sand and sea (not to mention holiday home!) But there is also a fairly recent addition, a sub-species commonly known as the 'golfing-grockle' who comes to Cornwall to seek out some of the finest golfing country in the Kingdom.

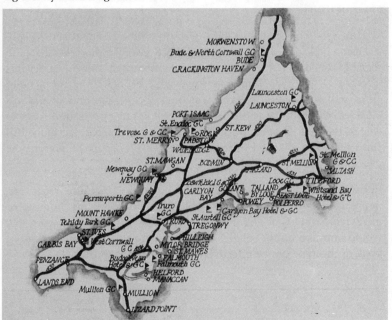

The South Coast

If one commences an imaginary tour by crossing the Tamar at Plymouth, **St Mellion** Golf and Country Club (0579) 50101 has surely to be the first port of call. It is one of the few places in Britain where one might bump into Jack Nicklaus. St Mellion, where there are two fine courses, one of which was designed by the great man, and plays host to tour events. Not far away in Saltash, a new course has recently opened called China Fleet, apparently the Navy (British—not Oriental) is the guiding force behind it.

Heading westwards **Looe** Golf Club (formerly, Looe Bin Down) is situated on high ground to the north of Looe, near Widegates. An 18 hole moorland course, it lies somewhat at the mercy of the elements and can get exceptionally windy. Not too far away at Portwinkle the **Whitsand Bay Hotel** (0503) 30276 is an ideal place to break a journey with its own gentle 18 hole golf course stretching out along the cliffs and looking down over Whitsand Bay.

We'll now, if you'll pardon the expression, leave the Looe area and, still heading in a clock-wise direction set sail for St Austell where we find a twin attraction for golfers: the redoubtable **Carlyon Bay** and the **St Austell Golf Club**. The St Austell course is situated on the western edge of the town off the A390. Rather shorter than Carlyon Bay but with an ample spread of gorse and numerous bunkers, it possesses plenty of challenges and attractions of its own.

Carlyon Bay is surely one of Britain's best loved Hotel courses. Not a Turnberry or a Gleneagles perhaps, but very pleasing with several challenging holes and views over a number of beaches—one of which is frequented by naturists!

Falmouth—a glorious harbour and seagulls aplenty. More good golf awaits. Like St Austell, there are two sets of fairways on which to exercise the swing. They are to be found at the **Falmouth** Golf Club, south west of the town (fine cliff-top views over Falmouth Bay) and at **Budock Vean Hotel**. This latter course has only nine holes but plenty of variety and is exceptionally well-kept.

Still heading down the coast, the course at **Mullion** is one of the short but sweet brigade. Situated seven miles south of Helston, it can lay claim to being the most southerly on the British mainland. Nestling around the cliff edges overlooking some particularly inviting sands and with distant views towards St Michael's Mount, Mullion typifies the charm of Cornish holiday golf.

Penzance is another place where people may wish to base themselves—golfers especially now that the 18 hole **Cape Cornwall** Golf and Country Club has been opened at nearby St Just.

North Cornwall
The **West Cornwall** Golf Club lies just beyond St Ives at Lelant. A beautiful and very natural old-fashioned type of links, it was laid out a hundred years ago by the then Vicar of Lelant. Like St Enodoc, it is a genuine links course—sand dunes and plenty of sea breezes!— and quite short. Jim Barnes, who won both the Open and US Open was born in Lelant village.

Passing numerous derelict tin and copper mines the inland course at **Tehidy Park** is soon reached. Located midway between Camborne and Portreath it presents a considerable contrast to the golf at Lelant:

here we are amidst the pine trees, rhododendrons and bluebells—hopefully not right amidst them! Getting back to the coast, **Perranporth** and **Newquay** look closer on the map than they are by road. Both are links type courses with outstanding sea views. Not far away at St Mawgan a new 9 hole course, **Treloy,** has recently opened.

Further along the coast lie two marvellous golfing challenges—**St Enodoc** at Rock and **Trevose** at Constantine Bay. They are often considered as a pair although they are quite different in appearance. Trevose is the longer course but much more open and it doesn't possess the massive sandhills that are the feature of St Enodoc's links.

Our coastal tour ends appropriately at Bude—a pleasant and unassuming seaside resort with a very good golf links, **Bude and North Cornwall,** situated almost in the town centre and renowned for its rolling fairways and excellent greens.

The golf course at Tehidy was mentioned on our coastal tour, but three other inland courses definitely merit attention: the first is **Truro,** a shortish parkland course, close to the lovely cathedral, the second is at **Launceston,** one of the best parkland courses in the county, and the third, the outstanding new course near Camelford, called **Bowood,** which we explore in some detail ahead.

KEY

*** Visitors welcome at all times
** Visitors on weekdays only
* No visitors at any time
(Mon, Wed) No visitors on specified days

GREEN FEES PER ROUND

A - £30 plus
B - £20 - £30
C - £15 - £25
D - £10 - £20
E - Under £10
F - Green fees on application

RESTRICTIONS

G - Guests only
H - Handicap certificate required
H(24) - Handicap of 24 or less required
L - Letter of introduction required
M - Visitor must be a member of another recognised club.

Bomin G. & C.C.
(0208) 73600
Bodmin
(18) 6137 yards/***/D

Bude and North Cornwall
G.C.
(0288) 352006
Burn View, Bude
Just outside town on A39.
(18)6202 yards/***/D

Budock Vean Hotel G.C.
(0326) 250288
Mawnan Smith, Falmouth
Between Falmouth and
Helston on A394.

(9)5007 yards/***/D

Cape Cornwall G. & C.C
(0736) 788611
St Just, Penzance
(18) 5788 yards/***/D

Carlyon Bay Hotel G.C.
(072681) 4228
Carlyon Bay, St.Austell.
(18)6463 yards/***/D/M

China Fleet G.C
(0752) 848668
Saltash
(18)6551 yards/***/F/H

Falmouth G.C.
(0326) 311262
Swanpool Rd. Falmouth
Just outside town centre.
(18)5581 yards/***/D/M

Launceston G.C.
(0566) 3442
St. Stephens, Launceston
Turn left opposite
church on B3254.
(18)6357 yards/***/D/H

Looe G.C.
(05034) 571
Widegates, Looe
Between Liskeard
and Looe on B3253.
(18)6104 yards/***/D

Lostwithiel G. & C.C.
(0208) 873550
Lostwithiel
(18)6500 yards/***/C

Mullion G.C.
(0326) 240276
Curry, Helston
5 miles from Helston on
B3296.
(18) 5616 yards/***/D/H

Newquay G.C.
(0637) 872091
Tower Rd. Newquay
Just outside town centre.
(18)6140 yards/***/F

Perranporth G.C.
(0872) 573701
Budnick Hill, Perranporth
Just outside town on B3285.
(18)6208 yards/***/D/H

Praa Sands G.C.
(0736) 763445
Germoe Crossroads,
Penzance
Between Helston and
Penzance
on A394.
(9)4036 yards/***/E/H

St.Austell G.C.
(0726) 74756
Tregongeeves Lane,
St.Austell
1 mile from St.Austell off
A390
(18)5725 yards/***/D/M/H

St.Enodoc G.C.
(020886) 3216
Rock, Wadebridge
(18)6207 yards/***/F/H(24)

St. Mellion G.& C.C.
(0579) 50101
St. Mellion, Saltash
3 miles from Callington on
A388
(18)6626 yards/***/A/H
(18)5927 yards/***/D

Tehidy Park G.C.
(0209) 842208
Cambourne
2 miles north of
Cambourne on B3300
(18)6222 yards/***/D/H

Tregana Castle Hotel
(0736) 795254
St Ives
(18) 3549 yards/***/E

Trevose G.& C.C.
(0841) 520208
Constantine Bay, Padstow
(18)6608 yards/***/F/H
(9)1357 yards/***/F

Truro G.C.
(0872) 72640
Treliske, Truro
(18)5357 yards/***/D/H

West Cornwall G.C.
(0736) 753401
Lelant, St Ives
(18)5854 yards/***/D/H

Whitsand Bay Hotel G.C.
(0503) 30470
Portwrinkle, Torpoint
Outside Crafthole on B3247
(18)5367 yards/***/D/L

'Glorious Devon' they call it—beaches to the north, beaches to the south and Dartmoor in the middle. Well, amidst all the glory are some thirty golf courses, the majority of which lie either directly on the coast or within a mile or so of it. The two most widely known are both located to the north of the county: **Royal North Devon** (or Westward Ho! as it is commonly known) and **Saunton**. The greater number of courses, however, are on the southern coast, or to put it another way, while North Devon may have the cream, most of the tees are to be found in the south.

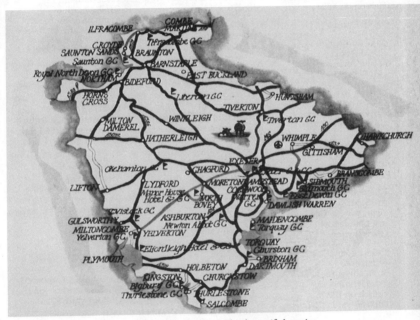

Firstly though, what about golf in the middle? The beautiful setting of the **Manor House** Hotel Golf Course at Moretonhampstead (see feature page) is known to many. However, it is not the sole course within Dartmoor; **Okehampton** is another moorland type course and whilst not overly long, has a number of interesting holes making it well worth a visit. Away from Dartmoor, but still fairly centrally located is the parkland course at **Tiverton**, easily reached from the M5 (junction 27), and a little closer to Exeter and adjacent to Woodbury Common is the highly acclaimed new development at **Woodbury Park**, where there is a very challenging 18 hole championship course designed by Hamilton Stutt plus a shorter 9 hole course and driving range. Note the spectacular par three 18th hole here—arguably the most dramatic closing hole in the South West.

With its many Tudor buildings, historic Guildhall and impressive Cathedral, Exeter makes an attractive county town. Golfwise, the city has an 18 hole course at Countess Wear, south of the town off the A377. A fairly short parkland course, **Exeter** Golf and Country Club has a very grand clubhouse and the course is renowned for its beautifully maintained greens, undoubtedly among the best in Devon.

South Devon

On the east side of the River Exe and only half an hour's drive from Exeter are the courses at Sidmouth and Budleigh Salterton (**East Devon**). Both are on fairly high ground providing panoramic views out to sea. **Sidmouth** is perhaps more of a typical cliff top course with well wooded fairways and 'springy' turf, while East Devon is a cross between downland and heathland with much heather and gorse. East Devon's delights are detailed ahead.

To the west of the Exe estuary, the friendly **Warren** Golf Club at Dawlish offers the only true links golf in South Devon. Laid out on a narrow hook-shaped peninsula and covered in gorse and numerous natural bunkers this is Devon's answer to St Andrews—and if this sounds a little far-fetched just inspect the aerial photographs at the 19th! It is a much improved course with an interesting finishing hole that will have the wayward hitter threatening both the Members in the Clubhouse and/or quite possibly the passengers on a passing London to Penzance 125. A fairly near neighbour of The Warren is **Teignmouth** Golf Club. It may be near, but Teignmouth offers a totally different challenge, being situated some 900 feet above sea level on Haldon Moor. Teignmouth can become shrouded in fog during the winter, but when all is clear, it's a very pleasant course and most attractive too.

The three handiest courses for those holidaying in the Torbay area are probably **Churston**, **Torquay** and **Newton Abbot**. The first two mentioned offer typical downland—clifftop type golf and a very different game from Newton Abbot's course at Stover where abundant heather, woods and a meandering brook are likely to pose the most challenges. Speaking of challenges, mention must also be made of the new **Dartmouth** Golf and Country Club at Blackawton, Totnes, which is set to rival the area's very best courses.

Heading further down the coast, the picturesque village of **Thurlestone** has one of the most popular courses in Devon. It is a superb cliff top course with several far-reaching views along the coast. **Bigbury** lies a short distance from Thurlestone and although perhaps a little less testing it is nevertheless equally attractive and looks across to Burgh Island, a favourite (or hopefully an ex-favourite) haunt of smugglers. Both Thurlestone and Bigbury can be reached from Plymouth via the A379, or from the Torbay region via the A381.

Golfers in Plymouth have probably been noting with interest the recent developments at nearby **St Mellion**, just over the border in Cornwall. Also not far from the great seafaring city, the **Elfordleigh Hotel's** 9 hole golf course at Plympton is very pleasant—and not as demanding as the Nicklaus course! and towards Dartmoor, **Yelverton** is certainly one not to be missed. Designed by Herbert Fowler, the architect of Walton Heath, Yelverton lies midway between Plymouth and Tavistock on the A386. It is a classic moorland course and very attractive too, with much gorse and heather.

Tavistock is also not far from Plymouth. **Tavistock** Golf Club is perhaps not as attractive as Yelverton, but worth a visit all the same. A second golf course in Tavistock, **Hurdwick** Golf Club has recently been opened.

North Devon
From Plymouth, the north coast of Devon is about an hour and a quarter's drive; from Exeter, a little less. Unless there is some urgency a leisurely drive is recommended for the scenery is truly spectacular.

North Devon can boast one of the oldest Golf Clubs in England, the **Royal North Devon** Club at Westward Ho!, founded in 1864, it can also claim to have seen the lowest known score for eighteen holes of golf. In 1936 the Woolacombe Bay professional recorded a 55 on his home course—29 out and 26 back, including a hole in one at the last! As this took place on the 1st January, one cannot help wondering quite what he did the night before! Unfortunately, this course closed long ago although there are 9 holes at **Morthoe & Woolacombe** and a very popular 18 hole test at nearby **Ilfracombe.** Situated several hundred feet above sea level, this latter course—offers many outstanding views of the North Devon coastline. The best hole is the par four 13th and there is an interesting selection of par three holes, one of which, the 4th, is played across a plunging ravine but measures a mere 80 yards. Yet another very recent addition to the county's golfing scene is the **Clovelly** Country Club near the famous 'sleepy village.'

Both **Saunton** and Westward Ho! deserve more than a fleeting visit: Westward Ho! is a place for pilgrimage, but Saunton provides the more modern championship challenge. There are two fine courses at Saunton, The East (which is the championship course) and the greatly improved West. Large sandhills dominate both courses, and when the wind blows. . . .

A final thought as we leave North Devon—should it actually happen and for some peculiar and presumably non-golfing reason (?!) you do get stranded in the dunes at Saunton, the chances are you will wake up to a glorious sunrise. If this is the case let's just hope the morning's golf is equally spectacular.

Axe Cliff G.C.
(0297) 24371
Axmouth, Seaton
1 mile east of Seaton.
(18)5000 yards/**/D

Bigbury G.C.
(0548) 810207
Bigbury-on-sea, Kingsbridge
(18)6076 yards/***/D/H

Chumleigh G.C.
(0769) 80519
Leigh Rd. Chumleigh
Between Exeter and
Barnstaple
on A377.
(18)1450 yards/***/E

Churston G.C.
(0803) 842218
Churston, Nr. Brixham
3 miles from Paignton on
A379
(18)6219 yards/***/F/H/M

Downes Crediton G.C.
(0363) 773991
Hookway, Crediton
(18)5868 yards/***/D/M

East Devon G.C.
(03954) 2018
North View Rd. Budleigh
5 miles from Exmouth on
A376.
(18)6214 yards/***/B/H/L

Elfordleigh Hotel G. and C.C.
(0752) 336428
Cobrook, Plympton,
Plymouth
Off A38, 5 miles N.of
Plymouth.
(9)56095 yards/**/D

Exeter G. & C.C.
(0392) 874139
Countess Wear, Exeter
On A379 to Exmouth.
(18)6061 yards/**/C/H

Great Torrington G.C.
(02372) 22229
Weare Trees, Torrington
1 mile north of Gt.
Torrington.
(9)4418 yards/***/E

Holsworthy G.C.
(0409) 253177
Kilatree, Holsworthy
Take A3072 to Bude.
(18)5935 yards/***/E

Honiton G.C.
(0404) 44422
Middlehills, Honiton
2 miles south of town.
(18)5931 yards/***/D/H/M

Ilfracombe G.C.
(0271) 863328
Hele Bay, Ilfracombe
On A399 past Hele.
(18)5857 yards/***/D/H

Manor House G. and C.C.
(0647) 40355
Moretonhampstead,
(18)6016 yards/***/D

Newton Abbot (Stover) G.C.
(0626) 52460
Bovey Rd. Newton Abbot
Take A382 to Bovey Tracey.
(18)5834 yards/***/C/M

Okehampton G.C.
(0837) 52113
Okehampton
(18)5163 yards/***/F

Royal North Devon G.C.
(0237) 473824
Westward Ho! Bideford
On Bone Hill Rd. near
Northam.
(18)6662 yards/***/C/H

Saunton G.C.
(0271) 812436
Saunton, Nr. Braunton
Take B3231 to Croyde Bay.
(18)6703 yards/***/C/H
(18)6356 yards/***/C/H

Sidmouth G.C.
(0395) 513023
Peak Hill, Cotmaston Rd.
(18)5166 yards/***/D/H

Staddon Heights G.C.
(0752) 402475
Staddon Heights, Plymstock
5 miles from Plymouth on
A379.
(18)5861 yards/***/D/H

Tavistock G.C.
(0822) 612049
Down Rd. Tavistock
(18)6250 yards/***/D/H

Teignmouth G.C.
(0626) 774194
Exeter Rd. Teignmouth
2 miles from
Teignmouth on B3192.
(18)6142 yards/***/C/H/M

Thurlestone G.C.
(0548) 560405
Thurlestone, Nr. Kingsbridge
Take A379 to Thurlesrtone.
(18) 6303 yards/***/C/H/M

Tiverton G.C.
(0884) 252187
Post Hill, Tiverton
(18) 6263 yards/***/C/H

Torquay G.C.
(0803) 37371
Petitor Rd. St. Marychurch
North of Torquay on A379
(18)6192 yards/***/C/H

Warren G.C.
(0626) 862255
Dawlish Warren, Dawlish
East of Dawlish on A379.
(18)968 yards/**/D/H

Somerset, Avon, Dorset and Wiltshire

From the wild beauty of Exmoor to the mystery of Stonehenge. The Quantocks and the Mendips; Lyme Regis and Bath; Avebury, Chesil Beach and Lulworth Cove. The West Country offers so much, no wonder those of us who do not live there are more than a little envious. The golf too can be equally spectacular. There may not be a Wentworth or a St George's here but the region offers a considerable variety and there is certainly no shortage of challenge. There is a true Championship links at Burnham and Berrow and a magnificent cliff top course at the Isle of Purbeck. Excellent downland golf can be enjoyed at Long Ashton and Bath while Bournemouth offers some majestic heathland and parkland type courses. We shall tee off in Somerset.

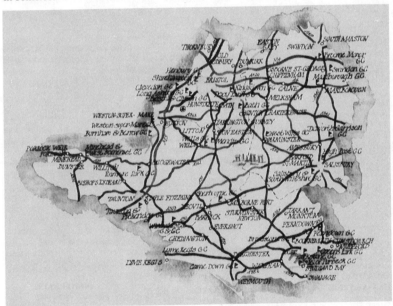

Somerset

Burnham and Berrow is without doubt the finest course in the county and the place where John H. Taylor wielded his famous mashie to great effect. The two holiday towns of **Minehead** and **Weston-Super-Mare** house the region's other two links courses. The Minehead and West Somerset Golf Club has more than a hundred years of history—it therefore remembers the quieter days in the years 'Before Butlins'. A fairly flat and windy course, it is situated on the eastern side of the town. Visitors are welcome, though during the peak season a quick telephone call to the Club is advisable. The same can be said of Weston—a slightly longer, well-maintained course, located just off the main A370 Bristol road. Perhaps a nearby course on which it may be easier to arrange a game is the attractive new 18 hole parkland layout at the **Ilse of Wedmore** Golf Club.

Taunton's golf course is at Corfe, the **Taunton and Pickeridge** Golf Club. It is located close to the town's race track and is fairly undulating.

More golf is found near Bridgwater. **Enmore Park,** located to the south of the town is a very pleasant medium length affair. The course enjoys a delightful setting and nestles around the foothills of the Quantocks. Moving from the Quantocks to the Mendips, the **Mendip** Golf Club at Gurney Slade offers possibly the most spectacular vistas of any course in the South West. From its 4th fairway, almost 1,000 feet above sea-level, on a clear day it is possible to sight the Cotswolds and the Quantocks, the Welsh Mountains and the Purbeck Hills, Glastonbury Tor and Westbury's White Horse…need I go on? Mendip is an enjoyable course and very visitor-friendly.

One final course to mention in Somerset is the magnificently titled **Windwhistle** Golf and Squash Club at Chard. The golf course is another laid out on high ground and offering extensive views. It's also close to the famous Cricket St Thomas Wildlife Park, where birdies and eagles abound.

Avon

The golf course at **Clevedon** stares spectacularly out across the mouth of the Severn. Clevedon is a cliff top course rather than a links and is well worth visiting. By travelling inland from Clevedon towards Bristol along the B3128, two of the city's best courses are reached before the famous Suspension Bridge. **Long Ashton** is actually immediately off the B3128, while to find **Bristol and Clifton** a left turn should be taken along the B3129. There is probably little to choose between the two, both being particularly attractive examples of downland golf. **Henbury** Golf Club is closer to the centre of Bristol, about 3 miles to the north to be precise, in the quiet suburb of Westbury-on-Trym. Henbury is a very mature parkland course with an abundance of trees making for some very attractive and challenging holes. One final club to recommend in Bristol is **Shirehampton**—always beautifully maintained.

Anyone travelling from Bristol to Bath (or vice versa) is likely to pass within a few miles of the **Tracy Park** Golf and Country Club at Wick. If possible a detour is recommended. Tracy Park is a newish course, built in the mid- seventies around a 400 year old mansion which acts as a rather impressive clubhouse. Although the course can get a little soggy in winter it offers a very good test of golf. Everybody, they say, falls in love with Bath—the Romans did, the Georgians did and the Americans think it's cute. For visiting golfers the City has two attractive propositions: **Bath** Golf Club and **Lansdown** Golf Club. The former, commonly known as Sham Castle because of its situation adjacent to Bath's greatest fraud (there is a beautiful castle frontage but nothing else!) is laid out high above the city and provides tremendous views over the surrounding countryside. Lansdown occupies flatter ground adjacent to Bath Races.

Wiltshire

Five years ago there were only a dozen or so golf courses in Wiltshire; by the end of 1993 there should be at least 20. Perhaps the two developments that have attracted most attention are the Dave Thomas designed Championship-styled course at **Bowood,** just off the A4 between Calne and Chippenham, and the dramatic layout at **Castle Combe** located to the north west of Chippenham, the handiwork of Peter Alliss and Clive Clark.

In **Wooton Bassett**, just west of Swindon, Alliss and Clark have constructed another new course, thus giving Swindon's golfers 3 courses close to the town; the 2 others are **Broome Manor** and the **Swindon** Golf Club, both are situated south of the town. The latter at Ogbourne St George, despite its name, is in fact closer to Marlborough than Swindon. It is an undulating, downland type course—very typical of the county's more established courses. Broome Manor is a public course and thus probably more accommodating to the visiting golfer.

Marlborough Golf Club is a near neighbour of Swindon Golf Club, being situated to the north west of the town on the Marlborough Downs. It offers similarly wide ranging views (and is similarly breezy!) Still further west there is a reasonable golf course at **Kingsdown.**

Dropping down the county, near Warminster, the **West Wilts** Golf Club is quite popular; the new 'pay and play' **Erlestoke Sands** course, south west of Devizes should prove to be, and t'other side of Stonehenge, **Tidworth Garrison** is certainly one of Wiltshire's top courses. It lies on Salisbury Plain and is owned by the Army. Salisbury offers two fine challenges, to the north, **High Post** and to the south west **Salisbury and South Wilts**. In the days before Bowood and Castle Combe appeared on the county's ever-changing golf map High Post was generally considered to be the leading course in the county. It's another classic downland type.

Dorset

The better golf courses in Dorset lie within a ten mile radius of the centre of Bournemouth. Having said all that, **Sherborne** in the far north of the county is undoubtedly one of the prettiest inland courses to be found anywhere in Britain.

Lyme Regis, famed for its fossils and more recently its French Lieutenant's Woman, has a fairly hilly 18 hole course which lies to the east of the town. The road between Lyme Regis and Weymouth provides dramatic views over Chesil Beach and passes through some of the most beautiful villages in England. The area north of Weymouth is Thomas Hardy country. Dorchester stands in the middle of it all and **Came Down** Golf Club is well worth noting when in these parts as is the **Mid Dorset** Golf Club at Blandford Forum.

Isle of Purbeck, Ferndown, Parkstone and **Broadstone** also fall in the 'must be visited' category. In addition to a game on one or more of these great courses, there are a handful of other easier-to-play courses around Bournemouth and Poole, including the new **Bulbury Woods** Golf Club at Lytchett Matravers west of Poole; Bournemouth's public courses shouldn't be overlooked either: **Meyrick Park** is very good while **Queens Park** is often described as the finest public course in England.

Somerset

Brean G.C.
(0278) 751595
Coast Rd. Brean, Burnham-on-Sea
Brean Leisure Centre.
(18)5436 yards/***/E/H

Burnham and Berrow G.C.
(0278) 785760
St Christophers, Burnham-on-Sea
1 mile north of town.
(18)6327 yards/***/B/M/H

Enmore Park G.C.
(0278) 67481
Enmore, Bridgwater
3 miles from Bridgwater
(18)6443 yards/D/M/H

Mendip G.C.
(0749) 840570
Gurney Slade, Bath
3 miles N. of Shepton Mallet on A37
(18)5982 yards/**/D

Minehead and West Somerset G.C.
(0643) 702057
The Warren, Minehead
Just outside Minehead town centre
(18)6130 yards/***/D

Taunton and Pickeridge G.C.
(0823) 42240
Corfe, Taunton
Just past Corfe on B31704
(18)5927 yards/**/D

Vivary Park G.C.
(0823) 289274
Taunton
Situated in town centre
(18)4620 yards/***/E

Wells G.C.
(0749) 72868
East Horrington Rd, Wells
1 mile east of the city.
(18)5354 yards/***/D/H

Windwhistle G.C.
(046030) 231
Cricket St. Thomas, Chard
3 miles from Chard on A30
(18)6055 yards/***/D

Yeovil G.C.
(0935) 22965
Sherborne Rd. Yeovil
1 mile from town on A30
(18)6139 yards/***/D/H

Weston-Super-Mare G.C.
(0934) 621360
Uphill Road North, Weston-Super-Mare
(18)6225 yards/***/B

Worlebury G.C.
Worlebury, Weston-Super-Mare
2 miles from Weston-Super-Mare
(18)5945 yards/**/C/H
Avon

Bath G.C.
(0225) 425182
Sham Castle, North Rd.
South of city off A36
(18)6369 yards/***/C/H

Bristol and Clifton G.C.
(0275) 393117
Beggar Bush Lane, Failand
Off A3969 to Bristol
(18)6270 yards/***/C/H

Chipping Sodbury G.C.
(0454) 319042
Chipping Sodbury, Bristol
Turn off Wickwar Rd. to
Horton
(18)6912 yards/***/D/H

Clevedon G.C.
(0275) 874057
Castle Rd. Clevedon
Just outside town
off Hodley Lane
(18)5887 yards/***/(Mon,
Wed)/D/H/M

Entry Hill G.C.
(0225) 834248
Entry Hill, Bath
South of the town on A367
(9)4206 yards/***/E

Filton G.C.
(0272) 694169
Golf Course Lane, Filton,
Bristol
(18)6277 yards/***/D

Fosseway G.C.
(0761) 412214
Charlton Lane, Midsomer
Norton
Take A367 to Charlton
(9)4246 yards/***/D

Henbury G.C.
(0272) 500044
Henbury Hill,
Westbury-on-Trym
3 miles north of Bristol
(18)6039 yards/**/D/H

Knowle G.C.
(0272) 770660
Fairway, Brislington
3 miles south of Bristol
(18)6016 yards/***/D/H

Landsdown G.C.
(0225) 422138

Landsdown, Bath
Next to Bath racecourse
(18)6267 yards/***/D/H

Long Ashton G.C.
(0275) 392316
Long Ashton, Bristol
Take B3128 to Long Ashton
(18)6051 yards/***/C/H

Mangotsfield G.C.
(0272) 565501
Carsons Rd. Mangotsfield
(18)5337 yards/***/E

Saltford G.C
(0272) 873220
Golf Club Lane, Saltford
Off A4 between Bath and
Bristol
(18)6081 yards/***/D/H

Shirehampton G.C.
(0272) 822083
Park Hill, Shirehampton
2 miles from village
(18)5493 yards/**/D/H

Tall Pines G.C.
(0275) 472076
Downside, Backwell
(18) 4250 yards/***/D

Tracy Park G.C.C
(027582) 2251
Bath Rd. Wick, Bristol
(18)6800 yards/***/D
(9)5200 yards/***/D
Dorset

Ashley Woods G.C.
(0258) 452253
Wimbourne Rd,
Blandford Forum
Take B3082 to
Wimbourne Minster
(18) 5246 yards/***/C/H

Bridport & West Dorset
G.C.
(0308) 22597
East Cliff, West Bay,
Bridport
Take A35 from Bridport
onto B3157
(18) 5246 yards/***/C/H

Broadstone G.C.
(0202) 692595
Wentworth Drive,
Broadstone
Between Wimbourne
and Poole on A349
(18)6151 yards/***/A/H

Bulbury Woods G.C.
(092945) 574
Nr Poole
(18)6020 yards

Came Down G.C.
(030581) 3494
Came Down, Dorchester
On A354 from Dorchester
to Wimbourne
(18)6224 yards/***/C/H

Chedington Court G.C.
(0935) 891413
Nr Beaminster, Dorset
Take A356
(9)3500 yards/***/E

East Dorset G.C.
(0929) 472244
(18)6640 yards/**/D/I
(9)2440 yards/*/D/I

Ferndown G.C.
(0202) 874602
119 Golf Links Rd,
Ferndown
Onto A348 from A31 to
Tricketts Cross
(18)6442 yards/***/A/H

Highcliffe Castle G.C.
(04252) 72210
107 Lymington Rd,
Highcliffe-on-Sea
Off A35 from
Bournemouth
(18)4732 yards/***/D/M

Isle of Purbeck G.C.
(092944) 361
On B3351 between Studland
and Swanage
(18) 6248 yards/***/C/H

(9) 2022 yards/***/E

Knighton Heath G.C.
(0202) 572633
Hyde, Wareham
(18)6108 yards/***/DLyme
Regis G.C.
(02974) 2963
Timber Hill, Lyme Regis
(18)6262 yards/***/C

Meyrick G.C.
(0202) 290871
Parks Dept. Bournemouth
(18) 5885 yards/***/E

Mid Dorset G.C.
(0258) 861386
Blandford Forum
(18)6500 yards/***/C

Parkstone G.C.
(0202) 707138
Links Road, Parkstone,
Poole
Turn south of A35
(18) 6250 yards/**/B/H

Queen's Park G.C.
(0202) 396198
Queen's Park, South Drive,
Bournemouth
(18) 6505 yards/***/E

Sherbourne G.C.
(0935) 812475
Higher Clatcombe,
Sherbourne
Take B3145 north of town
(18)5758 yards/***/D

Wareham G.C.
(09295) 54147
Sandford Rd. Wareham
(18) 5603 yards/**/C

Weymouth G.C.
(0305) 773981
Links Rd. Westham,
Weymouth
(18) 5979 yards/***/E

Wiltshire

Brinkworth G.C.
(066641) 277
Longman's Farm,
Brinkworth, Chippenham
(9)6086 yards/***/E

Bremhill G.C.
(0793) 782946
Shrivenham, Swindon
East of village
(18)5880 yards/***/E

Broome Manor G.C.
(0793) 532403
Piper's Way, Swindon
1 mile from Swindon old
town
(18)6359 yards/**/D

Chippenham G.C.
(0249) 652040
Malmebury Rd.
Chippenham
(18)5540 yards/***/C/M/H

High Post G.C.
(072273) 356
Great Durnford, Salisbury
Between Salisbury and
Amesbury on A345
(18)6267 yards/***/C/H

Kingsdown G.C.
(0225) 742 530
Kingsdown, Corsham
(18) 6254 yards/***/D/H

Marlborough G.C.
(0672) 512147
The Common, Marlborough
(18)6440 yards/B/H

North Wiltshire G.C.
(0380) 860257
Bishops Cannings, Devizes
(18)6450 yards/***/F/H

Salisbury and Wiltshire G.C.
(0722) 742645
Netherhampton, Salisbury
1 mile from Wilton on
A3094
(18)6146 yards/***/B/H

Shrivenham Park G.C.
(0793) 783853
Penny Hooks
(18)5899 yards/***/D

Swindon G.C.
(0672) 84217
Ogbourne St George
Take A345 towards
Marlborough
(18)6226 yards/**/C

West Wiltshire G.C.
(0985) 212702
Elm Hill, Warminster
Half a mile from
Warminster on A350
(18)5701 yards/***/B/H

Hampshire & the
Channel Islands

Even if the Isle of Wight and the Channel Islands were taken away from this region it would still score top marks, both for the quality of the golf and the quality of the accompanying scenery. With the New Forest to the south, the Downs to the north and Winchester Cathedral standing proudly in the middle, Hampshire is arguably the fairest of all English counties. And amongst all this finery stand the likes of Liphook, Old Thorns, North Hants, Blackmoor and Brokenhurst Manor—five of the country's leading inland courses.

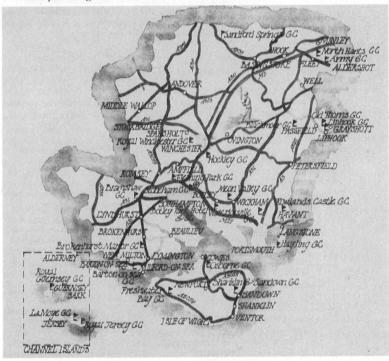

From Heathland to Links

Hampshire's traditional 'big three' of **Liphook**, **North Hants** and **Blackmoor**, lie towards the east of the county close to the boundary with Surrey. Not surprisingly they are staunch members of the heath-land club—silver birch and pine, fir, heather and a dash of gorse. Liphook is possibly the pick of the three, though it's a close thing. Each measures between 6,200 and 6,300 yards and is maintained in superb condition.

The Army Golf Club, just north of Aldershot is another fine and quite lengthy heathland type course with a reputation for separating the men from the boys although it is perhaps not quite in the same league as the illustrious trio above. The final mention in this area goes to one of the county's newest recruits, the **Old Thorns** Golf and Country Club, situated south of Liphook.

Basingstoke isn't Hampshire's most attractive town—too much London overspill. A very good and relatively new course nearby however is the **Sandford Springs** Golf Club at Wolverton, built on the site of a former Roman shrine, and officially opened in 1989 by Nick Faldo.

Winchester golfers, like those at Liphook, are doubly fortunate having two first class courses at hand: **Royal Winchester** and **Hockley,** which is located two miles south of the city on the A333. Both are well kept downland type courses. A recent, and most attractive addition to the Winchester/South Hampshire area is the **Botley Park** Hotel and Country Club Some excellent golfing weekend packages are offered.

Returning to the fairways, and switching nearer to the south coast, the **Rowlands Castle** parkland course occupies a peaceful setting. The course can play fairly long, especially from the back markers. While we're on the subject of length, a hundred years ago the links at **Hayling Island** is said to have measured 7,480 yards—so much for the modern-day monster courses! Today the course is less frightening but still quite a challenge and visitors are warmly received.

Southampton and the New Forest

Stoneham is without doubt the pick of the courses in the Southampton area, it is located just 2 miles north of the town. The venue of the first Dunlop British Masters tournament back in 1946, it is quite undulating with an ample sprinkling of gorse and heather which, though appealing to look at is often the curse of the wayward hitter. Just outside of Portsmouth a fine 18 hole course to note is **Waterlooville,** although there are in fact a number of courses (including some very reasonable public courses, such as **Fleming Park** at **Eastleigh**) in and around Southampton and Portsmouth. Midway between Portsmouth and Southampton (M27 junction 7) is the **Meon Valley** Golf and Country Club. A fairly new parkland course, designed by J. Hamilton Stutt, it too has an attractive setting, not a million miles from the New Forest.

I'm afraid I know very little about William the Conqueror but I understand there are at least two things we should thank him for—one is the Domesday Book and the other is the New Forest, without doubt one of the most beautiful areas in Britain. There are two real golfing treats in the New Forest, one is **Bramshaw** Golf Club—two fine 18 hole courses here, The Manor and The Forest courses, and the second is **Brokenhurst Manor,** a superb heathland course. Both venues are decidedly worth inspecting. A short distance from the New Forest, **Barton-on-Sea**'s exposed cliff top course is also worth a visit if in the area—it's not long, but with enough challenges and some spectacular views across to the Isle of Wight and Christchurch Bay.

Isle of Wight

There are no fewer than seven golf courses on the Isle of Wight. There are two 18 hole courses, **Shanklin and Sandown** is the better of the two (beautifully wooded with heather and gorse) and the other is **Freshwater Bay** (more of a downland/cliff top course.) Of the 9 holers, **Osborne** is the most scenic but a visit to any is appealing. All courses welcome visitors and green fees tend to compare favourably with those on the mainland—note that in summer, the courses can be very busy and so a pre-match telephone call is strongly advised.

The Channel Islands

If the Isle of Wight is good for golf, the Channel Islands are even better. Not that there is a proliferation of courses—indeed they could do with a couple more—but three of them, **La Moye, Royal Jersey** and **Royal Guernsey** are particularly fine. Unfortunately the German troops didn't share this opinion during the island's four year occupation: they demolished La Moye's Clubhouse and dug up the fairways at Royal Guernsey. Both have long since recovered though and all three provide tremendous holiday golf.

Hampshire

Alresford G.C.
(0962) 733746
Cheriton Rd. Alresford
1 mile south of the town.
(11)6038 yards/**/D

Alton G.C.
(0420)82042
Old Odiham Rd. Alton
(9)5744 yards/***/D

Ampfield Par Three G.C.
(0794) 68480
Winchester Rd. Ampfield,
Romsey
3 miles from Hursley on
A31.
(18)2478 yards/***/E/H

Army G.C.
(0252) 541104
Laffans Rd. Aldershot
(18)6579 yards/*G/F

Barton-on-Sea G.C.
(0425) 615308
Marine Drive, Barton-on-
Sea, New Milton
1 mile from New Milton.
(18)5565 yards/***/C/H

Basingstoke G.C.
(0256) 465990
Kempshott Park,
Basingstoke
3 miles west of town on
A30.
(18)6284 yards/**/C/H

Basingstoke Hospitals G.C.
(0256) 20347
Aldermaster Rd. Basingstoke
2 miles north of town centre
(9)5455 yards/****E

Bishopswood G.C.
(0734) 81513
Bishopswood Lane, Tadley
Off A340 west of Tadley.
(9)6474
yards/**(Mon,Wed)/E

Blackmoor G.C.
(04203) 2775
Golf Lane, Whitehill, Bordon
(18)6232 yards/**/C/H

Botley Park Hotel & G.C.
(0489) 780888
6 miles east of
Southampton on B3354
(18)6026 yards/***/C/H

Bramshaw G.C.
(0703) 813433
Brook, Lyndhurst
1 mile from Cadnam on
B3078.
(18)6233 yards/***/D
(18)5774 yards/***/D

Brokenhurst Manor G.C.
(0703) 23332
Sway Rd. Brockenhurst
1 mile outside village.
(18)6212 yards/**/D/H(24)

Burley G.C.
(04253) 2431
Burley, Ringwood
(9)6149 yards/**/D

Corhampton G.C.
(0489) 877279
Sheeps Pond Lane, Droxford
1 mile from Corhampton on
B3135
(18)6088 yards/**/D/H

Dibden G.C.
(0703) 845596
Dibden, Southampton
(18)6206 yards/***/E

Dunwood Manor G.C.
(0794) 40549
Shootash Hill, Romsey
(18)6004 yards/**/D

Fleming Park G.C.
(0703) 61297
Magpie Lane, Eastleigh
1 mile north of Eastleigh airport.
(18)4402 yards/***/F

Gosport and Stokes Bay G.C.
(0705) 527941
Military Rd. Halsar, Gosport
(9)5806 yards/**/E

Great Salterns G.C.
(0705) 664549
Portsmouth Golf Centre,
Eastern Rd.
(18)5970 yards/***/E

Hartley Whitney G.C.
(025126) 4211
London Rd. Hartley
Whitney
(9)6096 yards/**/D

Hayling G.C.
(0705) 464446
Ferry Rd. Hayling Island
(18)6489 yards/C/H/M/L

Hockley G.C.
(0962) 713165
Twyford, Winchester
(18)6279 yards/G/F

Leckford and Longstock G.C.
(0264) 810710
Leckford, Stockbridge
(9)3251 yards/*/F

Lee-on-the-Solent G.C.
(0705) 551170
Brune Lane, Lee-on-the-
Solent
(18)6022/**/C

Liphook G.C.
(0428) 723271
Wheatsheaf Enclosure,
Liphook
(18)6250 yards/**/B/H/M

Meon Valley G. and C.C.
(0329) 833455
Sandy Lane, Shedfield,
Southampton
(18)5748 yards/***/C

New Forest G.C.
(042128) 2450
Lyndhurst
(18)5748 yards/***/D

North Hants G.C.
(0252) 616443
Minley Rd Fleet
(18)6251 yards/***/H/M

Old Thorns G.C.
(0428) 724555
London Kasaido G. & C.C.
Longmoor Rd. Liphook
(18)5629 yards/***/B

Petersfield G.C.
(0730) 62386
Heath Rd. Petersfield
(18)5720 yards/***/D

Portsmouth G.C.
(0705) 372210
Crookhorn Rd. Widley,
Portsmouth
(18)6259 yards/***/E

Romsey G.C.
(0703) 734637
Nursling , Southampton
(18)5759 yards/**/F/H

Rowlands Castle G.C.
(0705) 412784
Links Lane, Rowlands Castle
(18)6627 yards/**/C

Royal Winchester G.C.
(0962) 52462
Sarum Rd. Winchester
(18)6218 yards/**/C/H

Sandford Springs G.C.
(0639) 297881
Wolverton, Basingstoke
Between Basingstoke and
Newbury on A339
(18)6064 yards/**/C/G

Southampton G.C.
(0703) 568407
Golf Course Rd. Bassett,
Southampton
(18)6218 yards/***/F

Southwick Park G.C.
(0705) 380131
Pinsley Drive, Soutwick,
Fareham
(18)5855 yards/**/E

Southwood G.C.
(0252) 548700
Ively Rd. Cove, Farnborough
(18)5553 yards/***/F

Stoneham G.C.
(0703) 768151
Bassett Rd, Bassett,
Southampton
(18)6310 yards/**/C/H

Tidworth Garrison G.C.
(0980) 4231
Tidworth
Tidworth 1 mile on Bulford
Road
(18) 5990 yards/**/C

Tylney Park G.C
(0256) 762079
Rotherwick, Basingstoke
(18)6138 yards/***/C/H

Waterlooville G.C
(0705) 263388
Cherry Tree Avenue,
Cowplain, Portsmouth
(18)6647 yards/**/C/H

Isle of Wight

Cowes G.C
(0983) 292303
Crossfield Avenue, Cowes
(9)2940 yards/***/D

Freshwater Bay G.C
(0983) 752955
Afton Down, Freshwater
Bay
2 miles from Yarmouth on
A3056
(18)5662 yards/***/D

Newport G.C
(0983) 525076
St Georges Down, Newport
(9)5704 yards/***/D/H

Osborne G.C
(0983)295421
Osborne, E Cowes
(9)6304 yards/**/D/H

Ryde G.C
(0983) 614809
Binstead Rd, Ryde
(9)5200 yards/***/F/H

Shanklin & Shandown G.C
(0983) 403217
The Fairway, Sandown
Near Sandown bus station
(18)5980 yards/C/H

Ventor G.C
(0983) 853326
Steephill Down, Ventor
North of Ventor on A3055
(9)5752 yards/***/E

Channel Islands

Alderney G.C
(048182) 2835
Routes des Carriers,
Alderney
1 mile E of St Annes
(9)2528 yards/***/D

La Moye G.C
(0534) 43401
La Moye, St Brelade
(18)6464 yards/***/A

Royal Guernsey G.C
(0481) 47022
LAncresse, Guernsey
3 miles from St Peter Port
(18)6206 yards/***(Thurs,Sat
pm,Sun(H))/F

Royal Jersey G.C
(0534) 54416
Grouville, Jersey
On coast, 4 miles from S
Helier
(18)6106
yards/***(W/Epm)/F

St Clements G.C
(0524) 21938
St Clements
Nr St Helier off A5
(9)3972 yards/***(Sunpm)/D

KEY

*** Visitors welcome at all times
** Visitors on weekdays only
* No visitors at any time
(Mon, Wed) No visitors on specified
days

GREEN FEES PER ROUND
A - £30 plus
B - £20 - £30
C - £15 - £25
D - £10 - £20
E - Under £10
F - Green fees on application

RESTRICTIONS
G - Guests only
H - Handicap certificate required
H(24) - Handicap of 24 or less
required
L - Letter of introduction required
M - Visitor must be a member of
another recognised club.

Sussex, where the South Downs tumble gently towards spectacular chalk cliffs or as Tennyson wrote, 'Green Sussex fading into blue'. Here is the county of downland and weald, of dramatic roller-coasting cliffs, the Seven Sisters and Beachy Head.

The situation in Sussex is superb. The golf is glorious as is the countryside all around, while at no time can you claim to be isolated—except perhaps when you visit the gorse at Ashdown Forest. West Sussex is as charming an area as one could find—the golf course of the same name is delightful and reflects the quality of some splendid nearby country house hotels. While in Rye, the golfer must visit with a packed wallet in order to seduce a member in a local drinking haunt and thus secure that elusive thing—a round of golf at Rye—a more spectacular day could not be wished for.

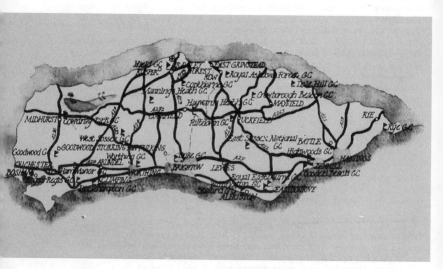

Close to the coast

On a selective tour of some of the better courses on or near the Sussex coast, there seems no more logical a place to commence than in the region's south west corner, and **Goodwood**—glorious Goodwood to racegoers, though the golf course is in a similarly idyllic spot, nestling in the southern foothills of the South Downs. Some four miles north of Chichester on the A286 it is in fact located just below the race course and has a magnificent 18th century clubhouse.

Staying in the south west of the region **Bognor Regis** is worth a visit—a flattish but attractive parkland course with several testing par fours. The course at **Littlehampton** lies about seven miles east of Bognor Regis off the A259. It is the nearest one gets to a true links course in West Sussex and is always kept in first class condition. Further along the A259 at Angmering is the friendly club of **Ham Manor,** like Bognor it is a parkland course with an interesting layout of two distinct loops. It also boasts a beautiful clubhouse.

As a town Worthing is somewhat overshadowed by neighbouring Brighton (though apparently it inspired Oscar Wilde)—overshadowed or not, it has one of the leading clubs in Sussex. **Worthing** has two eighteen hole courses, the Lower and the Upper. Both are exceptionally fine tests of golf. There is a reasonable public course too at Worthing, **Hill Barn**.

Moving into East Sussex and the town of Brighton; probably the best course in the area, and there are a number to choose from, is **The Dyke** Golf Club, located five miles north of the town centre. One of the more difficult courses in Sussex, it is on fairly high ground and provides some splendid views. A short distance along the ubiquitous A259 is **Seaford.** One of the older clubs in Sussex, the Seaford Golf Club at East Bletchington celebrated its centenary in 1987. A fair sprinkling of gorse and hawthorn is the feature of this outstanding downland course. The views too are quite spectacular being perched high above the town and overlooking the Channel.

As we continue to trek in an easterly direction, passing near to Beachy Head we arrive at Eastbourne where there are two fine courses—**Royal Eastbourne** and **Willingdon.** The former is situated very close to the town centre with the enviable address of Paradise Drive. Willingdon, north of the town off the A22, is quite a hilly course and very tough. Its interesting design has been likened to an oyster shell with the Clubhouse as the pearl. In the area around Bexhill, both **Cooden Beach** and **Highwoods** are well established courses.

Before heading inland a quick word on **Rye.** It is unquestionably one of the greatest and most natural links courses in Britain—in many people's opinion the equal of Deal and Sandwich. However, visitors are normally only permitted to play if accompanied by a Member—hence the rather flippant remark in the second paragraph!

Further Inland
If the majority of the leading courses in Sussex are located either on the coast or within a few miles of it, perhaps the most attractive courses are to be found a few more miles inland. **Piltdown,** two miles to the west of Uckfield, is a good example. Piltdown is a natural heathland course with a beautiful setting and somewhat unusually, though it shares the curiosity with Royal Ashdown, it has no

bunkers—though there are certainly enough natural hazards to set the golfer thinking.

Leaving the Piltdown Men and crossing the boundary from East to West, moving from Uckfield to Cuckfield, **Haywards Heath** stands right in the middle of Sussex. A very good heathland course this, but the pride of West Sussex is undoubtedly Pulborough—The **West Sussex** Golf Club.—suffice to say here that its reputation extends far beyond the bounds of East and West Sussex. Not too far from Pulborough, Brian Barnes has been the driving force behind the fine new development at **West Chiltington** and where the possibility for visitors of a weekend game is a definite bonus! Still in the West two more to note are in the north of the county, and very convenient for Gatwick, the **Ifield** Golf and Country Club and **Copthorne**. Another popular course is found at **Cowdray Park**—very pleasant and ideal should you happen to play polo as well! There is also a reasonable course at **Mannings Heath** (parkland golf despite the name.) The newest addition to the heart of Sussex is the magnificent **East Sussex National**.

Towards the north of East Sussex, **Dale Hill** is a much improved course with a new hotel attached. Considerable investment at this prestigious development have resulted in both a course of challenging quality and a hotel of the highest calibre. Next comes a classic pair: **Royal Ashdown Forest** and **Crowborough Beacon**—two wonderfully scenic courses where the heather and gorse simply run riot. Crowborough's course is situated some 800 feet above sea level and on clear days the sea can be glimpsed from the Clubhouse. Sir Arthur Conan Doyle would have taken in this view on many occasions for he lived adjacent to the course and was Captain of the Golf Club in 1910. It really is the most beautiful of courses and has in the par three 6th one of the best short holes in Britain.

Move over *Sunningdale, Wentworth and Walton Heath! These three great championship venues, all situated in the magnificent heathland belt of Surrey and Berkshire, are now having to make room for a newcomer from the heart of rural Sussex.*

East Sussex National has two great golf courses, the East and West which were officially opened for play as recently as April 1990. Both were designed by the American, Robert E Cupp, formerly Jack Nicklaus' Senior designer. For the first time in Great Britain, bent grasses have been used throughout from tee to green and the result is golf course conditioning of a type never witnessed before in this country. The fairways are genuinely carpet-like and the teeing areas are better than most golf course greens! Both courses measure in excess of 7,000 yards from their Championship tees and are similarly challenging but quite different in appearance. The East Course is the 'stadium' course, specifically designed with a view to staging big events, hence the gentle 'gallery mounding' evident around the 15th and the 18th greens. The West Course is more intimate. The landscape rises and falls quite sharply in parts; the surrounding woodland is more dense but because of the climbs there are many spectacular views over the South Downs.

Individuals, groups and corporate societies are welcome at East Sussex. Most visitors will play the East Course as the West is usually (but not always) reserved for members. Bookings can be made by telephoning **Reservations** on (0825) 880088. The visitors' green fee in 1993 was £65 for 18 holes and £85 per day. All membership and corporate enquiries can be dealt with through Corporate Hospitality on the above number. There are many outstanding holes

on the **East Course** but perhaps the par fives are especially memorable; three of the four, the 7th, 10th and 14th are as good a trio as one is likely to find on any course, anywhere.

Although the challenge isn't any greater on the **West Course**, in most people's minds it has the greater number of 'pretty' holes; in fact, 'provocatively spectacular' might be the description of some. Anyone wishing to put together a 'dream nine holes' could do worse than select the 1st, 2nd, 3rd, 9th, 10th, 12th, 13th, 14th and 18th on the East Sussex National West Course.

Many are likely to experience the full range of sensations in September 1993 when East Sussex stages the prestigious European Open. It is clearly a testimony to the quality of the Club's facilities, especially its two courses, that it has acquired a major event so soon. September 1993: The Ryder Cup at The Belfry and the European Open at East Sussex National—it's two months away as I write but my hands are already becoming clammy at the prospect!

***East Sussex National Golf Club,
Little Horsted, Uckfield,
East Sussex TN22 5ES.***

West Course

Hole	Yards	Par	Hole	Yards	Par
1	363	4	10	404	4
2	517	5	11	423	4
3	136	3	12	520	5
4	354	4	13	184	3
5	504	5	14	450	4
6	396	4	15	365	4
7	192	3	16	117	3
8	408	4	17	566	5
9	392	4	18	365	4
Out	3,262	36	In	3,394	36
			Out	3,262	36
			Totals	6,565	72

West Sussex

Bognor Regis G.C.
(0243) 821929
Downview Rd. Felpham,
Bognor Regis
(18)6238 yards/**/B/H

Copthorne G.C.
(0342) 712508
Bovers Arms Rd. Copthorne,
Crawley
(18)6550 yards/**/C

Cottesmore G.C.
(0923) 528256
Buchan Hill, Pease Pottage,
Crawley
1 mile from M23
on Horsham Rd.
(18)6100 yards/***/C
(18)5400 yards/***/D

Cowdray Park G.C.
(073081) 3599
Midhurst
1 mile east of Midhurst on
A272.
(18)5972 yards/***/C

Effingham Park G.C.
(0342) 716528
West Park Rd. Copthorne
(9)1749 yards/***/E

Goodwood G.C.
(0243) 774968
Goodwood, Chichester
Take A286 to Goodwood
racecourse.
(18)6318 yards/***/B/H

Goodwood Park G. & C.C.
(0243) 775987
4 miles north of Chichester
(18)6530 yards/***/D

Ham Manor G.C.
(0903) 783288
Angmering
Between Worthing and
Littlehampton on A259.
(18)6243 yards/***/B/H

Haywards Heath G.C.
(0444) 414457
High Beech Lane,
Haywards Heath
2 miles north of Haywards
Heath.
(18)6206 yards/***/C/H

Hill Barn G.C.
(0903) 237301
Hill Barn Lane, Worthing
N.of Worthing off the
Upper Brighton Rd.
(18)6224 yards/***/D

Ifield G. and C.C.
(0293) 520222
Rusper Rd. Ifield, Crawley
(18)6289 yards/**/C

Littlehampton G.C.
(0903) 717170
170 Rope Walk, Riverside,
Littlehampton
(18)6244 yards/***/C

Mannings Heath G.C.
(0403) 210228
Goldings Lane, Mannings
Heath
3 miles south of Horsham
off A281.
(18)6404 yards/**/C/H

Paxhill Park G.C.
(0444) 484467
1 mile north of Lindfield
(18) 6196 yards/***/D

Pycombe G.C.
(0273) 845372
Pycombe, Brighton
6 miles N of Brighton on
A272
(18) 6234 yards/***/C -

Selsey G.C.
(0243) 602203
Golf Links Lane, Selsey,
Chichester
7 miles south of Chichester
on B2145.
(9)5402 yards/***/D

Tilgate Forest G.C.
(0293) 530103
Titmus Drive, Tilgate,
Crawley
(18)6359 yards/***/D

West Chiltington G.C.
(0798) 813574
Broadford Bridge Road, W.
Chiltington
2 miles E of Pulborough
(18) 5969 yards/***/D

West Sussex G.C.
(0798) 872563
Pulborough
2 miles east of Pulborough
on A283
(18)6156 yards/**/F/H/L

Worthing G.C.
(0903) 260801
Links Rd. Worthing
At junction between
A27 and A24.
(18)6477 yards/***/B/H
(18)5243 yards/***/B/H

East Sussex

Aldershaw G.C.
(0424) 870898
Sedlescombe
(18) 6218 yards/***/D

Ashdown Forest Hotel G.C.
(0342) 824869
Chapel Lane, Forest Row
(18)5510 yards/***/C

Brighton and Hove G.C.
(0273) 556482
Dyke Rd, Brighton
2 miles north of Brighton.
(9)5722 yards/***/D

Cooden Beach G.C.
(04243) 2040
Cooden Sea Rd. Cooden
(18)6450 yards/***/C

Crowborough Beacon G.C.
(08926) 61511
Beacon Rd. Crowborough
8 miles south of Tunbridge
Wells on A26.
(18)6279 yards/**/B/H/L

Dale Hill G.C.
(0580) 200112
Ticehurst, Wadhurst
(18)6055 yards/***/C

Dyke G.C.
(0273) 857296
Dyke Rd. Brighton
4 miles north of Brighton.
(18)6212 yards/***(Sun)/C

Eastbourne Downs G.C.
(0323) 20827
East Dean Rd. Eastbourne
On A259 west of
Eastbourne.
(18)6635 yards/***/D

East Brighton G.C.
(0273) 604838
Roedean Rd. Brighton
Opposite Brighton
Marina off A259.
(18)6304 yards/***/C

East Sussex National G.C.
(0825) 75577
Little Horsted, Uckfield
(18)7081 yards/***/F
(18)7154 yards/*/F

Hastings G.C.
(0424) 852981
Battle Rd. St.Leonards-on-Sea
3 miles N.W. of Hastings
on A2100.
(18)6248 yards/***/E

Highwoods G.C.
(0424) 212625
Ellerslie Lane, Bexhill-on-Sea
2 miles west of Bexhill
on A259
(18)6218 yards/***/C

Hollingbury G.C.
(0273) 552010
Ditchling Rd. Brighton
(18)6502 yards/***/D

Horam Park G.C.
(04353) 3477
Chiddingly Rd. Horam,
Heathfield
(9)2844/***/D

Lewes G.C.
(0273) 473245
Chapel Hill, Lewes
Between Lewes and
Eastbourne on A27.
(18)5951 yards/**/D

Peacehaven G.C.
(0273) 514049
Brighton Rd. Newhaven
1 mile west of Newhaven
on A259.
(9)5007 yards/***/F/H

Piltdown G.C.
(082572) 2033
Piltdown, Uckfield
3 miles west of Uckfield.
(18)6059 yards/**/B/H/L

Royal Ashdown Forest G.C.
(034282) 2018
Chapel Lane, Forest Row,
E.Grinstead
(18)6439 yards/**/B/H

Royal Eastbourne G.C.
(0323) 30412
Paradise Drive, Eastbourne
Half-mile from town centre.
(18)6109 yards/***/C
(9)2147 yards/***/D

Rye G.C.
(0797) 225241
Camber, Rye
(18)6301 yards/*/F

Seaford G.C.
(0323) 892442
East Blatchington, Seaford
N of Seaford off A259
(18)6233 yards/**/F

Seaford Head G.C.
(0323) 890139
Southdown Rd, Seaford
12 miles from Brighton
(18)5348 yards/***/E

Waterhall G.C.
(0273) 508658
Mill Rd, Brighton
(18)5692 yards/***/D

West Hove G.C.
(0273) 413411
Old ShorehamRd, Hove
(18)6038 yards/**/C

Willingdon G.C.
(0323) 410983
Southdown Rd, Eastbourne
(18)6049 yards/**/C

From the mysterious and desolate lands of Romney Marsh to the famous White Cliffs of Dover. From the rich orchards of the Garden of England to the outskirts of Greater London. From the windswept links of Sandwich and Deal to the secluded Parks of Belmont and Knole, a county of great contrast.

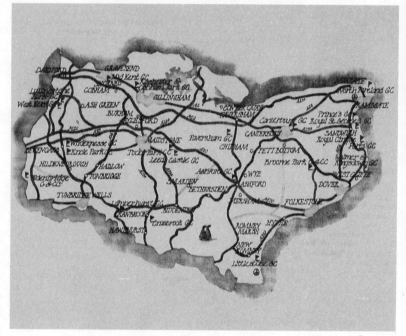

Kent's reputation as one of the country's greatest golfing counties has been built around a three mile stretch of links land lying midway between St Margaret's Bay and Pegwell Bay. Within this short distance lie three Open Championship courses: **Prince's** (1932), **Royal Cinque Ports** (1909 and 1920) and **Royal St George's** (too numerous to list!) Kent has a few other fine links courses but the golfer who sticks hard to the coast will be missing out on some of the most enjoyable inland golf Southern England has to offer.

Golfing Inland

In common with each of the counties that border Greater London many of Kent's courses are gradually finding themselves more in London than in Kent. When the Blackheath golfers left their famous Common and set up base at Eltham they were doubtless surrounded by the green fields of Kent. Even Charles Darwin's village of Orpington is now feeling the pinch but happily the **West Kent** Golf Club and nearby **Lullingstone Park** provide pleasant retreats.

Enough grousing! The ancient town of Sevenoaks is categorically in Kent and a very fortunate place too with **Wildernesse** Golf Club to the north and **Knole Park** to the south. The former is rated one of the finest inland courses in the county; with narrow fairways and quite thickly wooded, it is also one of the toughest. Knole Park is one of several Kentish courses that enjoy stately surroundings, being laid out in the handsome deer park of Lord Sackville. Both Wildernesse and Knole suffered during the great hurricane of October '87 but then so did many courses in southern England.

In the south west of the county, Tunbridge Wells is a very pretty, if congested, old town; **Nevil** Golf Club is nearby and there are 36 holes at the **Edenbridge** Golf and Country Club, but the most exciting of developments are the new **Hever** Golf Club which is located adjacent to the famous castle and the Anglo-Japanese creation **Moatlands** at Brenchley.

To the north of the county, both **Mid Kent's** downland course at Gravesend and **Rochester and Cobham** Park are handy for those travelling along the A2 although neither is outstanding. Further along this road is the attractive town of Faversham and south of the town off the A251 is Belmont Park, the estate of Lord Harris and the home of **Faversham** Golf Club. Here golf is played in the most tranquil of settings and can be particularly delightful in autumn when the fairways abound with countless strolling pheasants.

Leaving Faversham, famous pheasants and all, we must make a pilgrimage. The **Canterbury** Golf Club, situated to the east of the beautiful cathedral city along the A27 is well worth a visit. Surprisingly undulating, it is a first class parkland course—one of the best in the county. South of Canterbury (via A2 and A260) at Barham is the **Broome Park** Golf and Country Club, set in the grounds of yet another famous country house—this time a beautiful 300 year old mansion, the former home of Lord Kitchener. It too is a very pleasant parkland course and quite lengthy.

Maidstone may not have the appeal of Canterbury but to the south east of this busy commuter town is one of England's most attractive golf courses, **Leeds Castle.** The castle itself was described by Lord Conway as the most beautiful in the world and the setting really is quite idyllic. There are nine very individual holes and as it's a public course (like Lullingstone Park, mentioned above, and Cobtree Manor Park on the Chatham Road) there are no general restrictions on times of play although it can get very busy. Another recent golfing addition to the area is **Tudor Park** near Bearsted. Like Broome Park it is part of a Country Club; the golf course was designed by Donald Steel and is especially popular with golfing societies.

The golf course at **Ashford** is pretty much in the middle of the county, and is strongly worth inspecting. Ashford is a heathland

Royal St George's was founded in 1887, rather ironically by two Scottish gentlemen, Dr. Laidlaw Purves and Henry Lamb. Like all good Scotsmen they had been bitten by the bug; however, both were presently living in Victorian London. To them golf was meant to be played on a links by the sea. Hence the pair found themselves at Bournemouth setting off in an easterly direction looking for a suitable site, with patience no doubt wearing thin. Suddenly 'land ahoy!' Doctor Purves sights a vast stretch of duneland at Sandwich. The story is that he 'spied the land with a golfer's eye' from the tower of St Clement's Church. St George's had been located. Within seven short years the Open Championship had 'come south' and St George's was the first English venue.

More than one hundred years on **Gerald Watts** is the **Secretary** at St George's and he can be contacted by telephone on **(0304) 613090**. All written communication should be directed to him. As a general guide visitors are welcome between Mondays and Fridays; gentlemen must possess a handicap of no more than 18 and ladies no more than 15 and introductions are required. There are no ladies tees and other points to note are that the 1st tee is reserved daily for Members until 9.45am and between 1.15pm and 2.15pm; however, the 10th tee is usually free in the early mornings. St George's is essentially a singles and foursomes Club and three ball and four ball matches are only permissible with the agreement of the Secretary.

The green fees for 1993 were set at £50 per round, £70 per day. During the months of December, January and February the £50 fee is applicable for a full day's golf. Should there be a wish to hire golf clubs, a limited supply are for hire through the **professional**, Niall

Cameron, telephone **(0304) 615236**. Finally, the services of a caddie can be booked via the **Caddiemaster** on **(0304) 617380**.

Please excuse the awful pun but finding Sandwich should be a 'piece of cake.' The town is linked to Canterbury to the west by the A257, a distance of approximately 15 miles and to Deal, 6 miles south east of Sandwich by the A258. Motoring from London, the most direct route is to head for Canterbury using a combination of the A2 and M2 and thereafter following the A257 as above. For those coming from the south coast Ashford is the place to head for: Ashford is joined to Canterbury by the A28. Sandwich can also be reached by train.

Having done battle with the elements the golfer will find the Clubhouse welcoming. Excellent lunches are served daily and both breakfasts and dinners can be obtained with prior arrangement. A jacket and tie must be worn in all public rooms.

The Royal St George's Golf Club,
Sandwich,
Kent CT13 9PB.

Hole	Yards	Par	Hole	Yards	Par
1	448	4	10	401	4
2	377	4	11	218	3
3	215	3	12	367	4
4	471	4	13	445	4
5	422	4	14	509	5
6	157	3	15	468	4
7	532	5	16	165	3
8	420	4	17	427	4
9	391	4	18	470	4
Out	3,433	35	In	3,470	35
			Out	3,433	35
			Totals	6,903	70

type course, which in itself is fairly unique to Kent and where visitors are always made to feel welcome.

Cranbrook, a very pleasant and greatly improved parkland course, was the scene of Bing Crosby's last round in England. Apparently he was close to purchasing the course before his untimely death in Spain. .

The final inland course demanding a mention is to be found at Biddenden, the Nick Faldo-Steve Smyers designed course named **Chart Hills** which will be ready for play in late summer 1993, and for which many commentators are predicting great things. Chart Hills is Nick's first venture in golf course architecture.

Around the coast

Switching from the rich countryside of Kent we now visit the coast. **Littlestone** is the first port of call, and the contrast is a stark one. Situated on the edge of the flatlands of Romney Marsh, it enjoys a remote setting. Littlestone is a splendid links and an Open Championship qualifying course, which doesn't deserve to be overshadowed by Kent's more illustrious trio further along the coast. Littlestone's best holes are saved for near the end of the round—the par 4 16th and par 3 17th typify all that's best (and frightening!) about links golf.

North of Sandwich is the **North Foreland** Club at Broadstairs, also an Open qualifying course, although its 27 holes are more strictly clifftop than links in nature. To the south of Deal is **Walmer and Kingsdown**, a downland course providing splendid views.

Perhaps not surprisingly, where there is one great golf links there is often another nearby: Troon, Turnberry and Prestwick in Ayrshire; Birkdale, Hillside and Formby in Lancashire. Kent's famous three, **Royal St George's, Royal Cinque Ports** and **Prince's** are each in its own way deserving of a place in golfing history not to mention a visit.

Ashford G.C.
(0233) 622655
Sandyhurst Lane, Ashford
Off A20, 1/2 mile N.
of Ashford
(18)6246 yards/***/C/H

Austin Lodge G.C.
(0322) 863000
Off A225, nr Eynsford
Station
(18)6600 yards/***/D

Barnehurst G.C
(0322) 523 746
Mayplace Road, East
Barnehurst
(9)5320 yards/***/F

Bearsted G.C
(0622) 38198
Mill Lane, Enderby,
Leicester
Take junction 21 round-
about off M1/M69
(18)6253 yards/**/C/H/L

Broome Park Golf
& Country Club
(0227) 831701
Barham, Canterbury
Leave M2 for A2, turn onto
A260
(18)6610 yards/***/C/H

Canterbury G.C
(0227) 453532
Scotland Hills, Canterbury
1 mile from town centre on
A257
(18)6249 yards/**/C/H

Cherry Lodge G.C
(0959) 72250
Jail Lane, Biggin Hill
Leave Bromley on A233 to
Westerham
(18)6652 yards/**/B

Chestfield G.C
(022 779) 4411
103 Chestfield Road,
Whitstable
Take A229 to roundabout
nr. station, turn S.
(18)6080 yards/**/D

Cobtree Manor G.C
(0622) 53276
Maidstone
Leave M2 or M20 at A229
(18)5701 yards/***/E

Cranbrook G.C.
(0580) 712833
(18) 6351 yards/**/C

Cray Valley G.C
(0689) 831927
Sandy Lane, St. Pauls Cray,
Orpington
Leave A20 at Ruxley roundabout
(18)5624 yards/***/D

Darenth Valley G.C
(09592) 2944
Station Road, Shoreham
Take A225, club is 4 miles N.
of Sevenoaks
(18)6356 yards/***/E

Dartford G.C
(0322) 23616
Dartford Heath
On Dartford Heath, 2 miles
from city centre
(18)5914 yards/**/H/M

Deangate Ridge G.C
(0634) 251180
Hoo, Rochester
Take A228 from Rochester
to Isle of Grain
(18)6300 yards/***/E

Edenbridge Golf & Country
Club
(0732) 865097
Crouch House Road,
Edenbridge
From A25 at Westerham
take B2026
(18)6643 yards/***/D

Faversham G.C
(079589) 251
Belmont Park, Faversham
Leave M2 at junction 6
and take A251
(18)5979 yards/**/C

Gillingham G.C
(0634) 850999
Woodlands Road,
Gillingham
M2 to junction 4, north to
A2
(18)5911 yards/**/D

Hawkhurst G.C
(0580) 752396
High Street, Hawkhurst,
Cranbrook
On A268 2 miles from A21
at Flimwell
(9)5769 yards/**/D

Herne Bay G.C
(0227) 374097
Eddington, Herne Bay
Take A291 Thanet Way
Road to Herne Bay
(18)5466 yards/***/D/H

High Elms G.C
(0689) 58175
High Elms Road, Downe
Take A21 from Bromley,
right on Shire Lane
(18)5626 yards/***/E

Holtye G.C
(0342) 850635
Holtye Common, Cowden,
Edenbridge
On A264 near East
Grinstead
(9)5289 yards/***/D

Hythe Imperial G.C
(0303) 267441
Princes Parade, Hythe
Turn off M20 for Hythe
(9)5511 yards/***/D/H

Knole Park G.C
(0732) 452150
Seal Hollow Road,
Sevenoaks
On N.E of Seven Oaks,
down Seal Hollow
Road
(18)6249 yards/**/B/H

Lamberhurst G.C
(0892) 890241
Church Road, Lamberhurst
Take A21 S. from Tonbridge
towards
Hastings
(18)6277 yards/**/B

Leeds Castle G.C
(0622) 765400
Maidstone
M20 from Maidstone
and onto A20
(9)2910 yards/***/E

Littlestone G.C
(0679) 62310
St. Andrews Road,
Littlestone, New Romney
A20 to Ashford, B2070 to
New Romney
(18)6424 yards/**/F/H

Lullingstone Park G.C
(0959) 34542
Park Gate, Chelsfield,
Orpington
Take A20 to Swanley,
B258 to Park Gate
(18)6674 yards/***/E
(9)2445 yards/***/E

Mid Kent G.C
(0474) 568035
Singlewell Road, Gravesend
Off A2 S. of Gravesend
(18)6206 yards/**/F/H

Nevill G.C
(0892) 25818
Benhall Mill Road,
Tunbridge Wells
1 mile S.E of Tunbridge
Wells
(18)6336 yards/**/B/H

North Foreland G.C
(0843) 62140
Convent Road, Broadstairs
1 mile from Broadstairs station
(18)6382 yards/**/C/H

Poult Wood G.C
(0732) 364039
Higham Lane, Tonbridge
2 miles N. of town centre
off A227
(18)5569 yards/***/E

Princes G.C
(0304) 611118
Sandwich Bay, Sandwich
4 miles from Sandwich
through town centre
(27) (3x9)***/B

Rochester & Cobham Park
G.C
(047 482) 3411
Park Lane, by Rochester
South onto B2009 from A2
(18)6467 yards/**/B/H

Royal Cinque Ports G.C
(0304) 374007
Sandwich
Take A258 from Sandwich
to Upper Deal
(18)6744 yards/**/A/H

Royal St Georges G.C.
(0304) 613090
Sandwich Bay Rd, Sandwich
(18)6857 yards/**/A/H

Ruxley G.C.
(0689) 871490
Sandy Lane, St Pauls Cray,
Orpington
(18)4885 yards/***/E

St Augustines G.C.
(0843) 590333
Cottingham Road, Cliffsend,
Ramsgate
2 miles S W of Ramsgate
(18)5138 yards/***/C/H

Sene Valley G.C.
(0303) 68513
Sene, Folkestone
A20 from Folkestone
(18)6320 yards/***/C

Sheerness G.C
(0795) 662585
Power Station Rd, Sheerness
A249 then A250 towards
Seerness
(18)6500 yards/**/D/H

Sittingbourne & Milton
Regis G.C.
(0795) 842261
Wormdale, Newington,
Sittingbourne
Leave M2, exit 5 for A249
(18)6121 yards/**/D/H/L

Tenterden G.C.
(05806) 3987
Woodchurch Rd, Tenterden
1 mile E of Tenterden on
B2067
(18)6030 yards/**/D

Tudor Park G.& C.C.
(0622) 34334
Ashford Rd, Bearsted
Leave M20 at junction 8 for
A20
(18)6000 yards/**/B/H

Tunbridge Wells G.C.
(0892) 523034
Langton Rd, Tunbridge
Wells
Adjacent to Spa Hotel
(9)4684 yards/**/B/H

Upchurch River Valley
(0634) 360626
Upchurch, Sittingbourne
(18)6160 yards/***/E

Walmer & Kingsdown G.C.
(0304) 373256
The Leas, Kingsdown, Deal
Off A258, S of Deal
(18)6465 yards/***/C

Westgate & Birchungton
G.C.
(0843) 31115
Domneva Rd, Westgate On
Sea
A28 near Birchington
(18)4926 yards/***/D/L

West Kent G.C.
(0689) 853737
West Hill, Downe,
Orpington
A21 to Orpington and
Downe vill.
(18)6392 yards/**/C/H/L

West Malling G.C.
(0732) 844785
London Rd, Addington,
Maidstone
Take A20 from London to
Maidstone
(18)6142 yards/**/C
(18)6011 yards/**/C

Whitstable & Seasalter G.C
(0227) 272020
Collingwood Road,
Whitstable
Leave A299 for Thanet Way
at Borstal Hill
(9)5276 yards/**/D

Wildernesse G.C
(0732) 61526
Seal, Sevenoaks
Take A25 from Sevenoaks
towards
Maidstone
6478 yards/**/B/H/L

Woodlands Manor G.C
(09592) 3805
Tinkerpot Lane, Sevenoaks
Leave M25 at junction 3 and
take A20
(18)5858 yards/***/D/H

Wrotham Heath
(0732) 884800
Seven Mile Lane, Comp,
Sevenoaks
On B2016, S. of junction with
A20
(9) 5959 yards/**/C/H

Capital Golf

Records suggest that golf was first played in England in 1608; the venue was Blackheath in London but the participants were Scottish not English. James I (James VI of Scotland) and his courtiers are generally credited with bringing the game south of the border. The exact date that the English caught the bug is unclear, certainly in the 18th Century it was still pretty much an alien pastime—in his first English dictionary compiled in 1755 Dr Samuel Johnson described golf as, 'a game played with a ball and a club or bat'.

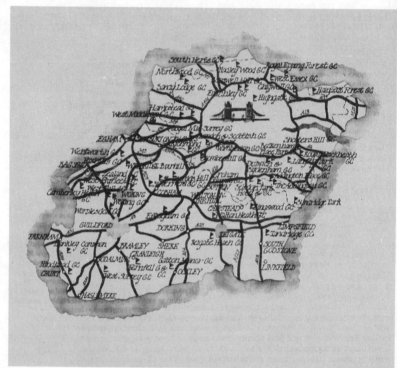

During its formative years golf in London was largely confined to the public commons such as those at Blackheath, Clapham, Chingford and Tooting Bec, the golfers having to share their rather crudely laid-out courses with 'nurse-maids, dogs, horses and stubborn old ladies and gentlemen'.

Not surprisingly when the first Golf Clubs started to form the tendency was to retreat from the public stage. The **Royal Blackheath** Golf Club, fittingly enough the first English Club to be founded (it dates from 1787)

eventually moved from the Heath and now plays on a private course at Eltham. Golf is no longer played (or at least shouldn't be!) on the commons at Clapham and Tooting Bec. However, golf does survive on those at **Wimbledon** and Chingford, the latter being the home of **Royal Epping Forest** and where golfers are still required to wear red clothing in order that they can be distinguished from other users of the common.

The majority of London Clubs are for obvious reasons set in deepest suburbia and with many it is often far from clear as to whether they fall within Greater London or not. In anyone's book **Muswell Hill** is in London, which for present purposes is just as well because it's an excellent course. Measuring close to 6,500 yards, and quite undulating, it represents a fairly stiff test from the back tees. Other good 18-hole courses to the north of London include **Finchley** (with its elegant Victorian clubhouse), **Mill Hill** (which has something of a heathland feel to it) and **Highgate** (which is particularly pretty), while **Hampstead** has an enjoyable 9 holes.

A cluster of fine courses lie a little further to the north west of the capital. Near neighbours of one another are **Northwood** and **Sandy Lodge**. The latter could be said to be Sandy by name, sandy by nature—a heathland course but it can play more like a golf links at times. Anyway, it's certainly an exceptionally fine course and hosts many top class events. Northwood is in parts parkland, in parts heathland with a very good back nine. A mention also for **West Middlesex**, one of West London's better parkland courses.

The other side of the M1 one finds **South Herts** and **Hadley Wood**. South Herts is somewhat tucked away in Totteridge but well worth finding. The Club can boast having both Harry Vardon and Dai Rees among its past professionals. Hadley Wood, near Barnet is a very beautiful course designed by Alister Mackenzie, with lovely tree-lined fairways. The Clubhouse is very elegant too. Over towards Essex, Royal Epping Forest has been mentioned; also within Epping Forest itself, **West Essex** is a fine parkland course and there are two first rate public courses at **Hainault Forest**.

Those looking for a game in south west London might consider looking in the Wimbledon area where there are several courses. **Royal Wimbledon** is just about the best in London but golfers may find it easier to arrange a game (during the week at any rate) on the nearby course at Wimbledon Common, home of the **London Scottish** Club, located two miles from Wimbledon railway station. **Coombe Hill** is another of the capital's most prestigious clubs—its well manicured fairways are just about visible from Royal Wimbledon. A little further out at Richmond, games can be enjoyed at **Royal Mid Surrey** (two courses here, an Outer and an Inner) and at **Richmond** Golf Club with its superb Georgian Clubhouse; there is also a public course at Richmond. Due West of London, **Ealing** offers a reasonable test and there are again a number of public courses in the vicinity.

South of London the Croydon area is yet another that is thick with Clubs. Althought difficult to arrange a game on, **Addington** is generally considered the best, a lovely heathland course covered in heather, pines and silver birch and has in the par 3, 13th one of golf's toughest and most beautiful short holes. **Addington Palace** is also well thought of, as indeed is **Croham Hurst**. To make up a four, especially if one requires a base, **Selsdon Park** must be the selection; a pleasant parkland course set around the Selsdon escarpment. Seldson Park is very popular with societies. Not far from Croydon, the course at **Coulsdon Court** has a welcoming reputation and an extraordinary selection of trees.Two of the better courses towards the south east of London are **Langley Park** (at Beckenham)—heavily wooded with a particularly good series of holes towards the end of the round including an attractive par 3 finishing hole featuring a fountain and small lake, and **Sundridge Park** where indeed there are two good courses, an East and West.

Elsewhere in the south east there is a popular public course at **Beckenham Place Park** (very cheap green fees) and there are interesting layouts at **Shooters Hill** and **Dulwich** and **Sydenham**, but the final mention goes to **Royal Blackheath**. The Club has a great sense of history and the course is full of character. Early in the round one may confront the famous Hamlet Cigar bunker' while its 18th isn't so much difficult as unusual, requiring a pitch over a hedge to the green. In some ways it's unfortunate that the Club ever had to leave its famous common—Blackheath village is quite charming—but then the author of this tome may just be a little biased!

Surrey

When Providence distributed land best suited for building golf courses it wasn't done in the most democratic of spirits. Take for instance the quite ridiculous amount of majestic links land to be found along the coast of Lancashire—its enough to make every good Yorkshireman weep. And then there's Surrey, blessed with acre upon acre of perfect inland golfing terrain—what a contrast to poor Essex!

Though very different in appearance, it is probably safe to suggest that **Walton Heath** and **Wentworth** are the county's two leading courses. (Sunningdale—at least according to the postman—being just over the border in Berkshire). But Walton and Wentworth are only two of Surrey's famous 'W Club'—there's also **Worplesdon** and **Woking, West Hill, West Surrey, West Byfleet** and to this list we can now add **Wisley** and **Wildwood**—two of the country's newest and most exclusive developments.

Located off the A32 to the west of Woking, Worplesdon, West Hill and Woking Golf Clubs lie practically next door to one another. Indeed it might be possible to devise a few dramatic cross—course holes—though in view of the value of some of the adjacent properties that would have to be driven over it's perhaps not such a good idea! West Hill is generally considered the most difficult of the three, the fairways at times being frighteningly narrow; Worplesdon with its superb greens is probably the most widely known (largely due to its famous annual foursomes event), while Woking, founded a century ago, perhaps possesses the greatest charm. Whatever their particular merits, all three are magnificent examples of the natural heathland and heather type course.

Marginally closer to the capital and still very much in the heart of stock-broker-belt country is a second outstanding trio of courses centred around Weybridge: **St George's Hill, New Zealand** and **West Byfleet**. Once again, these are heathland type courses where golf is played amidst heavily wooded surroundings, the combination of pines, silver birch, purple heather and, at New Zealand especially, a magnificent spread of rhododendrons, making for particularly attractive settings. St George's Hill is in fact one of the more undulating courses in Surrey and calls for several spectacular shots—indeed, many people rate it on a par with Wentworth and Walton Heath. No inland course in England however, I would suggest, has a better sequence of finishing holes than those at New Zealand, the 14th, 15th and 16th being especially memorable.

Golf in Surrey isn't of course all heathland and heather. **Tandridge** is one of the best downland courses in Southern England while just a short drive from Weybridge is the delightful parkland course at **Burhill**, situated some two miles south of Walton-on-Thames. Burhill's Clubhouse is a particularly grand affair—at one time it was the home of the Dowager Duchess of Wellington. Much less grand but to some of equal interest, is the Dick Turpin cottage sited on the course and reputed to have been used by the infamous highwayman. Also worth noting is a nearby public course, **Silvermere**, located midway between Byfleet and Cobham where it may be easier to arrange a game—at least in theory, as it does get very busy—and where green fees are naturally lower.

Generally speaking golf in the Home Counties and golf in America have precious little in common. However, the **Foxhills** Club at Ottershaw (off the A320) can make a genuine claim to have married the two successfully. A Jacobean-styled manor house run on American country club lines including an outstanding range of leisure facilities, it has two Championship length heathland type courses. Not surprisingly, Foxhills is a very popular haunt for golfing societies. Another fairly newish set up in this area is the highly recommended **Fernfell** Golf and Country Club at Cranleigh just south of Guildford.

The country club scene may not of course appeal to all types and excellent golf, in an extremely sedate atmosphere, can be enjoyed at **Gatton Manor** situated in Ockley near Dorking. The course has a very scenic layout running through woods and alongside lakes.

Heading towards Walton Heath, if a game cannot be arranged over one of its famous courses then there is golf of a similarly (if less challenging nature) at **Reigate Heath** and not too far away, at **Kingswood**, there is a fine parkland course.

The rich heathland seam runs the breadth of the county and over to the west, practically straddling the three counties of Surrey, Berkshire and Hampshire, lies the superb **Camberley Heath** course, (there is also a first rate public course in Camberley, **Pine Ridge**, which opened in 1992) while down in the south-west corner there is yet another outstanding trio of clubs: **Hindhead**, **West Surrey** and **Hankley Common**.

Hankley Common was for many years a favourite of the late South African Bobby Locke, four times Open Champion, who once owned a house adjacent to the course. Hankley Common is widely known for its spectacular 18th hole—one of the greatest closing holes in golf. A vast gulley which seems to possess magnetic powers looms in front of the green—nine out of ten first timers fail to reach the putting surface.

Greater London
(including Middlesex)

Arkley G.C.
(081) 4490394
Rowley Green Rd. Barnet
2 miles from Barnet.
(9)6045 yards/**/C/H

Ashford Manor G.C.
(0784) 252049
Fordbridge Rd. Ashford
2 miles east of Staines.
(18)6343 yards/***/B/H/M

Beckenham Place Park G.C.
(081) 6502292
Beckenham Hill Rd.
Beckenham
1 mile from Catford.
(18)5722 yards/***/E

Bexley Heath G.C.
(081) 3036951
Mount Row, Mount Rd.
Bexley Heath
(9)5239 yards/**/D

Brent Valley G.C.
(081) 5671287
Church Rd. Cuckoo Lane,
Hanwell
(18)5426 yards/***/E

Bushey G. and C.C.
(081) 9502283
High Street, Bushey
On the A411.
(9)3000 yards/***(Wed)/D

Bush Hill Park G.C.
(081) 3605738
Bush Hill, Winchmore Hill
(18)5809 yards/**/C

Chigwell GC.
(081) 5002059
High Rd. Chigwell
(18)6279 yards/**/A/H

Chingford G.C.
(081) 5292107
158 Station Rd. Chingford
(18)6336 yards/***/E

Chislehurst G.C.
(081) 4672782
Camden Park Rd.
Chislehurst
(18)5128 yards/**/C/H

Crews Hill G.C.
(081) 3636674
Cattlegate Rd. Crews Hill,
Enfield
(18)6230 yards/**/F/H/M

Dulwich and Sydenham Hill
G.C.
(081) 6933961
Grange Lane, College Rd.
(18)6051 yards/**/D/H(22)

Dyrham Park G.C.
(081) 4403361
Galley Lane, Barnet
2 miles from Barnet off A1.
(18)6369 yards/*/C/G

Ealing G.C.
(081) 9970937
Perivale Lane, Greenford
(18)6216 yards/**/B/H

Elstree G.C.
(081) 9536115
Watling Street, Elstree
1 mile north of Elstree on
A5183.
(18)6100 yards/***/B

Eltham Warren G.C.
(081) 8501166
Bexley Rd. Eltham
(9)5840 yards/**/B/H/M

Enfield G.C.
(081) 3633970
Old Park Road South,
Enfield
1 mile north east of Enfield.
(18)6137 yards/**/B/H/M

Finchley G.C.
(081) 3462436
Nether Court, Frith Lane,
Mill Hill
(18)6411 yards/***/A

Fulwell G.C.
(081) 9772733
Wellington Rd. Hampton
Hill
2 miles south of
Twickenham on A311.
(18)6490 yards/**/A/H

Grims Dyke G.C.
(081) 4284539
Oxhey Lane, Hatch End,
Pinner
2 miles west of Harrow on
A4008.
(18)5598 yards/**/B/H

Hadley Wood G.C.
(081) 4494486
Beech Hill, Barnet
(18)6473 yards/**/A/H/M

Hainault Forest G.C.
(081) 5002097
Chigwell Row, Hainault
(18)5754 yards/***/E
(18)6600 yards/***/E

Hampstead G.C.
(081) 4557089
Winnington Rd. Hampstead
(9)5821 yards/**/C/H

Harefield Place G.C.
(0895) 231169
The Drive, Harefield Place,
Uxbridge
2 miles north of Uxbridge
off A40.
(18)5753 yards/***/D/L

Hartsbourne G. and C.C.
(081) 9501133
Hartsbourne Ave. Bushey
Heath
(18)6305 yards/*/F/G
(9)5432 yards/*/F/G

Haste Hill G.C.
(09274) 22877
The Drive, Northwood
On A404.
(18)5753 yards/***/E

Hendon G.C.
(081) 3466023
Devonshire Rd, Mill Hill,
NW7
(18)6241 yards/***/B/M

Highgate G.C.
(081) 3403745
Denewood Rd. Highgate
(18)5982 yards/**(Wed)/B/H

Hillingdon G.C.
(0895) 33956
18 Dorset Way, Hillingdon
(9)5459
yards/**(Thu)/C/H/M

Home Park G.C.
(081) 9772423
Hampton Wick, Richmond-
upon-Thames
(18)6519 yards/***/C

Horsendon Hill G.C.
(081) 9024555
Woodland Rise, Greenford
(9)3236 yards/***/E

Hounslow Heath G.C.
(081) 5705271
Staines Rd. Hounslow
Adjacent to Hounslow
Heath.
(18)5820 yards/***/E

Ilford G.C.
(081) 5542930
291 Wanstead Park Rd.
Ilford
(18)5414 yards/***/D

Langley Park G.C
(081) 650 2090
Beckenham
(18) 6488 yards/**/A

London Scottish G.C.
(081)7897517
Windmill Enclosure,
Wimbledon Common
2 miles from Wimbledon
next to the windmill.
(18)5436 yards/**/D/H

Mill Hill G.C.
(081) 9592339
100 Barnet Way, Mill Hill
1 mile south of Stirling
Corner.
(18)6286 yards/***/A

Muswell Hill G.C.
(081) 8881764
Rhodes Ave. Wood Green
(18)6474 yards/**/B/H(24)

North Middlesex G.C.
(081) 4451604
Friern Barnet Lane,
Whetstone
5 miles north of Finchley on
A1000
(18)5611 yards/***/B

Northwood G.C.
(0923) 825329
Rickmansworth Rd.
Northwood
Between Rickmansworth
and North Hills on A404
(18)6493 yards/**/C/H

Old Fold Manor G.C.
(081) 4409185
Hadley Green, Barnet
Just outside Barnet on
Potters Bar Rd.
(18)6449 yards/**/B

Perivale Park G.C.
(081) 5758655
Ruislip Road East. Greenford
Between Greenford and
Perivale on Ruislip Rd. East
(9)2667 yards/***/E

Pinner Hill G.C.
(081) 8660963
South View Rd. Pinner Hill
1 mile west of Pinner Green.
(18)6293 yards/**(Wed,
Thurs)/F

Roehampton G.C.
(081) 8765505
Roehampton Lane SW15
(18)6011 yards/**/C/G

Royal Blackheath G.C.
(081) 8501795
Court Rd. Eltham SE9
(18)6214 yards/**/B/H

Royal Epping Forest G.C.
(081) 5292195
Forest Approach Chingford
E4
Just south of Chingford station.
(18)6620 yards/***/D/H

Royal Wimbledon G.C.
(081) 9462125
29 Camp Rd. Wimbledon
SW19
1 mile west of
Wimbledon village.
(18)6300 yards/**/A/H(18)/L

Ruislip G.C.
(0895) 632004
Ickenham Rd. Ruislip
(18)5500 yards/***/D

Shooters Hill G.C.
(081) 8546368
Eaglesfield Rd, SE18
1 mile from Welling.
(18)5718 yards/**/B/H/M

Shortlands G.C.
(081) 4602471
Meadow Rd. Shortlands,
Bromley
(9)5261 yards/*/D/G

Sidcup G.C.
(081) 3002150
7 Hurst Rd. Sidcup
Half a mile past Sidcup station.
(9)5692 yards/***/D/H

South Herts G.C.
(081) 4452035
Links Drive, Totteridge N20
(18)6432 yards/**/F/H

Stanmore G.C.
(081) 9542599
Gordon Ave. Stanmore
(18)5881 yards/**/D/H

Strawberry Hill G.C.
(081) 8940165
Wellesley Rd. Twickenham
Next to Strawberry Hill station.
(9)2381 yards/**/D

Sudbury G.C.
(081) 9023713
Bridgewater Rd. Wembley
(18)6282 yards/***/B/H/M

Sundridge Park G.C.
(081) 460278
Garden Rd. Bromley
1 mile from Bromley on
A2212.
(18)6410 yards/**/A/H
(18)6028 yards/**/A/H

Trent Park G.C.
(081) 3667432
Bramley Rd. Southgate N14
Opposite Oakwood tube.
(18)6008 yards/***/E

Twickenham G.C.
(081) 7831698
Staines Rd. Twickenham
Situated on A305.
(9)6014 yards/***/E

Wanstead G.C.
(081) 9893938
Overton Drive, Wanstead
(18)6211
yards/**(Wed,Thu)/B/H

West Middlesex G.C.
(081) 5743450
Greenford Rd. Southall
2 miles from Greenford.
(18)6242 yards/**/D

Whitewebbs G.C.
(081) 3634454
Beggars Hollow, Clay Hill,
Enfield
1 mile north of Enfield.
(18)5881 yards/***/F

Wimbledon Common G.C.
(081) 9467571
Camp Rd. Wimbledon
Common SW19
1 mile north west of
Wimbledon village.
(18)5486 yards/**/D

Wimbledon Park G.C.
(081) 9461250
Home Park Rd, Wimbledon
SW19
(18)5465 yards/***/B/H/L/M

Wyke Green G.C.
(081) 5608777
Syon Lane Isleworth
Just north of Gillette corner.
(18)6242 yards/***/A/H

Surrey

Addington G.C.
(081) 7771055
Shirley Church Rd, Croydon
(18)6242 yards/**/F

Addington Court G.C.
(081) 657 0281
Featherbed Lane, Addington
2 miles east of Croydon.
(18)5577 yards/***/D
(18)5513 yards/***/F

Addington Palace G.C.
(081) 6543061
Gravel Hill, Addington
Park,Croydon
2 miles from East Croydon
on A12.
(18)6282 yards/**/B

Barrow Hills G.C.
(0932) 848117
Longcross, Chertsey
4 miles west of Chertsey.
(18)3090 yards/*/F

Betchworth Park G.C.
(0306) 882052
Reigate Rd. Dorking
(18)6266
yards/**(Tue,Wed)/A

Bramley G.C.
(0483) 893042
Bramley, Guildford
4 miles south of Guildford
on A281.

(18)5910 yards/**/B/HBurhill
G.C.
(0932) 227345
Walton-on-Thames
(18)6224 yards/**/A/H/L

Camberley Heath G.C.
(0276) 23258
Golf Drive, Camberley
1 mile south of Camberley.
(18)6402 yards/**/C/H

Chipstead G.C.
(0737) 551053
How Lane, Coulsdon
Situated next to Chipstead
station.
(18)5454 yards/**/B

Coombe Hill G.C.
(081) 9422284
Kingston Hill.
(18)6286 yards/***/A

Combe Wood G.C.
(081) 9423828
George Rd. Kingston Hill
1 mile north of Kingston-on-
Thames.
(18)5210 yards/**/F/H
(9)1655 yards/***/E

Coulsdon Court G.C.
(081) 6600468
Coulsdon Rd. Coulsdon
2 miles south of Croydon.
(18)6030 yards/***/D

Crondall G.C.
(0252) 850880
Oak Park, Hoalte Lane,
Crondall, West Farnham
(18)6278 yards/***/C

Croham Hurst G.C.
(081) 6575581
Croham Rd. South Croydon
(18)6274 yards/**/C

Cuddington G.C.
(081) 3930952
Banstead Rd. Banstead
Next to Banstead station.
(18)6282 yards/**/A/H/L

Dorking G.C.
(0306) 889786
Chart Park, Dorking
1 mile south of Dorking on
A24.
(9)5210 yards/**/D

Drift G.C.
(04865) 4641
The Drift, East Horsley
(18)6404 yards/**/C

Effingham G.C.
(0372) 452203
Guildford Rd. Effingham
4 miles from Leatherhead.
(18)6488 yards/**/B/H

Epsom G.C.
(03727) 21666
Longdown Lane, Epsom
Just north of Epsom Downs
station.
(18)5668 yards/**/D

Farnham G.C.
(02518) 2109
The Sands, Farnham
1 mile east of Farnham off
A31.
(18)6313 yards/**/B

Farnham Park G.C.
(0252) 715216
Folly Hill, Farnham
1 mile north of Farnham.
(9)1161 yards/***/E

Fernfell G.C.
(0483) 268855
Barhatch Lane, Cranleigh
1 mile from Cranleigh off
A281.
(18)5561 yards/***/D

Foxhills G.C.
(093287) 2050
Stonehill Rd. Ottershaw
Behind St. Peters Hospital
(18)6880 yards/**/A
(18)6747 yards/**/A

Gatton Manor G.C.
(030679) 555
Ockley, Dorking
2 miles south west of
Ockley off A29.
(18)6902 yards/***/D

Goal Farm G.C.
(04867) 3183
Pirbright.
Between Woking and
Guildford on A322.
(9)1283 yards/***/E

Guildford G.C.
(0483) 575243
High Path Rd. Merrow,
Guildford
(18)6080 yards/**/C

Hankley Common G.C.
(025125) 2493
Tilford Rd. Tilford, Farnham
(18)6403 yards/**/B/H

Hindhead G.C.
(0428) 604614
Churt Rd. Hindhead
2 miles north of Hindhead
on A287.
(18)6349 yards/***/A

Hoebridge G.C.
(0483) 722611
Old Woking Rd. Old
Woking
Between Old Woking and
West Byfleet on B382.
(18)6536 yards/***/D
(18)2230 yards/***/E
(9)2900 yards/***/E

Kingswood G.C.
(0737) 832188
Sandy Lane, Kingswood
4 miles south of Sutton.
(18)6821 yards/***/B/H

Laleham G.C.
(0932) 564211
Laleham Reach, Chertsey
(18)6203 yards/**/C

Leatherhead G.C.
(037284) 3966
Kingston Rd. Leatherhead
(18)6088 yards/***/A
Leatherhead Golf Centre
(0372) 843453
Oaklawn Road, Leatherhead
(9)1752 yards/***/E

Limpsfield Chart G.C.
(0883) 723405
Limpsfield, Oxted
Between Oxted and
Westerham on A25.
(9)5718 yards/**(Thu)/F

Lingfield Park G.C.
(0342) 834602
M25 junction 6, beside racecourse
(18) 6500 yards/B

Malden G.C.
(081) 9420654
Traps Lane, New Malden
1 mile from New Malden
centre.
(18)6201 yards/**/B

Mitcham G.C.
(081) 6481508
Carshalton Rd. Mitcham
Junction
Next to Mitcham Junction
station.
(18)5935 yards/**/D/H(18)

Moore Place G.C.
(0372) 463533
Portsmouth Rd. Esher
1 mile from Esher on A3.
(9)3512 yards/***/E

New Zealand G.C.
(09323) 45049
Woodham Lane, Woodham,
Weybridge
(18)6012 yards/**/A

North Downs G.C.
(0883) 653298
Northdown Rd.
Woldingham, Caterham
(18)5787 yards/**/F/H

Oak Park G.C.
(0252) 850880
Crondall, nr Farnham
(18)6437 yards/***/D

Oak Sports Centre
(081) 643 8363
Woodmansterne Rd.
Carshalton
1 mile south of Carshalton
Beeches station on B2032.
(18)5975 yards/***/D
(9)1590 yards/***/E

Purley Downs G.C.
(081) 6578347
106 Purley Downs Rd.
Purley
(18)6243 yards/**/B/H/M/L

Puttenham G.C.
(0483) 810498
Heath Rd. Puttenham,
Guildford
4 miles west of Guildford
on A31.
(18)5367/**/B/H

R.A.C. Country Club
(03722) 763111
Woodcote Park, Epsom
1 mile from Epsom station.
(18)6702 yards/*/F/G
(18)5474 yards/*/F/G

Redhill and Reigate G.C.
(0737) 244626
Clarence Lodge,
Pendleton Rd. Redhill
(18)5238 yards/***/D

Reigate Heath G.C.
(0737) 242610
Reigate Heath, Reigate
(9)5554 yards/**/F

Richmond G.C.
(081) 9404351
Sudbrook Park, Richmond
(18)5965 yards/**/A

Richmond Park G.C.
(081) 876 3205
Roehampton Gate,
Richmond Park
(18)5940 yards/***/E
(18)5969 yards/***/E

Royal Mid Surrey G.C.
(081) 9401894
Old Deer Park, Richmond
(18)5544 yards/***/A/G/L
(18)6052 yards/***/A/G/L

St. Georges Hill G.C.
(0932) 842406
St. Georges Hill, Weybridge
(18)6492 yards/**/A/H

Sandown Park G.C.
(0372) 63340
Moor Lane, Esher
Situated in Sandown Park
racecourse.
(9)5656 yards/***/E
(9)1193 yards/***/E

Selsdon Park Hotel G.C.
(081) 6578811
Sanderstead, South Croydon
3 miles south of Croydon on
A2022.
(18)6402 yards/***/B

Shillingee Park G.C.
(0428) 653237
Chiddingford, Godalming
(9)2500 yards/***/D

Shirley Park G.C.
(081) 6541143
194 Addiscombe Rd.
Croydon
2 miles from East Croydon.
(18)6210 yards/**/B/H

Silvermere G.C.
(0932) 867275
Redhill Rd. Cobham
(18)6333 yards/***/D

Surbiton G.C.
(081) 3983101
Woodstock Lane,
Chessington
2 miles east of Esher off A3.
(18)6211 yards/***/A/H

Tandridge G.C.
(0883) 712273
Oxted
(18)6250 yards/**(Tue,Fri)/B

Thames Ditton and Esher
G.C.
(081) 3981551
Portsmouth Rd. Esher
Off A3 close to Sandown
racecourse.

(9)5606 yards/***/D

Tyrrells Wood G.C.
(0372) 376025
Tyrrells Wood, Leatherhead
(18)6219 yards/***/A/H

Walton Heath G.C.
(0737) 812060
Tadworth
(18)6813 yards/**/A/H/L
(18)6659 yards/**/A/H/L

Wentworth G.C.
(09904) 2201
Virginia Water
Just off the A30 near the
A329 junction.
(18)6945 yards/**/A/H
(18)6176 yards/**/A/H
(18)7000 yards/**/A/H

West Byfleet G.C.
(09323) 45230
Sheerwater Rd. West Byfleet
1 mile west of West Byfleet
on A245
(18)6211 yards/**/B

West Hill G.C.
(04867) 4365
Bagshot Rd. Brookwood
On A322 between Guildford
and Bagshot.
(18)6368 yards/**/B/H

West Surrey G.C.
(0483) 421275
Enton Green, Godalming
(18)6247 yards/**/B/H

Windlemere G.C.
(0276) 858727
Windlesham Rd. West End,
Woking Opposite Gordon
Boys School entrance.
(9)5346 yards/***/D

Wisley G.C.
(0483) 211022
1 mile from M25 junction 10
27 (3x9)/*/

Woking G.C.
(0483) 760053
Pond Rd, Hook Heath,
Woking
(18)6322 yards/**/B/H/M

Woodcote Park G.C.
(081) 6682788
Meadow Hill, Bridle Way,
Coulsdon
(18)6624 yards/**/B/H

Worplesdon G.C.
(0483) 489876
Heath House Rd. Woking
4 miles from Guildford.
(18)6422 yards/**/A/H/L

Herts, Beds & Essex

Unfortunately, for all too many the first and often lasting impression of a place can be determined by the great blue ribbons that now stretch the length and breadth of the country—Britain's ever expanding motorway network. The M1 (not to mention the M25) cuts through the heart of Hertfordshire and slices off the left ear of Bedfordshire. Between London and Luton it is a fearsome animal at the best of times and passing beyond these two counties one often draws a sigh of relief. The greater expanse of Essex fares a little better, escaping with a few nasty scratches, but in all three counties, the deeper realms are not as often explored as they might be, except needless to say by those who live there.

The golfing breed is a little more fortunate than most. In every county in Britain he, and she, can visit golf courses that are tucked away in the most secluded and tranquil of settings and even in the, 'there's an open space—lets build on it, 90s' Hertfordshire, Bedfordshire and Essex are not exceptions to the rule.

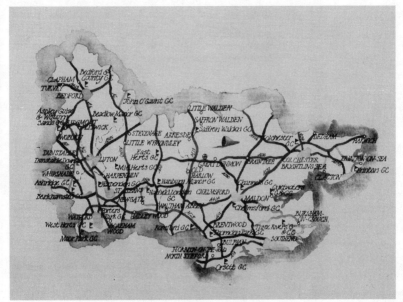

Hertfordshire

A glance at the map tells you that **Ashridge** in Hertfordshire isn't all that great a distance from London and the M1 but it occupies a particularly peaceful spot and the approach road which runs near

Berkhamsted Golf Club passes through some glorious countryside—the kind that once covered much of this part of the world. Both are delightful heathland/parkland courses. Berkhamsted is best known for its conspicuous absence of bunkers, though like Royal Ashdown Forest in Sussex has more than enough natural hazards to test the courage of any golfer, while Ashridge is perhaps most famed for its long association with Henry Cotton, for many years the Club's professional. There are many fine par fours at Ashridge, the 9th and 14th being two of the best; the approach to the latter bears an uncanny resemblance to the 17th at St. Andrews—the mischieviously positioned bunker front left and the road behind the green—though it's not quite as frightening! Both courses are decidedly worth a visit.

There is certainly no shortage of golf courses in Hertfordshire. In the upper realms of the county, Harpenden, convenient for those motoring along the M1, has two courses, **Harpenden** and **Harpenden Common**, the former at Hammonds End being perhaps the pick of the two. A short distance away at Wheathampstead is the **Mid Herts** Golf Club, while on the other side of the country's most famous blue ribbon lies **East Herts** near Buntingford, which is also worth noting if travelling along the A10. In the far north of the county a 45 hole development is taking shape at Malton near Royston and right in the heart of Hertfordshire stands the exclusive and very impressive new **Brocket Hall** Golf Club near Welwyn. The greater concentration of courses, however, perhaps not surprisingly, is in the area just north of London. **Moor Park** is the most widely known though nearby **Porters Park** (in the quiet of Radlett) and **West Herts** (on the edge of Watford, yet similarly peaceful) also strongly merit attention.

West Herts was once more commonly known as Cassiobury Park after its location. Bernard Darwin in his famous 'Golf Courses of the British Isles' sang its praises highly; 'Of all the race of park courses, it would scarcely be possible in point of sheer beauty, to beat Cassiobury Park near Watford.' One other course to note in Hertfordshire is the first class public course at Essendon, confusingly called **The Hatfield London Country Club.**

In Thundridge, near Ware, **Hanbury Manor** is a very fine Country House Hotel which can boast, among many things, a golf course first laid by Harry Vardon in the 1920s and recently completely redesigned by Jack Nicklaus Jnr, while **Hadley Wood** boasts a well established 18 hole course.

Bedfordshire

Arguably the two leading Clubs in Bedfordshire are **John O'Gaunt** at Sandy and **Beadlow Manor** near Shefford: both have more than one course. The former is more established, its two courses, the Championship John O'Gaunt course and the shorter Carthegena are curiously very different in character, the John O'Gaunt being a very pretty parkland type, the Carthegena, a heathland course.

Another of the better courses in Bedfordshire is **Dunstable Downs,** laid out on high ground, offering remarkably extensive views—both

Surrey to the south and Warwickshire to the north west can be sighted. It is a classic downland type course.

Elsewhere in the county, **Aspley Guise and Woburn Sands** (the more famous Woburn Golf and Country Club lies over the border in Buckinghamshire), is another that provides far reaching views and a word also for the **Bedford and County** Golf Club, just north of the county town off the A6, and near St Neots in Cambridgeshire. Just within Bedfordshire, **Wyboston Lakes** is a pleasant pay and play course.

Essex

Not much of Essex could be described as 'natural golfing country' yet of all England's counties this is the one witnessing perhaps the biggest explosion in golf course site applications. Strange, isn't it? Two of the top courses in the county are **Thorndon Park** (2 miles South of Brentford) and **Orsett** (2 miles East of Grays and in the wonderfully named area of Mucking and Fobbing). Neither is a great distance from the M25 and both can be reached via the A128. Thorndon Park, as its name suggests, is a parkland type course situated in a former deer park belonging to Thorndon Hall—a quite stunning mansion, whereas Orsett is much more of the heathland variety with sandy subsoil.

In a similar vein to neighbouring Hertfordshire, a number of the county's better courses are being gradually swallowed up by Greater London—the fine parkland course at **Abridge** with its splendidly luxurious Clubhouse being one of them, now lying the wrong side of the M25 (as does the famous course at **Epping Forest.**) **Romford** is one that holds its Essex identity. A well bunkered and fairly flat course, Romford was the home of James Braid before he moved to Walton Heath.

Further afield, both **Colchester** (the oldest town in England) and **Saffron Walden** have courses set in very pretty surroundings and for lovers of seaside golf there is a pleasant (though windy!) course at **Frinton-on-Sea.** One of the county's newest attractions is the beautifully named **Quietwaters Club** at Tolleshunt D'Arcy, not far from Maldon where there are 36 holes. Finally, for those visiting **Chelmsford,** both the Chelmsford Golf Club, to the south of the town and the **Channels** Golf Club to the north with its superb Elizabethan Clubhouse can be recommended, as can the nearby **Warren** Golf Club at Woodham Walter and **The Three Rivers** Golf and Country Club in Purleigh (two courses here).

Hertfordshire

Aldenham G. and C.C.
(0923) 853929
Radlett Rd. Aldenham,
Watford
(18)6344 yards/***/B

Ashridge G.C.
(044284) 2244
Little Gaddesden,
Berkhamstead
North of Northchurch on
B4506.
(18)6508 yards/***/A

Batchwood Hall G.C.
(0727) 52101
Batchwood Drive, St. Albans
North West St. Albans.
(18)6463 yards/***/E

Berkhamstead G.C.
(0442) 863730
The Common,
Berkhamstead
(18)6568 yards/***/A/H/M

Bishops Stortford G.C.
(0279) 654027
Dunmow Rd. Bishops
Stortford
Just to the east of Bishops
Stortford.
(18)6449 yards/**/C/H

Boxmoor G.C.
(0442) 242434
18 Box Lane, Hemel
Hempstead
2 miles from Hemel
Hempstead.
(9)4854 yards/***(Su)/D

Brickendon Grange G.C.
(099286) 228
Brickendon, Hertford
3 miles south of Hertford.
(18)6315 yards/**/C/H

Brookmans Park G.C.
(0707) 52487
Golf Club Rd. Hatfield
(18)6454 yards/**/C

Bushey Hall G.C.
(0923) 225802
Bushy Hall Drive, Bushey
1 mile south east of
Watford.
(18)6071 yards/**/C/H

Chadwell Springs G.C.
(0920) 463647
Hertford Rd. Ware
Between Hertford and Ware
on A119.
(9)3209 yards/**/C

Cheshunt G.C.
(0992) 24009
Park Lane, Cheshunt
(18)6608 yards/***/E

Chorleywood G.C.
(0923) 282009
Common Rd. Chorleywood
3 miles west of
Rickmansworth.
(9)2838
yards/**/(Tue,Thu)/D

East Herts G.C.
(0920) 821923
Hamels Park, Buntingford
1 mile north of
Puckeridge on A10.
(18)6449
yards/**(Wed)/B/H/M

Family Golf Centre
(0462) 482929
Jack's Hill, Graveley,
Stevenage
(18)6630 yards/***/D

Hanbury Manor Hotel &
G.C.
(0920) 487722
Thundridge, Ware
8 miles north of M25 junction 25
(18)6900 yards/***/A

Harpenden G.C.
(0582) 712580
Hammonds End, Redbourne
Lane, Harpenden
4 miles north of St. Albans.
(18)6363 yards/**/C/H

Harpenden Common G.C.
(0582) 712856
East Common, Harpenden
(18)5659 yards/**/C

Knebworth G.C.
(0438) 814681
Deards End Lane,
Knebworth
1 mile south of Stevenage
on B197.
(18)6428 yards/**/F/H

Letchworth G.C.
(0462) 683203
Letchworth Lane,
Letchworth
Near Willian Village.
(18)6181 yards/**/B/H/M

Little Hay G.C.
(0442) 833798
Box Lane, Hemel
Hempstead
(18)6610 yards/***/E

London Hatfield Country
Club
(0707) 32624
Essendon
(18)6500 yards/***/C

Mid Herts G.C.
(058283) 2242
Gustard Wood,
Wheathampstead, St. Albans
6 miles north of St. Albans.
(18)6060 yards/**/F

Moor Park G.C.
(0923) 773146
Moor Park Mansion, Moor
Park, Rickmansworth
Between Rickmansworth
and Northwood on A404.
(18)6713 yards/**/F
(18)5815 yards/**/F

Panshanger G.C.
(0707) 338507
Herns Lane, Welwyn
Garden City
1 mile north east of
Welwyn.
(18)6538 yards/***/E

Porters Park G.C.
(0923) 854127
Shenley Hill, Radlett
(18)6313 yards/**/A/H

Potters Bar G.C.
(0707) 52020
Darkers Lane, Potters Bar
North of Barnet off A1000
(18)6273 yards/**/F/H

Redbourn G.C.
(0582) 793493
Moor Lane, Rickmansworth
(18)6407 yards/**/D
(9)1361 yards/**/E

Rickmansworth G.C.
(0923) 775278
Moor Lane, Rickmansworth
(18)4412 yards/***/E

Royston G.C.
(0763) 242696
Baldock Rd. Royston
Between Baldock and
Royston on A505.
(18)6032 yards/**/C

Sandy Lodge G.C.
(0923) 825429
Sandy Lodge Lane,
Northwood
Next to Moor Park Station
(18)6340 yards/**/B/M/H

Stevenage G.C.
(043888) 424
Aston Lane, Aston,
Stevenage
(18)6451 yards/***/E

Verulam G.C.
(0727) 53327
London Rd. St. Albans
(18)6432 yards/**/C

Welwyn Garden City G.C.
(0707) 325243
Mannicotts, High Oaks Rd.
Welwyn
(18)6200 yards/**/B

West Herts G.C.
(0923) 224264
Cassiobury Park, Watford
2 miles south of Watford on
A412.
(18)6488 yards/**/C/H

Whipsnade Park G.C.
(044284) 2330
Studham Lane, Dagnall
Between Dagnall and
Studham.
(18)6735 yards/**/C

Bedfordshire

Aspley Guise and Woburn
Sands G.C.
(0908) 583596
West Hill, Aspley Guise,
Milton Keynes
Between Aspley Guise and
Woburn Sands on A5130.
(18)6248 yards/**/C/H

Aylesbury Vale G.C.
(0525) 240196
Wing, Leighton Buzzard
(18)6711 yards/***/C/H

Beadlow Manor Hotel G. &
C.C.
(0525) 60800
Beadlow, Shefford
(18)6238 yards/***/F
(9)6042 yards/***/F

Bedford and County G.C.
(0234) 352617
Green Lane, Clapham
Off A6 north of Bedford.
(18)6347 yards/**/B/H

Bedfordshire G.C.
(0234) 53241
Bromham Rd. Biddenham
2 miles from Bedford on
A428.
(18)6172 yards/**/B/H

Dunstable Downs G.C.
(0582) 604472
Whipsnade Rd. Dunstable
(18)6184 yards/**/F

John O'Gaunt G.C.
(0767) 260360
Sutton Park, Sandy
On B1040 to Potton.
(18)6513 yards/***/A/H
(18)5882 yards/***/A/H

Leighton Buzzard G.C.
(0525) 373811
Plantation Rd. Leighton
Buzzard
(18)5454 yards/**(Tue)/C/H

Millbrook G.C.
(0525) 404683
Millbrook, Ampthill
In Millbrook village.
(18)6473 yards/**(Thu)/D

Mowsbury G.C.
(0234) 216374
Cleat Hill, Kimbolton Rd
2 miles north of Bedford.
(18)6514 yards/***/E

South Beds G.C.
(0582) 591500
Warden Hill Rd. Luton
3 miles from Luton.
(18)6342 yards/**/C/H
(9)2590 yards/**/E/H

Stockwood Park G.C.
(0582) 413704
Stockwood Park,
London Rd. Luton
(18)5964 yards/***/E

Tilsworth G.C.
(0525) 219722
Dunstable Rd. Tilsworth,
Leighton Buzzard
(9)5443 yards/***/E

Wyboston Lakes G.C.
(0480) 212501
Wyboston Lakes, Wyboston
South of St. Neots off A1.
(18)5721 yards/***/C

Essex

Abridge G. and C.C.
(04028) 396
Epping Lane, Stapleford
Tawney, Abridge
(18)6703 yards/**/A/H

Ballards Gore G.C.
(07022) 58917
Gore Rd.Canedon, Rochford
2 miles east of Rochford.
(18)7062 yards/**/C

Basildon G.C.
(0268) 533297
Clay Hill Lane, Basildon
(18)6122 yards/***/E

Belfairs Park G.C.
(0702) 526911
Eastwood Road North,
Leigh-on-Sea
(18)5871 yards/***/E

Belhus Park G.C.
(0708) 854260
Belhus Park, South
Ockendon
(18)5900 yards/***/E

Bentley G.C.
(0277) 373179
Ongar Rd. Brentwood
4 miles north of Brentwood.
(18)6709 yards/**/C/H/L

Birch Grove G.C.
(0206) 34276
Layer Rd. Colchester
2 miles south of Colchester.
(9)4076 yards/***/E

Boyce Hill G.C.
(0268) 793625
Vicarage Hill, South Benfleet
7 miles west of Southend-
on-Sea.
(18)5882 yards/**/B

Braintree G.C.
(0376) 46079
Kings Lane, Sisted, Braintree
2 miles north of Braintree
on A120.
(18)6026 yards/**/C

Bunsay Downs G.C.
(0245) 412648
Little Baddow Rd.
Woodham Walter, Maldon
2 miles west of
Woodham Walter.
(9)2913 yards/***/D

Burnham-on-Crouch G.C.
(0621) 782282
Ferry Rd. Creeksea,
Burnham-on-Crouch
(9)5350 yards/**/C/M

Canons Brook G.C.
(0279) 421482
Elizabeth Way, Harlow
(18)6462 yards/**/B

Castle Point G.C.
(0268) 510830
Somnes Avenue, Canvey
Island
(18)5627 yards/***/E

Channels G.C.
(0245) 440005
Belsteads Farm Lane, Little
Waltham, Chelmsford
(18)6100 yards/**/B/H

Chelmsford G.C.
(0245) 256483
Widford Rd. Chelmsford
(18)5912 yards/**/B/M

Clacton-on-Sea G.C.
(0255) 421919
West Rd. Clacton-on-Sea
1 mile west of Clacton pier.
(18)6244 yards/***/B/H

Colchester G.C.
(0206) 853396
Braiswick, Colchester
1 mile north of town on
B1508.
(18)6319 yards/**/C

Earls Cone G.C.
(0787) 224466
Earls Cone, Colchester
(18)6842 yards/***/C

Fairlop Waters G.C.
081 500 9911
Barkingside, Ilford
(18)6288 yards/***/E

Forrester Park G.C.
(0621) 891406
Beckingham Rd. Great
Totham, Maldon
3 miles north of Maldon.
(9)2675 yards/***/D

Frinton G.C.
(0255) 674618
Esplanade, Frinton-on-Sea
(18)6259 yards/**/B/H

Gosfield Lakes G.C.
(0787) 474747
7 miles north of Braintree
(18)6512 yards/**/C/H
(9)1354 yards/***/E

Hanover G. & C.C.
(0702) 230033
Hullbridge Road, Rayleigh
(18)6800 yards/**/B

Hartswood G.C.
(0277) 218714
King George's Playing Fields,
Brentwood
(18)6238 yards/***/E

Harwich and Dovercourt
G.C.
(0255) 3616
Station Rd. Parkeston,
Harwich
(9)5692 yards/***/F/H

Havering G.C.
(0708) 741429
Risebridge Chase, Lower
Bedfords Rd. Romford
2 miles from Gallows
Corner
off A12.
(18)5237 yards/***/D

Langdon Hills G.C.
(0268) 548061
Bulphan
SW of Basildon, M25 junction 29
(18)6485 yards/***/B/H

Maldon G.C.
(0621) 853212
Beeleig, Langford, Maldon
2 miles north of Maldon on
B1019.
(9)6197 yards/**/C/H

Maylands G. and C.C.
(04023) 73080
Colchester Rd. Harold Park,
Romford
Between Romford and
Brentwood on A12.
(18)6182 yards/**/C/M

Orsett G.C.
(0375) 891352
Brentwood Rd. Orsett
(18)6614 yards/**/B/H

Pipps Hill G.C.
(0268) 23456
Cranes Farm Rd. Basildon
(9)2829 yards/***/F

Quietwaters Hotel & C.C.
(0621) 860410
Tolleshunt Knights, nr
Maldon
(18)6194 yards/***/C
(18)6765 yards/***/A

Rochford Hundred G.C.
(0702) 544302
Rochford Hall, Hall Rd.
Rochford
4 miles north of Southend.
(18)6255 yards/**/B/H

Romford G.C.
(0708) 740007
Heath Drive, Gidea Park,
Romford
2 miles from Romford off
A12.
(18)6365 yards/**/B/H/M

Saffron Walden G.C.
(0799) 522786
Windmill Hill, Saffron
Walden
(18)6608 yards/**/B/H

Skips G.C.
(04023) 48234
Horsemanside, Tysea Hill,
Stapleford
(18)6146 yards/*/F

Stapleford Abbots G.C.
(04023) 81108
3 miles north of Romford
(18)6487 yards/**/C
(18)5965 yards/**/C
(9)1140 yards/**/C

Stoke-by-Nayland G.C.
(006) 262836
Keepers Lane, Leavenheath,
Colchester
(18)6471 yards/***/B/H/M
(18)6498 yards/***/B/H/M

Theydon Bois G.C.
(0992) 813054
Theydon Rd. Epping
1 mile south of Epping off
B172.
(18)5472 yards/***/A/H/M

Thorndon Park G.C.
(0277) 810345
Ingrave, Brentwood
2 miles south of Brentwood
on A128.
(18)6455 yards/**/A

Thorpe Hall G.C.
(0702) 582205
Thorpe Hall Ave. Thorpe
Bay
(18)6286 yards/**/B/H

Three Rivers G. and C.C.
(0621) 828631
Stow Rd. Purleigh, Nr.
Chelmsford
(18)6609 yards/**/C/H
(9)2142 yards/**/C/H·

Toot Hill G.C.
(0277) 365523
Toot Hill, Ongar
(18)6013 yards/*/G

Towerlands G.C.
(0376) 552487
Panfield Rd. Braintree
Just out of town on B1053.
(9)2698 yards/***/E
(18)5406 yards/***/D

Upminster G.C.
(04022) 20249
114 Hall Lane, Upminster
(18)5926 yards/**/C/M

Warley Park G.C.
(0277) 224891
Magpie Lane, Little Warley
M25 junction 29
(27)(3 x 9)/**/B

Warren G.C.
(024541) 3258
Woodham Walter, Maldon
6 miles east of Chelmsford
on A414.
(18)6211 yards/**/B

West Essex G.C.
081-5290928
Sewardstonebury, Chingford
(18) 6289 yards/**/B/H

Woodford G.C.
081 5040553
2 Sunset Ave. Woodford
Green
10 miles from London.
(9)5806 yards/**/C

Berkshire, Buckinghamshire and Oxfordshire—three very English counties, don't you think? From Burnham Beeches to Banbury Cross, the region extends from the edge of the Chilterns to the edge of the Cotswolds and occupies a very prosperous part of southern Britain.

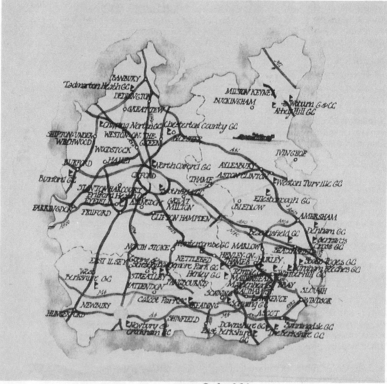

Oxfordshire

We start at **Huntercombe,** a charming Golf Club which has enjoyed an interesting history. In the early years of the century three rather old Daimler motor cars were used to ferry Members to and from the local station and later a thirty seater bus was acquired for the same purpose. The course itself has passed through various owners—at first a property company, then an insurance company (the Norwich Union) and later Viscount Nuffield before finally becoming a Members Club in 1963. Situated on the edge of the Chilterns at some 700 feet above sea level there are some marvellous views across the Oxford Plain. The course itself is fairly flat and is always kept in first class condition. Nearby in Henley there are two courses worth inspecting, the more established **Henley** Golf Club and **Badgemore Park**, a fairly new course but one that has settled down quickly.

As The Berkshire has a Red and Blue, so **Frilford Heath** has a Red and a Green. Both of Frilford's 18 hole challenges—and challenge is certainly the word—are exceptionally fine heathland courses and the Club can proudly and justly boast the best golf in the county.

Oxford is actually not all that far away. There are two courses either side of the town—**North Oxford** and **Southfield** and although the neither is in the Frilford Heath league both are certainly worth a game. The latter is the home of Oxford University.

Beyond Oxford, there is a flattish parkland course near Bicester, the **Chesterton** Golf Club and a much improved course at **Burford**. Inching up towards the Cotswolds there is a pleasant course at **Chipping Norton** but the best in the north of the county, although it may be a little more difficult to arrange a game upon, is clearly **Tadmarton Heath**. At less than 6000 yards in length, it is fairly short by modern standards, but the narrow fairways and a great spread of gorse can make it a very difficult test. It also has a wonderfully remote setting.

Buckinghamshire

Moving into Buckinghamshire, the magnificence of **Woburn** stands rather alone in the far north of the county. Heading 'down the county' **Ellesborough's** golf course is another with rather stately surroundings being located on part of the property of Chequers. Quite a hilly course and rather testing, it is well worth inspecting and not only because there are some commanding views across the Buckinghamshire countryside. Elsewhere in the centre of the county, there is a less attractive but fairly lengthy parkland course at **Weston Turville**, south of Aylesbury.

It is in southern Buckinghamshire where most of the county's better courses are to be found. **Stoke Poges** has staged many leading amateur events, not at all surprisingly, this being one of the finest parkland courses in the south of England. In this area note also **Farnham Park**, a nearby public course.

Denham Golf Club is a close neighbour of Stoke Poges lying some 3 miles north of Uxbridge, and as an old Club handbook will tell you 'half an hour's drive from Marble Arch'. (Add an extra sixty minutes nowadays if you're attempting the journey during 'Rush Hour'). It is worth making the escape though for Denham enjoys a beautiful setting, deeply secluded amidst some glorious countryside. The Clubhouse is a most unusual building having been built around a 16th century tithe barn.

In equally beautiful surroundings is the **Burnham Beeches** Golf Club, situated approximately 4 miles west of Slough. Others to note in southern Buckinghamshire include **Beaconsfield, Wycombe Heights** (an outstanding new municipal complex in the Chilterns) **Harewood Downs** (at Chalfont St. Giles), **Gerrards Cross** and at Denham Court the new **Buckinghamshire** Golf Club designed by John Jacobs.

Berkshire

Berkshire—or should one say 'Royal Berkshire'—is often described as being cigar-shaped. Now whilst this may not say much for the present day talents of cigar-makers it does serve as a fairly rough description in as much as the county is indeed peculiarly long and thin. When it comes to surveying the county's twenty or so golf courses it is tempting to adopt another cigar analogy in that one end could be said to glow rather more brightly than the other.

To the east of the county there is a famous heathland belt and it is here that the twin pearls of **Sunningdale** and **The Berkshire** are to be found. Both Clubs possess two 18 hole courses which for sheer enjoyment can stand comparison with anything that golf has to offer.

Sunningdale is better known than The Berkshire but it is difficult to imagine a more delightful setting than the tranquil, tree-lined fairways of The Red and The Blue Courses at The Berkshire—and so close to London too. **Swinley Forest** is the other outstanding heathland course in the area, a veritable paradis terrestre indeed. However this is a very private club and visitors are only permitted to play as guests of Members. Still in heather and pine country is the very attractive **East Berkshire** course at Crowthorne. Also in close proximity is the popular **Downshire** public course where the green fees are naturally less expensive than the above mentioned courses.

Time for some more golf and **Temple's** fine course can be glimpsed from the main A23 Maidenhead to Henley Road. It has an interesting layout with many fine trees and lush fairways. Designed by Willie Park early this century, it was for a number of years the home of Henry Cotton. The course is always maintained in first class condition.

The golf course at **Winter Hill** is on fairly high ground—apparently its name derives from the particularly chilling winds that sweep across in winter (I have no explanation for nearby Crazies Hill!) From the course there are some spectacular views over the Thames—definitely worth a visit. So for that matter is classy **Sonning,** situated further towards Reading. There is a reasonable course in (or on the outskirts of) **Maidenhead** and just beyond the boating villages of Goring and Streatly, lies the fairly tough **Goring and Streatly** course.

On the western edge of Reading **Calcot Park** golf course poses many interesting challenges; it can boast Guinness Book of Records fame too in that one sterling fellow sprinted round the course in a motorised cart in just over 24 minutes—a more leisurely round is suggested!

Berkshire

Bearwood G.C
(0734) 760060
Mole Road, Sindlesham
Leave M4 at junction 10 for
B3030
(9) 2814 yards/**/D/H

The Berkshire G.C
(0344) 21495
Swinley Road, Ascot
Leave M3 at junction 3 or
M4 at junction 10
(18) 6356 yards/**/A/L
(18) 6258 yards/**/A/L

Calcot Park G.C
(0734) 427124
Bath Road, Calcot, Reading
Leave M4 at junction 12 for
A4 to Reading
(18) 6283 yards/**/F

Donnington Valley G.C
(0635) 32488
Old Oxford Road,
Donnington
North of Newbury
(18) 4002 yards/***/F

Downshire G.C
(0344) 424066
Easthampstead Park,
Wokingham
Take M3 or M4 to Bracknell
& to Easthampstead Park
(18) 6382 yards/***/E

East Berkshire G.C
(0344) 772041
Ravenswood Avenue,
Crowthorne
Take M3 or M4 to
Bracknell, onto A3095 then
B3348
(18) 6315 yards/**/B/H

Goring & Streatley G.C
(0491) 873229
Rectory Road, Streatley-on-
Thames
10 miles N.W of Reading
(18) 6255 yards/**/B

Hawthorn Hill G.C
(0628) 771030
Drift Road, Nr Maidenead
Leave M4 at exit 8/9, take
A330 to Bracknell
(18) 6212 yards/***/E

Hurst G.C
(0734) 345143
Sandford Lane, Hurst,
Wokingham
3 miles from Wokingham
on B3030
(9) 3013 yards (men)/ 2906
(ladies)/***/E

Lavender Park G.C
(0344) 884074
Swinley Road, Ascot
4 miles S.W of Ascot on
A332
(9) 1104 yards/***/E

Maidenhead G.C
(0628) 24693
Shoppenhangers Road,
Maidenhead
Take A4 or M4 to
Maidenhead, onto A308
(18) 6360 yards/**/B/H

Mill Ride G.C
(0344) 886777
Mill Ride, North Ascot
(18) 6639 yards/***/A/H

Newbury & Crookham G.C
(0635) 40035
Burys Bank Road,
Greenham, Newbury
2 miles S.E of Newbury off
A34
(18) 5880 yards/**/B/M

Reading G.C
(0734) 472909
17 Kidmore End Road,
Emmer Green, Reading
2 miles N. of Reading off
B481
(18) 6212 yards/**(not
Friday)/B

Royal Ascot G.C
(0344) 25175
Winkfield Road, Ascot
Leave M3 at junction 3, take
A332 N.
(18) 5653 yards/***/F

Newbury is of course better known for its racing than its golf, but
the **Newbury and Crookham** Golf Club close to Greenham Common
is one of the oldest Clubs in Southern England and is strongly recommended. The course is hilly and well-wooded, though not overly
long.

Before leaving Berkshire it is worth noting one of the county's more
recent additions, **West Berkshire**, situated just south of the village of
Chaddleworth. It is a splendid downland course, but not exactly one
for the weak-kneed—it stretches to around the 7000 yard mark with
one par five measuring well over 600 yards—a hearty breakfast
before playing here is a must!

Sunningdale

On seeing the spectacularly beautiful 18th hole at Killarney during one of his visits to Ireland, the late Henry Longhurst declared, 'What a lovely place to die'. Now whilst one rarely wishes to dwell on the subject of meeting our maker, golfers have been known to indulge in a considerable amount of speculation as to the type of course they might find on the arrival of such an occasion.

The gentleman in charge of the terrestrial Sunningdale is the **Secretary, Stewart Zuill**. Mr. Zuill may be contacted on **(0344) 21681. Keith Maxwell** is the Club's resident **professional** and he can be reached on **(0344) 20128**. Unless accompanied by a Member visitors are restricted to weekdays and must make prior arrangement with the Secretary. A letter of introduction is also required. All written communications should be addressed to Mr. Zuill. In 1993 the green fee was set at £80. This entitled the visitor to a full day's golf, enabling a round over both courses.

Sunningdale is situated just off the A30, about 28 miles West of London. Motoring from the South and West the M3, (leaving at junction 3) and the M4 (junction 10) may be of assistance, while from the North both the A332 and the A330 pass through nearby Ascot. The Club's precise location is some 300 yards from Sunningdale Railway Station.

When golfers talk of Sunningdale, invariably it is the Old Course they have in mind, this despite the fact that a large number of people consider the New to be its equal. The former has acquired such pre-eminence largely as a result of the many major professional and amateur tournaments that have been staged there. However the Old Course is perhaps best known for a single round of golf played by the legendary Bobby

Jones. In qualifying for the 1926 Open Championship, which he in fact went on to win, the great man put together what has often been described as the finest 18 holes of golf ever seen.

At 6341 yards (par 70) the Old Course is more than three hundred yards shorter than the New (6676 yards, par 70). The respective distances from the Ladies tees are 5825 yards and 5840 yards (both being par 74). It seems somehow wrong to single out individual holes, each course possessing its own wealth of variety and charm. The views from the 5th and 10th tees on the Old Course are, however, particularly outstanding and the 18th also provides a spectacular closing hole as it gently dog-legs towards the green and the giant spreading oak tree, very much the symbol of Sunningdale.

The Sunningdale Golf Club,
Ridge mount Road,
Sunningdale,
Berkshire SL5 9RW

Old Course

Hole	Yards	Par	Hole	Yards	Par
1	494	5	10	463	4
2	456	4	11	299	4
3	296	4	12	423	4
4	161	3	13	178	3
5	400	4	14	477	5
6	388	4	15	226	3
7	383	4	16	423	4
8	172	3	17	421	4
9	267	4	18	414	4
Out	3,017	35	In	3,324	35
			Out	3,017	35
			Totals	6,341	70

Sonning G.C
(0734) 693332
Duffield Road, Sonning-on-
Thames
Take A4 from Reading to
Maidenhead
(18) 6345 yards/**/F/H

Sunningdale G.C
(0990) 21681
Ridgemount Road,
Sunningdale, Ascot
28 miles W. of London off
A30
6586 yards/**/A/H
6676 yards/**/A/H

Sunningdale Ladies G.C
(0990) 20507
Cross Road, Sunningdale
Off A30 from M3 or M4
(18) 3622 yards/***/D (men
extra)

Swinley Forest G.C
(0344) 20197
Coronation Road, S. Ascot
Take M3 or M4 to Ascot
(18) 6011 yards/*/F/G/H

Temple G.C
(0628) 824248
Henley Road, Hurley,
Maidenhead
1 mile E. of Hurley on A423
(18) 6206 yards/**/A/H

West Berkshire G.C
(048 82) 574
Chaddleworth, Newbury
Leave M4 at junction 14,
take A338 N.
(18) 7053 yards/**/C

Winter Hill G.C
Grange Lane, Cookham,
Maidenhead
4 Miles from Maidenhead
via M4 (junction 9)
(18) 6408 yards/**/C

Buckinghamshire

Abbey Hill G.C.
(0908) 563845
Monks Way, Two Mile Ash,
Stony Stratford
2 miles south of Stony
Stratford.
(18) 6193 yards/***/E

Beaconsfield G.C.
(0494) 676545
Seer Green, Beaconsfield
(18)6469 yards/**/A/H

Buckingham G.C.
(0280) 815566
Tingewick Rd. Buckingham
2 miles from town on A421.
(18) 6082 yards/**/B/M

Burnham Beeches G.C.
(0628) 661448
Green Lane, Burnham
(18) 6415 yards/**/A/H

Chesham and Ley Hill G.C.
(0494) 784541
Ley Hill, Chesham
(9) 5240 yards/**/D

Chiltern Forest G.C.
(0296) 630899
Aston Hill, Halton,
Aylesbury
5 miles south of Aylesbury
off A41.
(18) 6038 yards/**/D

Datchet G.C.
(0753) 43887
Buccleuch Rd. Datchett,
Slough
2 miles from Slough.
(9) 5978 yards/**/C/H

Denham G.C.
(0895) 832022
Tilehouse Lane, Denham
(18) 6451 yards/**(Fri)/A

Ellesborough G.C.
(0296) 622114
Butlers Cross, Aylesbury
1 mile west of Wendover on
A413.
(18) 6271 yards/**/F/H

Farnham Park G.C.
(0753) 647065
Park Rd. Stoke Poges
(18) 5787 yards/***/E

Flackwell Heath G.C.
(06285) 520929
Treadaway Rd. Flackwell
Heath, High Wycombe
(18) 6150 yards/**/B/H

Gerrards Cross G.C.
(0753) 885300
Chalfont Park, Gerrards
Cross
(18) 6021 yards/**/A/H

Harewood Downs G.C.
(0494) 762308
Cokes Lane, Chalfont St.
Giles
3 miles south of Amersham
off A413.
(18) 5448 yards/**/B/H

Hazelmere G. and C.C.
(0494) 718298
Penn Rd. Hazelmere, High
Wycombe
3 miles from High
Wycombe on B474.
(18) 6039 yards/***/B

Iver G.C.
(0753) 655615
Hollow Hill Lane, Langley
Park Rd. Iver
(9) 6214 yards/***/E

Little Chalfont G.C.
(0494) 764877
Lodge Lane, Little Chalfont
(9) 2926 yards/***/E

Stoke Poges G.C.
(0753) 526385
Stoke Park, Park Rd. Stoke
Poges
3 miles from Slough on
B416.
(18) 6654 yards/**/B/H

Stowe G.C.
(0280) 813650
Stowe, Buckingham
4 miles from Buckingham
on A413.
(9) 4573 yards/**/E/G

Wavendon Golf Centre
(0908) 281811
Wavendon, Milton Keynes
1 mile from M1 junction 13
(18) 5800 yards/***/E

- - -

Weston Turville G.C.
(0296) 24084
New Rd. Weston Turville,
Aylesbury
(18) 6782 yards/***/D

Wrexham Park G.C.
(0753) 663271
Wrexham Street, Wrexham,
Slough
(18) 5836 yards/***/D
(9) 2383 yards/***/E

Whiteleaf G.C.
(08444) 3097
The Clubhouse, Whiteleaf,
Aylesbury
(9) 5391 yards/**/C/H

Windmill Hill G.C
(0908) 378623
Tannenhoe Lane, Bletchley
(18) 6773 yards/***/E

Woburn G. and C.C.
(0908) 370756
Bow Brickhill, Milton
Keynes
2 miles from Woburn.
(18) 6913 yards/**/F/H
(18) 6641 yards/**/F/H

Wycombe Heights G.C
(0494) 816686
Rayners Avenue,
Loudwater, High Wycombe
(18) 6300 yards/***/E

Oxfordshire

Badgemore Park G.C.
(0491) 572206
Badgemore Park, Henley-on-
Thames
1 mile from Henley.
(18) 6112 yards/***/B/H

Burford G.C.
(099382) 2583
Burford
(18) 6405 yards/**/B/H

Cherwell Edge G.C
(0295) 711591
Chacombe, Banbury
East of Banbury on B4525
(18) 5925 yards/***/E

Chesterton G.C.
(0869) 241204
Chesterton, Bicester
(18) 6224 yards/***/C/H

Chipping Norton G.C.
(0608) 2383
Southcombe, Chipping
Norton
1 mile south of Chipping
town centre.
(18) 6283 yards/**/C

Frilford Heath G.C.
(0865) 390864
Frilford Heath, Abingdon
3 miles west of
Abingdon off A338.
(18) 6768 yards/***/A/H
(18) 6006 yards/***/A/H

Hadden Hill G.C
(0235) 510410
Wallingford Road, Didcot
(18) 6563 yards/***/D

Henley G.C.
(0491) 575742
Harpsden, Henley-on-

Thames
1 mile from Henley.
(18)6330 yards/**/A/H

Huntercombe G.C.
(0491) 641207
Nuffield, Henley-on-Thames
6 miles from Henley off
A423.
(18) 6108 yards/**/A/H

North Oxford G.C.
(0865) 54415
Banbury Rd. Oxford
3 miles north of City centre.
(18) 5805 yards/***/B/H

Southfield G.C.
(0865) 242158
Hill Top Rd. Oxford
(18) 6230 yards/**/B/H

Tadmarton Heath G.C.
(0608) 737278
Wiggington, Banbury
5 miles west of Banbury on
B4035.
(18) 5917 yards/**/B/H

KEY

*** Visitors welcome at all times
** Visitors on weekdays only
* No visitors at any time
(Mon, Wed) No visitors on specified
days

GREEN FEES PER ROUND
A - £30 plus
B - £20 - £30
C - £15 - £25
D - £10 - £20
E - Under £10
F - Green fees on application

RESTRICTIONS
G - Guests only
H - Handicap certificate required
H(24) - Handicap of 24 or less
required
L - Letter of introduction required
M - Visitor must be a member of
another recognised club.

Glos, Hereford &
Worcester

A hush descends as you ponder your first swing in old Worcestershire. Apple and cherry trees are in blossom and in the distance a herd of white faced Herefords appraise your stance. You're fortunate, for several hundred years ago the air in these parts was thick with the clatter of sword against sword but now there is peace. Crack! Straight down the fairway—the echo resounds and then dies—you're on your way.

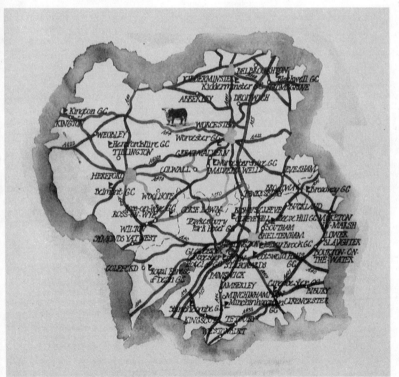

Herefordshire, Worcestershire and Gloucestershire—what a lovely trio! Bordering the Principality the region is arguably the most tranquil in England. It is an area of rich pastures and cider orchards, of small market towns and sleepy villages rather than crowded cities and encompasses the Cotswolds and the Malverns, the beautiful Wye Valley and the splendid Vale of Evesham. Truly a green and pleasant land!

Hereford & Worcester

Herefordshire and Worcestershire are no more—at least according to the modern county boundaries—Hereford and Worcester it is now, no doubt a compromise to the two county towns.

Golf courses aren't exactly plentiful, but those there are tend to be very scenic, often hidden away deep in the glorious countryside. To the north west of Hereford, **Kington** and **Herefordshire** are two typical examples and both clubs warmly welcome visitors. Kington is further towards Wales and is reputed to be the highest course in either country. It is a place where poor golf can always be blamed on the rarefied atmosphere. To the south of Hereford is another attractive course, **Belmont,** one of the newer courses in the region, but one that has already gained a good reputation.

Ross-on-Wye is a renowned beauty spot and the town's golf course reflects the reputation. Set in the heart of the Wye Valley and surrounded by a blaze of colour, it's hard to believe that the M50 is under a mile away (junction 4).

Worcester is an attractive city with a very beautiful Cathedral which overlooks the famous old county cricket ground. Only a mile from the town centre off the A4103 is the **Worcester** Golf and Country Club. The oldest course in the county, and possibly the finest is the appropriately name **Worcestershire** Golf Club, situated two miles south of Great Malvern. There are extensive views from the course towards the Malverns, the Severn Valley and the Cotswolds. Elsewhere in the county, **The Vale** Golf and Country Club near Pershore has recently opened to generous acclaim and boasts twenty-seven testing holes and a driving range and there is a reasonable course at **Kidderminster.** One prestigious new development to experience in 1994 will be the Bank House project with golf, bowling and a host of other sporting activities at this first class hotel in Bransford. The final recommendation in Worcestershire is the popular **Blackwell** Golf Club near Bromsgrove.

Gloucestershire

Heading into Gloucestershire, I trust that when Doctor Foster went to Gloucester he wasn't a well travelled golfer. Again the county has very few courses and Gloucester itself didn't possess one at all until as recently as 1976. Neighbouring Cheltenham has been a little more fortunate but granted one or two exceptions, the quality of the golf in the county doesn't exactly match up to the undeniable quality of its scenery.

The county's two best known courses are probably **Cotswold Hills** and **Lilley Brook,** located to the north and south of Cheltenham respectively. Both offer commanding views of the Gloucestershire countryside, especially perhaps Lilley Brook, one of southern England's most undulating courses.

Cleeve Hill is Cheltenham's third 18 hole course. Situated on high ground to the north of the town it can get rather cold in winter. One anonymous person said that when visiting Cheltenham he enjoyed a game at Lilley Brook in the summer as half of him was mountain goat, and at Cleeve Hill in the winter because the other half of him was eskimo!

Outside of Cheltenham, **Minchinhampton** has perhaps the biggest golfing reputation. A Club of great character, it celebrated its centenary in 1989. There are two courses here, an Old and a New, the latter was constructed in the 1970s. A quick word for another course in the south of the county, **Stinchcombe Hill** which is also very well thought of. The 18 hole course at **Cirencester** is probably the nearest one gets to golf in the Cotswolds. Cirencester is certainly a pleasant enough place but to most of us the real Cotswolds are the many wonderfully named villages: Bourton-on-the-Water, Stow-on-the-Wold, Upper Slaughter and Lower Slaughter.

Gloucester's newish course lies within the grounds of **The Gloucester Hotel** at Robinswood Hill. A luxurious Country Club, there are in fact 27 holes here plus all manner of accompanying leisure facilities. The 18 hole course enjoys a pleasant setting and has matured very rapidly. The same can be said of **Tewkesbury Park Hotel's** golf course which is laid out on the site of the famous Roses Battle of 1471. Both hotels are comfortable and their courses are open to residents and non-residents alike, although booking in advance is preferred. However, for a special occasion, we can recommend a stay at **Puckrup Hall** (previously known as Tewkesbury Hall), an elegant Regency house set in 40 acres of parkland with an adjacent new 18 hole golf course and at Upton St Leonards, near Gloucester, Hatton Court is most relaxing.

The Forest of Dean is our next port of call—another beauty spot and some good golf too at the **Royal Forest of Dean** Golf Club in Coleford. In Coleford itself, there is the lovely 16th century Poolway House which is well worth more than an overnight treat as there are some exceptional value golfing breaks available through the hotel.

Last but not least, **Broadway** Golf Club—the course being a mile and a half or so from 'the loveliest village in England'. It really is a beautiful part of the world and those wishing to do some exploring will find several superb hotels, any of which will make an ideal base.

Gloustershire

Cirencester G.C.
(0285) 2465
Cheltenham Rd. Bagendon, Cirencester
2 miles from Cirencester on A435.
(18)6100 yards/***/C/H

Cleeve Hill G.C.
(024267) 2592
Cleeve Hill, Nr. Prestbury, Cheltenham
3 miles north of Cheltenham on A46.
(18)6217 yards/***/D

Cotswold Hills G.C.
(0242) 515264
Ullenwood, Cheltenham
3 miles south of Cheltenham.
(18)6716 yards/***/F/H/M

Gloucester Hotel G. and C.C.
(0452) 411331
Matson Lane, Robinswood Hill
2 miles south of Gloucester on B4073.
(18)6135 yards/***/B/H

Lilley Brook G.C.
(0204) 526785
Cirencester Rd. Charlton Kings
3 miles from Cheltenham on A435.
(18)6226 yards/***/B/H/M

Lydney G.C.
(0594) 842614
Lakeside Ave. Lydney
(9)5382 yads/**/D

Minchinhampton G.C.
(045383) 3866
Minchinhampton, Stroud
5 miles south of Stroud.
(18)6675 yards/***/C/H
(18)6295 yards/***/C/H

Painswick G.C.
(0452) 812180
Painswick, Stroud
1 mile north of
Painswick on A46.
(18)4780 yards/**/D

Royal Forest of Dean G.C.
(0594) 32583
Lords Hill, Coleford
(18)5519 yards/***/D

Stinchcombe Hill G.C.
(0453) 2015
Stinchcombe Hill, Dursley
1 mile from Tetbury.
(18)5710 yards/**/C

Tewkesbury Park Hotel G.C.
(0684) 295404
Lincoln Green Lane,
Tewkesbury
1 mile south of town on
A38.
(18)6533 yards/***/B/H

Westonbirt G.C.
(0666) 88242
Westonbirt, Tetbury
(9)4504 yards/***/E

Hereford & Worcester

Abbey Park G.C.
(0527) 63918
Abbey Park,
Dagnell End Rd. Redditch
North of Redditch on B4101.
(18)5857 yards/***/D

Belmont G.C.
(0432) 35266
Belmont House, Belmont
2 miles south of Hereford
on A465.
(18)6448 yards/***/F

Blackwell G.C.
(021445) 1994
Blackwell, Bromsgrove
3 miles east of Bromsgrove.
(18)6202 yards/**/A/H

Broadway G.C.
(0386) 853683
Willersey Hill, Broadway
3 miles east of Broadway
off A44.
(18)6122 yards/***(Sat)/B/H

Churchill and Blakedown
G.C.
(0562) 700200
Churchill Lane, Blakedown,
Kidderminster
3 miles north of
Kidderminster.
(9)5399 yards/**/D

Droitwich G. and C.C.
(0905) 774344
Westford House,
Ford Lane, Droitwich
1 mile north of Droitwich.
(18)6040 yards/**/C/H

Evesham G.C.
(0386) 860395
Cray Combe Links,
Fladbury, Pershore
4 miles west of Fladbury.
(9)6415 yards/**/C/H

Habberley G.C.
(0562) 745756
Habberley, Kidderminster
3 miles north of
Kidderminster.
(9)5104 yards/**/D/M

Herefordshire G.C.
(0432) 71219
Ravens Causeway,
Wormsley
(18)6200 yards/***/C

Kidderminster G.C.
(0562) 822303
Russel Rd. Kidderminster
1 mile south of town off
A449.
(18)5659 yards/**/C/M

Kington G.C
(0544) 230340
Bradnor Hll, Kington,
1 mile north of
Kington on B4355.
(18)5726 yards/***/D

Leominster G.C.
(0568) 2863
Ford Bridge, Leominster
(9)5250 yards/***/F

Little Lakes G.C.
(0299) 266385
Lye Head, Rock, Bewdley
3 miles west of Bewdley.
(9)6247 yards/**/D

Pitcheroak G.C.
(0527) 41054
Plymouth Rd. Redditch
(9)4724 yards/***/E

Redditch G.C.
(0527) 43309
Lower Grintsy, Green Lane,
Callow Hill
3 miles west of Redditch.
(18)6671 yards/**/F/M

Ross-on-Wye G.C.
(098982) 267
Two Park, Gorsley, Ross-on-
Wye
(18)6500 yards/***/B/H/M

Tolladine G.C.
(0905) 21074
Tolladine Rd. Worcester
1 mile east of Worcester.
(9)5134 yards/**/D

Worcester G.and C.C.
(0905) 422555
Boughton Park, Worcester
Just east of Hereford city
centre.
(18)5946 yards/**/B/H

Worcestershire G.C.
(0684) 575992
Wood farm, Malvern Wells
(18)6449

East & West Midlands

Greater Birmingham

Golfers in the City of London have often been known to get frustrated at having to travel many a mile for a decent game of golf. In 1919 one obviously disgusted individual teed up at Piccadilly Circus and proceeded to play along The Strand, through Fleet Street and Ludgate Hill firing his last shot at the Royal Exchange. Such behaviour is, as far as I'm aware, unknown in Birmingham—the Bull Ring and the NEC in their admittedly shorter existence, have never been peppered with golf balls, this I suspect may be because the needs of its golfing citizens have been properly attended to.

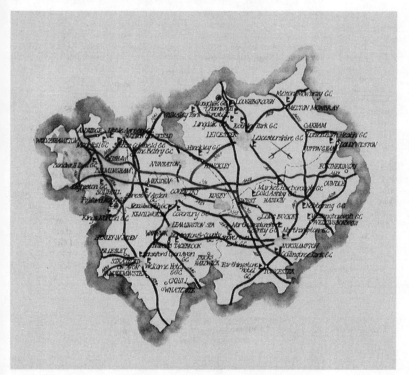

Within a sensible distance (ie. easy access) of the town centre lie the likes of **The Belfry** and **Little Aston** to the North, **Fulford Heath**, **Copt Heath** and **Kings Norton** to the South, and **Sandwell Park** and **Edgbaston** lying somewhere in the middle. Golfers north of Birmingham are indeed particularly fortunate for in addition to The

Belfry and Little Aston there is also **Sutton Coldfield** and **Moor Hall**. All provide extremely pleasant retreats from the noise and confusion of England's second largest city. One need hardly add that there are also a number of public courses dotted around the outskirts of Birmingham.

Despite its relative youth, **The Belfry** has become the area's best known golfing attraction thanks largely of course to the thrilling Ryder Cup encounters staged there. However, **Little Aston** has long been regarded as one of Britain's finest inland courses and has hosted numerous major events—both amateur and professional.

Coventry

Like Birmingham, the city of Coventry has been removed from Warwickshire and now bears the West Midlands label. **Coventry** Golf Club enjoys a decidedly peaceful setting at Finham Park, two miles south of the city along the A444. The course is good enough to have recently staged the British Seniors Championship. To the north west of Coventry at Meriden, the **Forest of Arden** Golf and Country Club offers a marvellous day's golf—36 holes to savour here with the beautiful Aylesford and Arden courses—while the leisure facilities at the Country Club Hotel are outstanding. In 1993 the Forest of Arden staged the Murphy's English Open Championship.

Warwickshire

Birmingham and Coventry removed, Warwickshire has been left with only a handful of courses. The county's two most popular towns (tourist wise) are unquestionably Stratford and **Warwick**. Until recently Warwick had only a nine hole course located inside its race track, but now, not far away from Warwick at Leek Wooton, (close to jct 15 of the M40) is **The Warwickshire** where 36 holes of modern 'Championship Golf' await. Shakespeare-spotters who've sneaked the clubs into the boot will also be well rewarded. There are two fine 18 hole courses in Stratford, **Stratford** Golf Club and the **Welcombe Hotel** Golf Course, and a little beyond the town there are plans to build a 27 hole course at Bidford on Avon.

Lastly we visit Leamington Spa. It may not have the attractions of a Stratford or a Warwick but it does have a very fine golf course. **Leamington and County** is a hilly parkland course, situated to the south of Leamington.

Leicestershire

As we move from the West to the East Midlands let us start with the best course in Leicestershire.

Luffenham Heath lies over to the far east of the county within what was formerly Rutland and very close to the border with Lincolnshire. It is without question one of the most attractive heathland courses in England and being in a conservation area something of a haven for numerous species of wildlife. It isn't the longest of courses but then, thankfully, golf isn't always a question of how far you can belt the ball!

Rothley Park Golf Club is one of Leicestershire's most picturesque parkland courses and is within easy access of Leicester, lying some seven miles to the north west of the city, off the A6. Leicester is well served by golf courses and there are no fewer than three 18 hole municipal courses within four miles of the centre of Leicester, **Western Park** perhaps being the best of these. **Leicestershire** Golf Club is situated just two miles from the city centre along the A6. It is one of the top courses in the county; try to avoid the ubiquitous stream that runs through it. Leicester may not be the country's most attractive city but it does have its good points.

Looking further afield, in the north of the county the ancient town of **Melton Mowbray** has a fine nine hole course sited on high ground to the north east of the town and Loughborough possesses an 18 hole heathland type course, **Longcliffe,** which is heavily wooded with a particularly testing front nine.

In the south of the county, **Market Harborough's** nine hole course offers extensive views across the surrounding countryside. Northwest of Leicester, Charnwood Forest is one of the Midland's most pleasant retreats, an area where heath and woodland confront rocky craggs and granite outcrops. The village of Woodhouse Eaves lies on the eastern edge of the Forest and has two extremely pleasant courses at hand, **Lingdale** and **Charnwood Forest.** Though they are less than two miles apart they offer quite different challenges. Lingdale (which has recently been extended from 9 holes to 18) has a parkland setting with a trout stream flowing through it, while Charnwood Forest is another heathland type course—nine holes, no bunkers but several outcrops of granite to negotiate.

Hinckley is linked to the centre of Leicester by the A47. Hinckley's golf course is a fairly new creation, built over the original nine hole Burbage Common layout. Several lakes and much gorse have to be confronted making this potentially the toughest in the county. The final mention for a round in Leicestershire goes to **Willesley Park** at Ashby-de-la-Zouch. A parkland-heathland mix this and well worth a visit.

Northamptonshire

The much admired **Northamptonshire County** course is situated some five miles north of Northampton at Church Brampton, and indeed is often referred to locally as Church Brampton. Famed for its many testing par fours, it is a splendid heather and gorse type with a fair few undulations in its 6,500 yards. Rather like Liphook in Hampshire a railway line bisects the course. In the past it has staged the British Youths Championship. Though not as good as Church Brampton, **Northampton** Golf Club can also be recommended while nearby at **Collingtree Park** Johnny Miller's spectacularly designed course has recently been opened to the public. One final mention for visitors to the county town is the **Delapre** Golf Complex where a game should be easily arranged.

Elsewhere in the county there is a reasonable course at **Kettering** and not far away there is a better course at **Wellingborough,** two miles east of the town and set around the former Harrowden Hall. Quite hilly, it has several lakes and a mass of mature trees. It is certainly one of the best courses in the county. Others include **Staverton Park** at Daventry, **Cold Ashby** (near the site of the famous Battle of Naesby of 1645) with its superb views across the Northamptonshire Uplands, and the popular **Farthingstone Hotel** Golf and Leisure Centre near Towcester.

Northamptonshire

Cherwell Edge G.C.
(0295) 711591
Chacombe, Banbury
3 miles east of Banbury on A442.
(18)5322 yards/***/D

Cold Ashby G.C.
(0604) 7400548
Cold Ashby, Northampton
(18)5898 yards/***/C

Collingtree Park G.C
(0604) 700000
Windingbrook Lane, Northampton
(18)6692 yards/***/A

Daventry and District G.C.
(0327) 702829
Norton Rd. Daventry
1 mile north of Daventry.
(9)5582 yards/***/D

Delapre G.C.
(0604) 764036
Eagle Drive, Nene
Valley Way, Northampton
Just south of town.
(18)6293 yards/***/D

Farthingstone Hotel G. C
(0327) 36291
Farthingstone, Towcester
(18)6500 yards/***/C

Hellidon Lakes Hotel & CC
(0327) 62550
Hellidon
(18)6691 yards/***/B

Kettering G.C.
(0536) 512074
Headlands, Kettering
(18)6036 yards/**/C/H

Kingsthorpe G.C.
(0604) 710610
Kingsley Rd. Northampton
2 miles from town off A508.
(18)6006 yards/**/B/H

Northampton G.C.
(0604) 845155
Kettering Rd. Northampton
Just north of town on A43.
(18)6002 yards/**/C/H

Northamptonshire County G.C.
(0604) 843025
Sandy Lane, Church Brampton, Northampton
5 miles from Northampton off A50.
(18)6503 yards/***/A/H

Oundle G.C.
(0832) 273267
Benefield Rd. Oundle, Peterboro
2 miles west of Peterborough.
(18)5507 yards/**/F

Priors Hall G.C.
(0536) 60756
Stamford Rd, Weldon
2 miles east of Weldon off A43.
(18)6677 yards/***/E

Rushden and District G.C.
(0933) 312581
Kimbolton Rd. Chelveston, Wellingborough
2 miles east of Higam Ferrers on old A45.
(9)6381 yards/**/C

Staverton Park G.C.
(0327) 705911
Staverton, Daventry
1 mile south of Daventry on A425.
(18)6204 yards/***/C

Wellingborough G.C.
(0933) 677234
Horrowden Hall, Great Horrowden
North of Wellingborough on A509.
(18)6604 yards/**/C/H

Woodlands Vale G.C.
(032736) 291
Woodlands Vale,
Farthingstone, Towcester
3 miles west of Weedon.
(18)6330 yards/***/C

Leicestershire

Birstall G.C.
(0533) 674322
Station Rd. Birstall, Leicester
3 miles north of Leicester
off A6.
(18)5988 yards/***/B/H

Charnwood Forest G.C.
(0509) 890259
Breakback Lane,
Woodhouse Eaves,
Loughborough
(9)6202 yards/***/C/H

Cosby G.C.
(0533) 864759
Chapel Lane, Cosby
(18)6277 yards/**/F/H

Enderby G.C.
(0533) 849388
Mill Lane, Enderby
(9)4356 yards/***/E

Glen Gorse G.C.
(0533) 714159
Glen Rd. Oadby
Just outside Oadby on A6.
(18)6641 yards/**/F/H

Greetham Valley G.C.
(078086) 666
Off B668 in Greetham
(18) 6656 yards/***/C

Hinckley G.C.
(0455) 615124
Leicester Rd. Hinckley
1 mile north of Hinckley on
A47.
(18)6592 yards/**(Tue)/F/H

Humberstone Heights G.C.
(0533) 764674
Gipsy Lane, Leicester
3 miles east of Leicester on
A47.
(18)6444 yards/***/D

Kibworth G.C.
(0533) 792301
Weir Rd. Kibworth
Beauchamp
8 miles south of Leicester on
A6.
(18)6282 yards/**/C

Kirby Muxloe G.C.
(0533) 393457
Station Rd. Kirby Muxloe
4 miles west of Leicester on
A47.
(18)6303 yards/**/F/H

Leicestershire G.C.
(0533) 738825
Evington Lane, Leicester
2 miles south of Leicester.
(18)6312 yards/***/B

Leicestershire Forest G.C
(0455) 824800
Markfield Rd, Botcheston
(18)6111 yards/***/D

Lingdale G.C.
(0509) 890703
Joe Moores Lane,
Woodhouse Eaves
(9)6114 yards/***/C

Longcliffe G.C.
(0509) 239129
Shells Nook Lane,
Nanpantan, Loughborough
(18)6551 yards/**/B/H]

Luffenham Heath G.C.
(0780) 720205
Ketton, Stamford
6 miles south of Stamford.
(18)6254 yards/***/A/H

Lutterworth G.C.
(0455) 552532
Rugby Rd. Lutterworth
(18)5570 yards/**/C

Market Harborough G.C.
(0858) 463684
Oxendon Rd. Market
Harborough
1 mile south of Market
Harboro on A508.
(9)6080 yards/**/D

Melton Mowbray G.C.
(0664) 62118
Waltham Rd. Thorpe
Arnold, Melton Mowbray
2 miles north of Melton
Mowbray on A607.
(9)6200 yards/***/C/M

Oadby G.C.
(0533) 700326
Leicester Rd. Oadby
1 mile south of Leicester on
A6.
(18)6228 yards/***/E

Rothley Park G.C.
(0533) 302809
Westfield Lane, Rothley
6 miles north of Leicester
off A6.
(18)6487 yards/***/B/H/M

R.A.F. North Luffenham G.C.
(0780) 720041
North Luffenham, Oakham
(9)5998 yards/*/E/G

Scraptoft G.C.
(0533) 418863
Beeby Rd. Scraptoft,
Leicester
(18)6146 yards/***/B/H

Ullesthorpe G.C.
(0455) 209023
Frolesworth Rd. Ullesthorpe
(18)6206 yards/**/C/H

Western Park G.C.
(0533) 872339
Scudmore Rd. Braunstone
Frith
2 miles west of Leicester on
A47.
(18)6532 yards/***/E

Whetstone G.C.
(0533) 861424
Cambridge Rd. Cosby
Just south of Leicester.
(18)5795 yards/***/D

Willesley Park G.C.
(0530) 414596
Tamworth Rd. Asby-de-la-
Zouch
2 miles south from Asby-de-
la-Zouch on A453.
(18)6304 yards/***/B/H/M

West Midlands

Belfry G.C
(0675) 70301
Lichfield Road, North
Wishaw, Sutton Coldfield
On junction of A4091 and
A446
(18) 6975 yards/***/A
(18) 6077 yards/***/D

Bloxwich G.C
(0922) 405724
Stafford Road, Bloxwich,
Walsall
4 miles from Walsall centre
off A34
(18) 6286 yards/**/D/H

Boldmere G.C
021-354 3379
Monmouth Drive, Sutton
Coldfield
6 miles N.E of
Birmingham on A452
(18) 4463 yards/***/E

Brand Hall G.C
021-552 2195
Heran Road, Oldbury,
Warley
Leave M5 at junction 2 for
A4123
(18) 5813 yards/***/E

Calderfields G.C
(0922) 640540
Aldridge Road, Walsall
Leave M6 at junction
7 for the A454
(18) 6700 yards/***/E

City of Coventry G.C
(Brandon Wood)
(0203) 543133
Brandon Lane,
Brandon, Coventry
6 miles S. of Coventry on
A45
(18) 6530 yards/***/F

Cocks Moor Woods G.C
021-444 3584
Alcester Road South, Kings
Heath, Birmingham
On A435 near city boundary
(18) 5742 yards/***/E

Copt Heath G.C
(0564) 772650
Warwick Road, Knowle,
Solihull
Leave M42 at junction 5 for
A41
(18) 6504 yards/**/B/H/M

Coventry G.C
(0203) 414152
Finham Park, Coventry
2 miles S. of Coventry on
A444
6613 yards/**/C/H

Dartmouth G.C
021 588 2131
West Bromwich
Off the West Bromwich-
Walsall Road
(9) 6060 yards/**/D

Druids Heath G.C
(0922) 55595
Stonnal Road, Aldridge
Between Sutton Coldfield
and Walsall off A452
(18) 6914 yards/**/C/H

Dudley G.C
(0384) 233877
Turners Hill, Rowley
Regis, Warley
One mile from town centre
(18) 5715 yards/**/E

Edgbaston G.C.
021 454 1736
1 mile south of city centre
(18) 6118 yards/***/B

Enville G.C
(0384) 872074
Highgate Common, Enville,
Stourbridge
Take A458 Bridgnorth Road
(18) 6541 yards/**/C/H
(18) 6207 yards/**/C/H

Forest of Arden Golf &
Country Club
(0676) 22335
Maxstoke Road, meriden,
Coventry
10 miles W. of Coventry off
A45
(18) 6962 yards/***/B/H
(18) 6500 yards/***/B

Fulford Heath
(0564) 822806
Tanners Green Lane,
Wythall, Birmingham
1 mile from main Alcester
road
(18) 6216 yards/**/D/H

Gay Hill G.C
021 430 6523
Alcester Road, Hollywood,
Birmingham
7 miles from city centre on
A435
(18) 6522 yards/**/C/H

Grange G.C
(0203) 451465
Copsewood, Coventry
3 miles from city centre on
A428
(9) 3001 yards/**/E

Great Barr G.C
021 358 4376
Chapel Lane, Great Barr,
Birmingham
Adjacent to exit 7 of M6
(18) 6546 yards/**/D/H

Hagley G.C
(0562) 883701
Wassel Grove, hagley,
Stourbridge
Off A456 Kidderminster-
Birmingham Road
(18) 6353 yards/**/D

Halesowen G.C
021-501 3606
The Leasowes, Halesowen
(18) 5754 yards/**/D

Handsworth G.C
021 554 0599
11 Sunningdale Close,
Handsworth, Birmingham
3 miles N.W of city centre
off A41
(18) 6312 yards/**/C/H

Harborne G.C
021 427 3058
40 Tennal Road,
Birmingham
3 miles W. of city centre
off A4040
(18) 6240 yards/**/C/H

Harborne Church Farm G.C
021 427 1204
Vicarage Road, Harborne,
Birmingham
Follow harborne Road to
Vicarage Lane
(9) 4514 yards/***/F

Hatchford Brook G.C
021 743 9821
Coventry Road, Sheldon,
Birmingham
On A45 road to Coventry
(18) 6164 yards/***/F

Hearsall G.C
(0203) 713470
Beechwood Avenue,
Coventry
Off A45, 2 miles S. of city
centre
(18) 5963 yards/**/C/H

Hilltop G.C
021 554 4463
Park Lane, Handsworth,
Birmingham
Take Birmingham road
from M5
(18) 6114 yards/***/E

Himley Hall G.C
(0902) 895207
Log Cabin, Himley Hall Park,
Dudley
Turn onto B4176 from A449
(9) 3090 yards/***/E

Kings Norton G.C
(0564) 826789
Brockhill Lane, Weatheroak,
Alvechurch, Birmingham
2 miles from junction 3 of
M42
(27) **/D/H

Ladbrook Park G.C
(05644) 2264
Poolhead lane, Yanworth-in-
Arden, Solihull
4 miles from Hockley Heath
on A4023
6407 yards/***(prior arrangement)/D/H

Lickey Hills G.C
(021) 453 3159
Rose Hill, Old Birmingham
Road, Rednal, Birmingham
Road
10 miles S.E of city centre
(18) 6010 yards/***/E

Little Aston G.C
021 353 2066
Streetly, Sutton Coldfield
3 miles N. of Sutton
Coldfield
(18) 6724 yards/**/F

Maxstoke Park G.C
(0675) 64915
Castle lane, Coleshill,
Birmingham
From A446 take B4147
to Nuneaton
(18) 6437 yards/**/D

Moor Hall G.C
021 308 6130
Moor Hall Drive, Four Oaks,
Sutton Coldfield
2 miles from Sutton
Coldfield on A453
(18) 6219 yards/**/B

Moseley G.C
021 444 2115
Springfield Road,
Kings Heath, Birmingham
E. of Alcester Road on
Birmingham ring-road
(18) 6227 yards/B/H/L

North Warwickshire G.C
(0676) 22259
Hampton Lane, Meriden
1 mile from Stourbridge on
B4102
(9) 3186 yards/**(not
Thurs)/C

North Worcestershire G.C
021 475 1047
Frankley Beeches Road,
Northfield, Birmingham
(18) 5919 yards/**/D

Olton G.C
021 705 1083
Mirfield Road, Solihull
7 miles S. of Birmingham on
A41
(18) 6229 yards/**(not
Weds)/D/H

Oxley Park G.C
(0902) 20506
Bushbury, Wolverhampton
2 miles from town centre
off A449
(18) 6168 yards/***/D

Patshull Park
(0902) 700100
Burnhill Green, Pattingham,
Wolverhampton
Take exit 3 from M54 to
Albrighton and Patshull
(18) 6460 yards/***/F

Penn G.C
(0902) 341142
Penn Common, Penn,
Wolverhampton
2 miles S.W of town off
A449
(18) 6465 yards/**/D

Pype Hayes G.C
021 351 1014
Eaglehurst Road, Walmley,
Sutton Coldfield
Take junction 6 from M6,
take Tyburn road to
Eaglehurst
(18) 5811 yards/***/E

Robin Hood G.C
021 706 0061
St. Bernards Road, Solihull
6 miles S. of Birmingham on
A41
(18) 6609 yards/**/F/H

Rose Hill G.C
021 453 3159
Lickey Hills, Rednal,
Birmingham
Leave M5 by junction 4
to Lickey Hills
(18) 6006 yards/***/E

Sandwell Park G.C
021 553 4637
Birmingham Road, West
Bromwich
(18) 6470 yards/**/F

Shirley G.C
021 744 6001
Stratford Road, Solihull
7 miles S. of Birmingham on
A34
(18) 6445 yards/**/C

South Staffordshire G.C
(0902) 751065
Tettenhall
(18) 6653 yards/**/B

Stourbridge G.C
(0384) 395566
Pedmore
(18)6178 yards/**/C

Sutton Coldfield G.C
021 353 9633
Streetly
(18)6541 yards/***/B

Swindon G.C
(0902) 897031
Bridgnorth Rd, Swindon
(18) 6042 yards/**/C

Walmley G.C
021 373 0029
Wylde Green
(18)6537 yards/**/B

Walsall G.C
(0922) 613512
The Broadway, 0ff A34
(18) 6243 yards/**/A

Windmill Village Hotel &
G.C
(0203) 407241
Birmingham Rd, Coventry
(18) 5200 yards/***/D

Warwickshire

Atherstone G.C
(0827) 713110
The Outwoods, Atherstone
Half mile out of Atherstone
on Colehill Road
(18) 6239 yards/**/C/H

Kenilworth G.C
(0926) 58517
Crew Lane, kenilworth
Off A429 from Kenilworth
to Coventry
(18) 6408 yards/***/F/H

Leamington & County G.C
(0926) 425961
Golf Lane, Whitnash,
Leamington Spa
2 miles from town centre
on A452
(18) 6425 yards/***/F

Newbold Comyn G.C
(0926) 421157
Newbold Terrace East,
Leamington Spa
Off B4099 Willes Road
(18) 6259 yards/***/D

Nuneaton G.C
(0203) 347810
Golf Drive, Whitestone,
Nuneaton
2 miles from town centre
off B4114
(18) 6412 yards/**/C/H

Purley Chase G.C
(0203) 393118
Ridge lane, Atherstone,
Nuneaton
Take A5 to Mancetters
Island and onto Pipers Lane
(18) 6604 yards/***/F/H

Rugby G.C
(0788) 542306
Clifton Road, Rugby
Off the Rugby-Market
Harborough Road
(18) 5457 yards/***/E

Stratford-Upon-Avon G.C
(0789) 205749
Tiddlington Road,
Stratford-upon-Avon
Half-mile from River bridge
on B4089
(18) 6309 yards/**/F/H

Warwick G.C
(0926) 494396
The Racecourse, Warwick
Half-mile pat junction
of A41 and A46
(9) 2682 yards/***(not
Sundays)/E

Welcombe Hotel G.C
(0789) 295292
Warwick Road,
Stratford-Upon-Avon
2 miles from Stratford
on A46 to Warwick
(18) 6600 yards/**/C/H

The Belfry

The 'Belfry project' involved not only a plan to build a Championship course on American lines where in due course the Ryder Cup could be staged, but also the siting of a new headquarters for the P.G.A. Peter Alliss and Dave Thomas were given the task of designing the show piece and a very great task it was, for the land they were given was flat, uninteresting and comprised one small lake, a stream and numerous acres of potato fields.

Well, the boys didn't hang about: earth mountains were moved, the potatoes disappeared and hundreds of trees were planted—the end result in fact produced two 18 hole courses, opened in June 1977. The feature course was named the **Brabazon**, after Lord Brabazon a former President of the P.G.A. and the shorter, easier course, the **Derby**.

A key feature of The Belfry is that it is a Club without any Members. Both courses open their doors to the general public at all times all the year round. Not surprisingly the Brabazon is particularly busy and before setting off it is important to telephone and book a starting time. The **Golf Manager**, **Robert Maxfield**, and the two resident golf **professionals**, **Peter McGovern** and **Simon Wordsworth** run the show efficiently. They can be contacted on **(0675) 470301**.

In 1993 the green fees payable for a round on the Brabazon course were £50 (seven days a week) This contrasted with £25 for a round on the Derby course; a day ticket (one round on both courses) was priced at £75 (again the same rate being applicable throughout the week).

Situated close to the country's industrial heart there is surely no golfing complex in Britain better served by communication networks. The Belfry is one mile

from the M42 (junction 9), five miles from the M6 (junction 4), nine miles from Birmingham city centre and less than ten minutes from Birmingham International Airport and the N.E.C. Railway Station. The exact positioning of the Golf Club is at the apex of the A446 and A4091.

Apart from the sheer length of the Brabazon Course the many water hazards are likely to present the greatest challenge. Two of its holes are guaranteed to excite; the short par four 10th where almost everyone tries to be famous for five seconds before spending five minutes trying to fish his or her ball out of the lake, and the thrilling 18th where Christy O'Connor Jnr hit that magnificent 2 iron in the 1989 Ryder Cup, and where American dreams of victory in the same match met a watery grave.

The Belfry,
Lichfield Road,
Wishaw,
North Warwickshire, B76 9PR.

Brabazon Course

Hole	Yards	Par	Hole	Yards	Par
1	408	4	10	301	4
2	340	4	11	365	4
3	455	4	12	225	3
4	569	5	13	364	4
5	389	4	14	184	3
6	386	4	15	540	5
7	173	3	16	400	4
8	476	5	17	555	5
9	390	4	18	455	4
Out	3,586	37	In	3,389	36
			Out	3,586	37
			Totals	6,975	73

The counties of East Anglia, which for our purposes comprise Norfolk, Suffolk and Cambridgeshire, stretch from Constable Country in the south, through the Fens and the Broads to the tip of the Wash. For golfers this means it stretches from Felixstowe Ferry, through Thetford to Hunstanton. There are numerous other combinations capable of whetting the golfing appetite, for East Anglia is one of the game's richest regions; certainly for quality and variety it has few equals. It is also a corner of Britain where golf has long been a popular pastime.

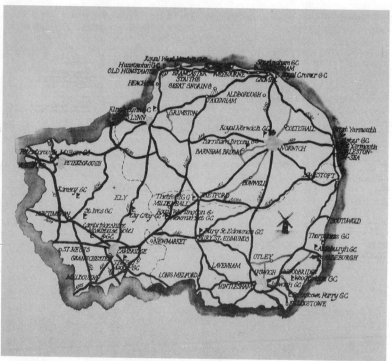

Norfolk

It is doubtful whether any county in England can surpass Norfolk's great range of outstanding courses. In short it offers the golfer a bit of everything. There are the magnificent links courses at **Hunstanton** and **Brancaster**, some terrifically scenic golf along the cliffs at **Sheringham** and **Cromer** and a number of superb inland courses of which **Thetford, Barnham Broom** and **Kings Lynn** are prime examples.

However, the title of 'Oldest Club' in Norfolk goes to **Great Yarmouth and Caister**, founded in 1882. A fine seaside links, it is located to the north of Great Yarmouth close to the old Roman town of Caister-on-Sea and near to the start of the A149 coastal road. Punters may wish to note that the golf course is actually situated inside part of Great Yarmouth race course.

Cromer, some twenty-five miles north along the A149 is apparently famed for its crabs—the town, not the golf course I hasten to add—and also for its 150 year old lighthouse. The latter is a feature of **Royal Cromer's** attractive cliff top course. The 14th, the 'Lighthouse Hole', was played by Tony Jacklin during his '18 holes at 18 different courses helicopter round'. Several elevated tees and a generous spread of gorse makes for a very interesting game.

Sheringham is only five miles further along the coast and is Norfolk's other great cliff top course. Founded some three years after Cromer in 1891 it is perhaps less exacting than its neighbour but certainly no less scenic. The view from the 5th hole is particularly stunning looking out across the rugged north Norfolk.

Kings Lynn is our next port of call, and another very good golf course. Although the **Kings Lynn** Golf Club was founded back in 1923, it has played at Castle Rising to the north of the town since 1975. An Alliss-Thomas creation, it's very heavily wooded and quite a demanding test of golf.

The golfing visitor to Norwich, one of England's more attractive county towns, should have little difficulty in finding a game. **Sprowston Park** is a welcoming club on the edge of the city while for a fine combination of the old and the new try **Royal Norwich** and **Barnham Broom**. Both clubs have excellent parkland courses. Barnham Broom is part of an Hotel and Country Club complex and has two courses with numerous accompanying leisure facilities.

Last but not least we must visit **Thetford,** right in the very heart of East Anglia and close to the Norfolk-Suffolk boundary. Thetford is surely one of England's most beautiful inland courses. Set amid glorious oaks, pines and silver birch trees it is also a great haven for wildlife (rather like Luffenham Heath in Leicestershire). Golden pheasant abound and one can also sight red deer and even, so I'm told, Chinese Water Deer (whatever they may be!) The green fee here is always money well spent.

Suffolk

Of the twenty or so Golf Clubs in Suffolk, about half were founded in the nineteenth Century and the **Felixstowe Ferry** Golf Club which dates from 1880 is the fifth oldest club in England. Given its antiquity, and the fact that it was here that the 'father of golf writers' Bernard Darwin began to play his golf, Felixstowe Ferry is as good a place as any to begin our brief golfing tour of Suffolk.

The course lies about a mile to the north east of Felixstowe and is a classic test of traditional links golf. This part of Suffolk is fairly remote and at times it could easily be imagined that one was playing one of the better Scottish links courses. The greens are first class and the wind is often a major factor.

The A45 links Felixstowe with Suffolk's largest town. The **Ipswich** Golf Club at Purdis Heath, three miles east of Ipswich, was designed by James Braid and is a fine heathland course. Always well-maintained, the fairways wind their way between two large ponds and are bordered by heather and an attractive assortment of hardwood trees and silver birches. **Woodbridge** offers a similar type of challenge. Like the Ipswich course it's beautifully mature but is much more undulating. The Golf Club is located two miles east of Woodbridge along the B1084 Orford road.

A little further up the Suffolk coast lie two delightful holiday courses: **Thorpeness** and **Aldeburgh**. Although close to the sea both are again heather and gorse types. The town of Aldeburgh is of course famed for its annual music festival and Benjamin Britten once lived next to the Club's 14th fairway. Thorpeness, yet another James Braid creation, is about two miles north of Aldeburgh and is especially scenic. One hole that everyone remembers is the par three 7th, played across an attractive pond. On the 18th an unusual water tower (the 'House in the Clouds') and a restored windmill provide a unique background.

Over to the west of Suffolk the two courses that stand out are **Bury St. Edmunds** and **Royal Worlington**. The former is a fairly tough parkland course. Royal Worlington and Newmarket, to give the latter its full title, is located two miles from Mildenhall, midway between Cambridge and Bury St. Edmunds. A marvellous course, essentially heathland but with an almost links feel it was once generously described as the finest nine hole course in the world, visitors should note, however, that it can be very difficult to arrange a game here.

Cambridgeshire

Having ventured west it is time to inspect the land of the fens and the courses of Cambridgeshire. Not exactly a county renowned for its golf, the courses tending, as one might expect, to be rather flat. One great exception though is the **Gog Magog** Golf Club situated to the south east of Cambridge which offers a tremendously enjoyable test of golf. The Club takes its name from the ridge of low hills on which it lies. Apparently taking a line due east from here the next range of hills one comes across is the Ural Mountains! Among many fine holes, the par four 16th stands out and is surely one of the best (and toughest!) two-shot holes in the country. A second good course, though not in the same league as Gog Magog, close to the famous University City belongs to the **Cambridgeshire Moat House Hotel**. It is a particularly tough course when played from the back tees with a lake and several ditches providing the challenges.

Cambridgeshire
Abbotsley G.C.
(0480) 215153
Eynesbury Hardwicke, St.
Neots
(18)6150 yards/***/C

Cambridgeshire Moat
House Hotel G.C.
(0954) 780555
Bar Hill 4 miles north of
Cambridge off A604.
(18)6734 yards/***/B/L/M

Ely City G.C.
(0353) 662751
Cambridge Rd. Ely
Just south of Ely on A10.
(18)6686 yards/**/B

Girton G.C.
(0223) 276169
Dodford Lane, Girton
3 miles north of Cambridge
off A604. (18)6085
yards/**/C

Gog Magog G.C.
(0223) 247626
Shelford Bottom
2 miles south of Cambridge
on A13107. (18)5354
yards/**/F/H
(9)5833 yards/**/F/H

Hintlesham Hall G.C.
(047387) 334
Hintlesham
(18)6630 yards/***/A

March G.C.
(0354) 52364
Frogs Abbey, March
(9)6200 yards/**/D

Orton Meadows G.C.
(0733) 237478
Ham Lane, Peterborough
2 miles west of Peterboro.
(18)5800 yards/***/D

Peterborough Milton G.C.
(0733) 380489
Milton Ferry, Peterborough
2 miles west of Peterboro
on A47.
(18)6431 yards/**/F/H

Ramsey G.C.
(0487) 812600
4 Abbey Terrace, Ramsey,
Huntingdon
(18)6136 yards/**/C/H

St. Ives G.C.
(0480) 68392
Westwood Rd. St. Ives
5 miles east of Huntingdon
off A604. (9)6052
yards/**/C/H

Lakeside Lodge G.C.
(0487) 740540
Fen Road, Pidley
(18)6600 yards/E/***

St. Neots G.C.
(0480) 72363
Crosshall Rd. St. Neots
2 miles west of St. Neots off
A1. (18)6027 yards/**/F

Thorpe Wood G.C.
(0733) 267701
Thorpe Wood,
Peterborough
(18)6595 yards/***/D

Suffolk
Aldeburgh G.C.
(0728) 452890
Saxmundham Rd.
Aldeburgh
1 mile from town on A1094.
(18)6330 yards/***/F/H
(9)4228 yards/***/F/H

Beccles G.C.
(0502) 712244
The Common, Beccles
(9)2696 yards/**/C

Bungay and Waveney
Valley G.C.
(0986) 892337
Outney Common, Bungay
Outside Bungay on A143.
(18)6615 yards/**/C/H

Bury St. Edmunds G.C.
(0284) 755979
Tuthill, Bury St. Edmunds
2 miles from Bury on A45.
(18)6615 yards/***/B/H

Cretingham G.C.
(0728) 685275
Cretingham, Woodridge
(9)1955 yards/***/D

Felixstowe Ferry G.C.
(0394) 286834
Ferry Rd. Felixstowe
(18)6042 yards/***/C/H

Flempton G.C.
(0284) 728291

Flempton, Bury St.
Edmonds
4 miles from Bury.
(9)6074 yards/**/C

Fornham Park G.C.
(0284) 706777
Fornham St. Genevive,
Bury St. Edmunds
2 miles from Bury.
(18)6212 yards/***/F

Haverhill G.C.
(0440) 61951
Coupals Rd. Haverhill
(9)5680 yards/***/C

Ipswich G.C.
(0473) 728941
Purdis Heath, Bucklesham
Rd.
3 miles east of Ipswich off
A45.
(18)6405 yards/**/B/H(18)
(9)3860 yards/***/D

Links G.C.
(0638) 663000
Cambridge Rd. Newmarket
1 mile south of Newmarket
opposite racecourse.
(18)6162 yards/***/F/H

Newton Green G.C.
(0787) 77217
Newton Green, Sudbury
3 miles east of Sudbury on
A134.
(9)5488 yards/**/D/H

Rookery Park G.C.
(0502) 560380
Beccles Rd. Carlton
Coleville, Lowestoft
2 miles west of Lowestoft
on A146.
(18)6649 yards/***/C/H

Royal Worlington and
Newmarket G.C.
(0368) 71226
Worlington, Bury St.
Edmonds
(9)3105 yards/**/B

Rushmere G.C.
(0473) 725648
Rushmere Heath, Ipswich
East of Ipswich off A1214.
(18)6287 yards/***/C/H

Southwold G.C.
(0502) 723234

The Common, Southwold
(9)6001 yards/***/C/H

Stowmarket G.C.
(0449) 736473
Lower Rd. Onehouse,
Stowmarket
(18)6101 yards/***/C/H

Thorpeness G.C.
(072845) 2176
Thorpeness
(18)6241 yards/**/B/H

Waldringfield Heath G.C.
(0473) 36768
Newbourne Rd.
Waldringfield
5 miles north of Ipswich
off A12.
(18)5837 yards/***/C

Woodbridge G.C.
(03943) 2038
Bromeswell Heath,
Woodbridge
2 miles east of Woodbridge
off A12. (18)6314
yards/**/B/H
(9)4486 yards/**/B/H

Wood Valley G.C.
(0502) 712244
The Common, Beccles
(9)2781 yards/**/D/H

Norfolk
Barnham Broom G. and C.C.
(060) 545393
Norwich, Norfolk
8 miles south of Norwich.
(18)6603 yards/**/B

Bawburgh G.C.
(0603) 746390
Long Lane, Bawburgh,
Norwich
Behind Royal Norfolk
Showground.
(9)5278 yards/***/D

Costessey Park G.C.
(0603) 746333
Costessey Park, Costessey,
Norwich
3 miles west of Norwich.
(18)5853 yards/***/C

Dereham G.C.
(0362) 695900
Quebec Rd. Dereham
1 mile from Derehamon.
(9)6225 yards/**/C/H

Diss G.C.
(0379) 642847
Stutson Rd. Stutson
Common, Diss 1 mile town
centre.
(9)5900 yards/***/D

Eaton G.C.
(0603) 51686
Newmarket Rd. Norwich
(18)6125 yards/**/B/H

Fakenham G.C.
(0328) 2867
Sports Centre, The
Racecourse, Fakenham
1 mile south of Fakenham
off A1065.
(9)5879 yards/***/C

Gorlestone G.C.
(0493) 661911
Warren Rd. Gorlestone,
Gt.Yarmouth
3 miles south of Gt.
Yarmouth off A12.
(18)6400 yards/***/C/H

Great Yarmouth and
Caister G.C.
(0493) 728699
Beech House, Caister-on-
Sea, Gt.Yarmouth
2 miles north of
Gt.Yarmouth on A149.
(18)6235 yards/***/F

Hunstanton G.C.
(0485) 532811
Golf Course Rd. Old
Hunstanton
(18)6670 yards/***/A/H

Kings Lynn G.C.
(0553) 631654
Castle Rising, Kings Lynn
(18)6646 yards/**/A/H

Links Country Park Hotel
(026375) 691
West Runton
Betweeen Cromer and
Sheringham on A149.
(9)2407 yards/***/C

Mundesley G.C.
(0263) 720279
Links Rd. Mundesley
1 mile from Mundesley.
(9)5410 yards/***/C

R.A.F. Marham G.C.
(0760) 337261
RAF Marham, Kings Lynn
(9)5244 yards/*/D/G

Richmond Park G.C.
(0953) 881803
Saham Rd, Watton
(18)6300 yards/***/D/H

Royal Cromer G.C.
(0263) 512884
145 Overstrand Rd. Cromer
1 mile east of Cromer on
B1159.
(18)6508 yards/***/B/H

Royal Norwich G.C.
(0603) 429928
Drayton High Rd.
Hellesdon
(18)6603 yards/**/F/H

Royal West Norfolk G.C.
(0485) 210087
Brancaster, Kings Lynn
(18)6428 yards/**/A/H

Ryston Park G.C.
(0366) 383834
Denver, Downham Maret
1 mile south of Downham
on A10.
(9)6292 yards/**/D

Sheringham G.C.
(0263) 823488
Weybourne Rd.
Sheringham
1 mile from town on A149.
(18)6464 yards/***/F/H

Sprowston Park G.C.
(0603) 410657
Wroxham Rd. Sprowston
(18)5985 yards/**/B/H

Swaffham G.C.
(0760) 721611
Cley Rd. Swaffham
1 mile from Swaffham.
(9)6252 yards/**/C

Thetford G.C.
(0842) 752169
Brandon Rd. Thetford
(18)6879 yards/**/B/H

Derbyshire, Nottinghamshire & Lincs

Derbyshire

Not wishing to be unkind but Derby the town isn't one of Earth's more inspiring places—nor for that matter are most of the Midland's industrial sprawls—but Derbyshire the county is a different matter altogether. The Peak District is without question one of the most scenic regions in Britain and commencing only a short distance north of Derby, it covers the greater part of the county—the Pennine Way of course starts in Derbyshire.

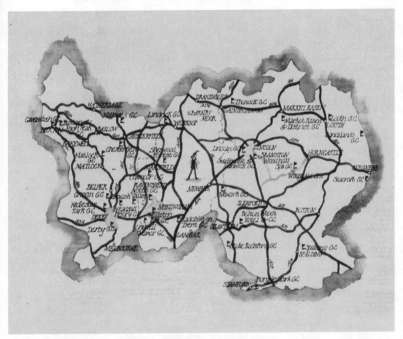

As well as being the beginning of all things beautiful the area just north of Derby is where three of the county's leading golf courses are to be found: Kedlestone Park, Breadsall Priory and Chevin. Located approximately four miles from Derby off the A111 (and well signposted) **Kedleston Park** golf course occupies a beautiful situation and is generally rated as the finest course in Derbyshire. Quite lengthy from the back tees, it has a variety of challenging holes. Eyeing the course from across a lake is the impressive Kedleston Hall, historic home of Lord Scarsdale.

I'm not sure what the 13th century monks would have made of the **Breadsall Priory** Golf and Country Club, 3 miles north east of Derby at Morley, but for heathens of the 20th century it provides an ideal setting for one of the most enjoyable games in the Midlands. Golfwise Breadsall Priory has only been on the map since 1976 but the undulating parkland course with its imported Cumberland turf greens has matured rapidly; indeed a second 18 holes have recently been completed and they admirably complement a new plush leisure centre.

Chevin lies slightly further north off the A6 at Duffield; it has an interesting layout, the first ten holes are a steady climb towards a spectacular vantage point after which holes eleven to eighteen gently bring you down to earth (or at least to Duffield!) Another course to recommend in the south of the county and over towards Nottingham is the wooded layout at **Erewash Valley**, noted for its two quarry holes.

Moving 'up country', the picturesque town of **Matlock** has a fairly short but pleasant course situated north of the town off the Chesterfield road, and if heading in that direction **Chesterfield's** course at Walton is also well worth a visit and there are two public courses also close to the town centre.

The town of Buxton lies in the heart of the Peak District and is for many people their idea of the perfect town. This may have something to do with the fact that some of the finest pubs in England are located round about, but it is also helped by the fact that there are two excellent golf courses either side of the town—Buxton and High Peak and Cavendish. Of similar length it is difficult to say which is the better, in any event both warmly welcome visitors at green fees that should leave a few pennies for celebrating nearby.

Nottinghamshire

Moving into Nottinghamshire, the famous **Notts** Golf Club at Hollinwell is a rather splendid 'Nottingham gorse affair'. In addition those visiting the county town should strongly consider the merits of **Wollaton Park**, an attractive course set amidst the deer park of a stately home, surprisingly close to the centre of Nottingham, and the city's two 18 hole municipal courses are also fairly good. Slightly further afield but well worth noting are the parkland courses at **Chilwell Manor** (A6005) and **Radcliffe on Trent** (A52 East of the town).

Two of the county's finest courses lie fairly close to one another near the centre of Nottinghamshire, **Coxmoor** and **Sherwood Forest**. The former is a moorland type course situated just south of Mansfield at Sutton-in-Ashfield. The Sherwood Forest course is more of a heathland type—well wooded, (as one might expect given its name) with much tangling heather. Measuring over 6,700 yards it is quite a test too.

Over towards the border with Lincolnshire is the attractive town of Newark with its twelfth century castle and cobbled market square.

Newark Golf Club lies four miles east of the town off the A17. Reasonably flat and quite secluded the golf is a little less testing than at some of the county's bigger clubs. .

Before inspecting Lincolnshire, a brief word on the delights of **Lindrick**. Diplomats take note, it is a source of aggravation to many proud Yorkshiremen that this fine course which lies for the most part in their county has a Notts postal address.

Lincolnshire

Lincolnshire is a large county. It used to be even larger before Grimsby, Scunthorpe and Cleethorpes were all snatched away by that upstart Humberside. Still, by my reckoning there are at least twenty golf courses left. **Woodhall Spa** is of course head and shoulders above the rest but although the county as a whole is unlikely to be the venue for many golfing holidays there are certainly a handful of courses well worth a visit.

Woodhall Spa is one of the country's greatest, (and most beautiful) heathland courses. **Burghley Park** Golf Club is noted for its greens and its links with Mark James, while just over the county boundary in Leicestershire lies **Luffenham Heath**, a truly splendid golf course.

Lincoln was briefly mentioned, it really is an attractive city—a beautiful cathedral, a castle and a wealth of history. The best golf to be found in **Lincoln** is at Torksey just to the north west of the city. It's a fairly sandy, heathland type course with a lovely selection of trees. **Southcliffe and Canwick**, on the opposite side of Lincoln is a shorter parkland course, but challenging in its own way.

Three courses of note towards the north of the county are at **Gainsborough** (Thonock), **Market Rasen** and **Louth**. All are very welcoming, Thonock is a classic parkland layout, Market Rasen is a very good woodland type course while Louth has an attractive setting in a local beauty spot, the Hubbards Hills. A second course near Louth, **Kenwick Park**, recently opened and already promises to be one of the region's top courses.

Skegness is a famous resort, perhaps not everyone's cup of tea, but a game here is certainly recommended for those who like their links golf. **Seacroft** is the place; flattish, windy and plenty of sand dunes. Further up the coast, a less severe challenge is offered at **Sandilands**. The south of the county comprises much rich agricultural land but not too much in the way of golf. **Stoke Rochford** however is a popular parkland course and **Spalding** is worth inspecting particularly at the time of year when the famous bulbs have flourished. An 18 hole course here, and in the south west, the new **Belton Woods** Hotel & Country Club has a delightfully peaceful setting outside Grantham. It has two eighteen hole courses, (as well as a multitude of other facilities) the Lancaster and Wellington, and there is a lot of water to be negotiated—a few Barnes Wallis type shots may be called for!

Derbyshire

Alfreton G.C
(0773) 832070
Wingfield Rd, Oakesthorpe
1 mile N of Alfreton
(9) 5012 yards/**/D

Allestree Park G.C
(0332) 550616
Allestree Hall, Derbyshire
3 miles N of Derby off A6
(18) 5749 yards/***(Sun
am)/E

Ashbourne G.C
(0335) 42078
Clifton, Ashbourne
1 mile S of Ashborne
(9) 5359 yards/***/D

Bakewell Golf Club
(062981) 2307
Station Rd, Bakewell
E of Bakewell off A619
(9) 4808 yards/***/E

Breadshall Priory G.& CC
(0332) 832235
Moor Rd, Morley, Derby
3 miles N of Derby off A61
(9) 6402 yards/***/C

Burton On Trent G.C
(0283) 44551
Ashby Road East,
Burton On Trent
(18) 6555 yards/***(H)/F

Buxton & High Peak G.C
(0298) 23453
Fairfield, Buxton
N of Buxton off A6
(18) 5954 yards/***/F

Cavendish G.C
(0298) 23494
Gadley Lane, Buxton
1 mile W of Buxton
(18) 5815 yards/***/C

Chapel en le Frith G.C.
(0298) 812118
Manchester Road
(18)6089 yards/***/D

Horsley Lodge G.C.
(0332) 780838
Smalley Mill Road
(18)6434 yards/***/C

Chesterfield G.C
(0246) 279256
Walton, Chesterfield
(18) 6326 yards/**/C

Chesterfield Municipal G.C
(0246) 73887
Crow Lane, Chesterfield
(18) 6044 yards/***/E

Chevin G.C
(0332) 841864
Golf Lane, Duffield
5 miles N of Derby, off A6
(18) 6043 yards/**/C

Craythorne G.C
(0293) 64329
Stretton, Burton On Trent
Off A38
(18) 5164 yards/***/D

Derby G.C
(0332) 766323
Sinfin, Derby
(18) 6183 yards/***/E

Erewash Valley G.C
(0602) 323258
Stanton By Dale, Ilkeston
Junction 25 off M1
(18) 6444 yards/**/C

Glossop & District G.C
(04574) 3117
Sheffield Rd, Glossop
1 mile from Glossop of A57
(18) 5726 yards/***/E

Ilkeston Borough G.C
(0602) 320304
West End Drive, Ilkeston
(18) 6636 yards/***/E

Kedleston Park G.C
(0332) 840035
Kedleston, Quarndon,
Derby
4 miles N of Derby off A11
(18) 6636 yards/**(H)/B

Matlock G.C
(0629) 582191
Chesterfield Road,
Matlock Off A632
(18) 5871 yards/**/C

Mickleover G.C
(0332) 518662
Uttoxeter Rd, Mickleover
3 miles W of Derby off
A516
(18) 5621 yards/***(Sun)/D

Ormonde Fields G & CC
(0773) 742987
Nottingham Rd, Codnor,
Ripley
Off A610
(18) 6007 yards/***/B

Pastures G.C
(0332) 513921
Pastures Hospital,
Mickleover
3 miles W of Derby
(9) 5005 yards/*/F

Renishaw Park G.C
(0246) 432044
Station Rd, Renishaw
(18) 6253 yards/***/C

Shirland G. & C C
(0773) 834935
Lower Delves, Shirland
(18) 6021 yards/***/D

Sickleholme G.C
(0443) 51306
Barnford
(18) 6064 yards/***/C

Stanedge G.C
(0246) 566156
Walton, Chesterfield
5 miles S of Chesterfield
(9) 4867 yards/**(pm)/D

Tapton Park G.C.
(0246) 239500
Murray House, Tapton
(18)6010 yards/***/E

Nottinghamshire

Beeston Fields G.C
(0602) 257062
Beeston Fields, Nottingham
4 miles W of Nottingham
(18) 6404 yards/***/F

Bulwell Forest G.C
(0602) 278008
Huchnall Rd, Bulwell
4 miles N of Notts off A611
(18) 572 yards/***/C

Chilwell Manor G.C
(0602) 258958
Chilwell, Nottingham
(18) 6379 yards/**/C

Coxmoor G.C
(0623) 557359
Coxmoor Rd, Sutton In
Ashfield
3 miles SW of Mansfield
(18) 6501 yards/**(H)/B

Edwalton Municipal G.C
(0602) 234775
Edwalton, Nottingham
(9) 6672 yards/***/E

Kilton Forest G.C
(0909) 472488
Blyth Rd, Worksop
2 miles N of Worksop
(18) 6772 yards/***(Sun)/E

Lindrick G.C
(0909) 475282
Lindrick Common,
Worksop
4 miles W of Worksop off
A57
(18) 6615 yards/***/Winter
B/A

Mapperley G.C
(0602) 265611
Mapperley Plains,
Nottingham
5 miles NE of Notts
(18) 6224 yards/***/D

Newark G.C
(0636) 626282
Coddington, Newark
(18) 6486 yards/**/C

Nottingham City G.C
(0602) 278021
Bulwell, Nottingham
NW of city
(18) 6120 yards/***/E

Notts G.C
(0623) 753225
Hollinwell, Kirkby In
Ashfield
3 miles N of Notts of A611
(18) 7020 yards/**(H)/A/B

Oakmere Park G.C
(0602) 653545
Oaks Lane
(18) 7100 yards/***/C
(9) 3400 yards/***/E

Oxton G.C
(0602) 653545
Oxton, Southwell
(18) 6630 yards/***/D

Radcliffe On Trent G.C
(0602) 333000
Cropwell Road,
Radcliffe On Trent
7 miles W of Notts
(18) 6423 yards/**(Tues)/C

Retford G.C
(0777) 703733
Ordsall, Retford
Off A620
(9) 6230 yards/**/F

Ruddington Grange G.C
(0602) 846141
Wilford Road
5 miles south of
Nottingham
(18) 6500 yards/**/C

Sherwood Forest G.C
(0623) 26689
Eaking Road, Mansfield
3 miles S of Mansfield
(18) 6709 yards/***(Mon,
Thurs, Fri)/B

Ruchcliffe G.C.
(0509) 852959
Stocking Lane
(18)6020 yards/**/B

Stanton On The Wolds G.C
(06077) 2006
Stanton On The Wolds,
Keyworth
7 miles S of Notts off A606
(18) 6379 yards/**(Tues)/C

Wollaton Park G.C
(0602) 787574
Wollaton Park, Nottingham
(18) 6494 yards/**/D

Worksop G.C
(0909) 472696
Windmill Lane, Worksop
S of Worksop, off A57
(18) 6651 yards/***/C

Lincolnshire

Belton Park G.C
(0476) 67399
Belton Lane, Grantham
2 miles from Grantham.
(18) 6420 yards/***/C

Belton Woods G.C
(0476) 593200
(18) 7021 yards/***/D
(18) 6875 yards/***/D
(9) 1184 yards/***/E

Blankney G.C
(0526) 20263
Blankney, Lincoln
1 mile S of Metheringham
on B1188.
(18) 6402 yards/**/C

Boston G.C
(0205) 350589
Cowbridge,
Horncastle Rd. Boston
2 miles N of Boston on
B1183.
(18) 5825 yards/***/B

Burghley Park G.C
(0780) 53789
St. Martins Without,
Stamford
(18) 6200 yards/***/B

Canwick Park G.C
(0522) 522166
Canwick Park,
Washingborough Rd.
2 miles S of Lincoln on
A158. (18) 6257 yards/**/D

Carholme G.C
(0522) 23725
Carholme Rd. Lincoln
1 mile from Lincoln on A57.
(18) 6114 yards/***(Sun)/F

Gainsborough G.C
(0427) 613088
Thonock, Gainsborough
1 mile NE of Gainsboro.
(18) 6504 yards/***/B

Horncastle G.C.
(0507) 526800
West Ashby
(18) 5782 yards/***/D

Lincoln G.C
(042771) 210
Torksey, Lincoln
(18) 6400 yards/***/B/H/L

Louth G.C
(0507) 603681
Crowtree Lane, Louth
(18) 6502 yards/***/C/M

Market Rasen and District
G.C
(0673) 842416
Legsby Rd. Market Rasen
(18) 6043 yards/**/F

Millfield G.C
(042771) 255
Laughterton, Lincoln
(18) 5583 yards/***/E

North Shore G.C
(0754) 763298
North Shore Rd. Skegness

1 mile N of Skegness.
(18) 6134 yards/***/C/M

R.A.F. Waddington G.C
(0552) 720271
Waddington, Lincoln
(18) 5223 yards/***/E/L

Sandilands G.C
(0521) 41432
Sea Lane, Sandilands,
Sutton-on-Sea.
4 miles S of Mablethorpe
on A52. (18) 5995
yards/***/C/H

Seacroft G.C
(0754) 3020
Drummond Rd. Skegness
1 mile S of Skegness.
(18) 6478 yards/***/C/H/M

Sleaford G.C
(05298) 273
South Rauceby, Sleaford
W of Sleaford off A153.

(18) 6443 yards/***/C/H
Spalding G.C
(077585) 474
Surfleet, Spalding
4 miles N of Spalding off
A16.
(18) 5847 yards/***/C/M

Stoke Rochford G.C
(047683) 275
Stoke Rochford, Grantham
5 miles S of Grantham off
A1.
(18) 6204 yards/***/B/H

Sutton Bridge G.C
(0406) 350323
New Rd. Sutton Bridge,
Spalding (9) 5804
yards/**/C/H

Woodhall Spa G.C
(0526) 52511
The Broadway, Woodhall
Spa 6 miles S of Horncastle
on B1191. (18) 6866
yards/***/B/H

Staffs, Shropshire & Cheshire

Staffordshire, Shropshire and Cheshire: three essentially rural counties. Staffordshire shares a boundary with the West Midlands and Cheshire has two rather ill-defined borders with Greater Manchester and Merseyside. As for Shropshire it enjoys a splendid peace, broken only perhaps by the mooing of cows and the cries of fore! from the county's many lush fairways.

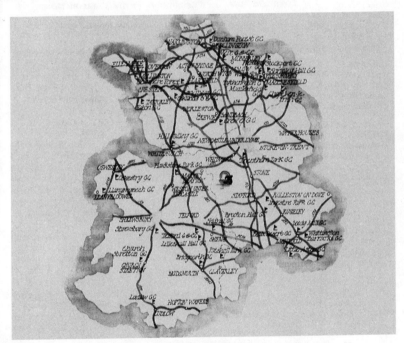

Each of the three has a great deal to offer the visiting golfer: in Staffordshire, **Beau Desert** and **Whittington Barracks** are two of the best (and prettiest) courses in the Midlands; Cheshire offers **Tytherington, Mere, The Portal** and some heathland gems (we have described Hoylake and the Wirral courses in the 'Lancashire' section) while Shropshire, in addition to possessing the likes of **Hawkstone Park** and **Patshull Park** can boast of having produced two US Masters champions—both Sandy Lyle and Ian Woosnam who were bred if not born in the county.

Staffordshire

Making a start in Staffordshire, **Whittington Barracks** and **Beau Desert** have already been mentioned. The former, located near Lichfield off the A51 is a heathland type course with fine views towards the three spires of Lichfield Cathedral; it is quite possibly the county's toughest challenge. Beau Desert Golf Club near Hazel Slade occupies an unlikely setting in the middle of Cannock Chase. Surrounded by fir trees and spruces it is, as its name implies, quite a haven. Perhaps a mixture of heathland and woodland, and less testing than Whittington Barracks, it is nonetheless equally enjoyable.

From the heart of Cannock Chase to the heart of the Potteries, there are a number of courses in and around Stoke-on-Trent. **Trentham** and **Trentham Park**, near neighbours to the south of the city, are both well worth a visit, particularly perhaps the latter where the course is well-wooded and there are many delightful views.

Stafford, the county town, is pretty much in the middle of things. Once again a pair of 18 hole courses to note here; to the south of Stafford is **Brocton Hall** and to the north east, set in the grounds of the former home of the Earl of Shrewsbury is **Ingestre Park**. Both offer a very relaxing game. There is also an enjoyable 9 holer at **Stafford Castle.**

Shropshire

Moving into Shropshire, many will wish to head straight for **Hawkstone Park** and its fine hotel—note the superb Terrace Restaurant here. Shropshire has a lot more than Hawkstone Park on the menu. **Patshull Park** makes a marvellous starter, especially considering its closeness to the Midlands—an ideal retreat in fact. As at Hawkstone golf is played amid very peaceful and picturesque surroundings and overnight accommodation is immediately at hand.

Shrewsbury is a pleasant county town with many charming half-timbered buildings. **Shrewsbury** Golf Club is situated about five miles from the town centre off the A49. It is an interesting course with a railway track running through the middle.

Travelling a little further down the A49 into southern Shropshire, **Church Stretton**, set amidst the Long Mynd Hills, is well worth a visit. Not the longest course in Britain but one that offers quite outstanding views.

The largest town in Shropshire is Telford. It's a strange mixture of the old and the new: a modern centre yet surrounded by a considerable amount of history—Brunel's famous Ironbridge is here. The popular **Telford Hotel** Golf and Country Club is situated near to the Ironbridge Gorge, high above it in fact, and is easily accessible from the M54 (junction 4 or 5). Full leisure facilities are offered at the Hotel. Further south of Telford, towards Bridgnorth, **Lilleshall Hall** offers a pleasant game. To the east of Telford, **Shifnal** Golf Club is set in a glorious park and an old manor house serves as an impressive Clubhouse.

In the middle of Shropshire, **Bridgnorth** is one of the oldest and longest courses in the county, and in the far south is historic **Ludlow**. It's now a fairly quiet market town but in former times was the capital of the West Marches. The golf course takes you around the town's race course—or is it vice versa?

To the north west of Shropshire three courses are strongly recommended. **Oswestry** is one clearly to note—if only because this is where Ian Woosnam relaxes when he's not winning The Masters. Close to the Welsh border, **Llanymynech** (Woosie's first course) lies on high ground and is very scenic. On the 4th hole you stand on the tee in Wales and drive into England (always good for the ego). **Hill Valley** near Whitchurch, brings us down to earth. We may get wet as well with water affecting many holes on this fairly new American-style course.

Cheshire

Cheshire could be described as the 'Surrey of the North'. In many parts it's decidedly affluent, with a great band of commuter towns lining its northern fringes. There's also a sand belt where heathland golf is found—no Sunningdale here perhaps but **Delamere Forest** and **Sandiway** would certainly be at home in either Surrey of Berkshire. Delamere is particularly good. A creation of Herbert Fowler, who also designed Walton Heath and The Berkshire, it's a marvellous heather and gorse type course—some superb trees also. The words 'temporary green' do not exist at Delamere Forest (something winter-golfers might wish to bear in mind) nor apparently does the word 'par'—the old fashioned term 'bogey' being preferred as a more realistic yardstick of a hole's difficulty—at least for the non-pro.

Mere is certainly one of the leading courses in Cheshire. Although fairly close to Sandiway and Delamere, Mere is a classic parkland course, and a beautiful one too with a testing closing stretch including the spectacular par five 18th, where a new green has been built on the edge of a small lake.

The area around Wilmslow is fairly thick with Clubs. **Wilmslow** itself and **Prestbury** have two of the better courses. For many years the former was the venue of The Greater Manchester Open. Both are extremely well kept. While in the area **Mottram Hall** at Mottram St Andrews— is quite magnificent. The hotel now also boasts a challenging 18 hole course, designed in fine style by Dave Thomas.

Stockport provides a dramatic contrast to rural Cheshire—not the prettiest of places perhaps but full of character (with a wonderful market my mother tells me). Offerton is where **Stockport** Golf Club is found. It's a good test and well worth visiting; so for that matter are the two courses at Bramhall, **Bramhall** and **Bramhall Park**. **Macclesfield's** course offers some extensive views and between Macclesfield and Prestbury is the fairly new, but highly acclaimed **Tytherington** Club. **Shrigley Hall** in Pott Shrigley, again near to both Prestbury and Macclesfield, has another newish golf course in a wonderful setting with extensive views over the Cheshire Plain.

Over to the far east of Cheshire, close to the Derbyshire border and the splendid Peak District is **Chapel-en-le-Frith**. A really friendly Club this and some enjoyable golf too. From the far east to the far west, Chester demands inspection—a fascinating Roman city with all manner of attractions. Two of the best places to swing a club are at Upton, namely the delightful **Upton-by-Chester** Golf Club and at **Eaton**, a parkland course to the south of the city. Just 15 minutes drive from Chester an impressive Golf and Leisure Complex is set to open in 1994 at **Carden Park**—watch this space! South East of Chester near Tarporley much has been happening and two courses have recently appeared on the county's ever-changing golf map, namely the highly acclaimed **Portal** Golf Club and the **Oaklands** Golf and Country Club.

In the middle of the county, **Crewe** offers a pleasant 18 holes and a few miles outside of the town Weston Hall is being converted into a £50 million golf complex which promises to include a 'European Tour' purpose built stadium course. Back towards the north of the region, **Ringway** Golf Club is a good parkland challenge and our final visit takes us to the end of a very leafy lane in Altrincham—the impressive **Dunham Forest** Golf and Country Club. Only two miles from the M56 (junction 7) and not all that far from the whirl of Manchester it nonetheless delights in an incredibly tranquil setting. The beautifully mature tree-lined fairways are a sheer delight to play on and if you cannot enjoy your golf here, well, let's just say you've got problems!

KEY

*** Visitors welcome at all times
** Visitors on weekdays only
* No visitors at any time
(Mon, Wed) No visitors on specified days

GREEN FEES PER ROUND
A - £30 plus
B - £20 - £30
C - £15 - £25
D - £10 - £20
E - Under £10
F - Green fees on application

RESTRICTIONS
G - Guests only
H - Handicap certificate required
H(24) - Handicap of 24 or less required
L - Letter of introduction required
M - Visitor must be a member of another recognised club.

Staffordshire

Alsager G. and C.C.
(0270) 875700
Andley Rd. Alsager, Stoke-on-Trent
(18)6206 yards/**/C/M

Barlaston G.C.
(078139) 2795
Meaford Rd. Barlaston, Stone
1 mile north of Stone off A34.
(18)5800 yards/***/C

Beau Desert G.C.
(0543) 422626
Hazelslade, Hednesford, Cannock
(18)6300 yards/**/B/H

Branston G.C.
(0283) 43207
Burton Rd. Branston, Burton-upon-Trent
(18)6458 yards/**/C/H

Brocton Hall G.C.
(0785) 661901
Brocton
4 miles south of Stafford off A34.
(18)6095 yards/***/B/H

Burslem G.C.
(0782) 837006
Wood Farm, High Lane, Tunstall
(9)5527 yards/**/D

Burton-upon-Trent G.C.
(0283) 4451
43 Ashby Road East, Burton-uponTrent
3 miles from Burton on A50.
(18)6555 yards/***/B/H/L/M

Craythorne G.C.
(0283) 64329
Craythorne Rd. Stretton
2 miles north of Burton off A38.
(18)5230 yards/***/D/H

Drayton Park G.C.
(0827) 251139
Drayton Park, Tamworth
(18)6414 yards/**/B/H

Golden Hill G.C.
(0782) 784715
Mobberley Rd. Golden Hill, Stoke-on-Trent
Between Tunstall and Kidgrove on A50.
(18)5957 yards/***/D

Greenway Hall G.C.
(0782) 503158
Stockton Brook, Stoke-on-Trent
5 miles from Stoke off A53.
(18)5676 yards/*/F/G

Ingestre Park G.C.
(0889) 270304
Ingestre, Stafford
6 miles east of Stafford off A51.
(18)6376 yards/**/B/H

Lakeside G.C.
(0889) 583181
Rugeley Power Station, Rugeley
2 miles south off Rugeley on A513.
(9)4768 yards/*/E/G

Leek G.C.
(0538) 384779
Cheddleton Rd. Leek
1 mile from Leek on A520.
(18)6229 yards/**/B/H

Newcastle Municipal G.C.
(0782) 627596
Keele Rd. Newcastle
(18)6256 yards/***/E

Newcastle-under-Lyme G.C.
(0782) 618526
Whitmore Rd.
Newcastle-under-Lyme
2 miles south of
Newcastle-under-Lyme on A53.
(18)6427 yards/**/B/H

Patsull Park Hotel & G.C
(0902)700100
Beside A464
(18)6400 yards/***/B

Perton Park G.C.
(0902) 380103
Wrottesley Park Road
West of Wolverhampton
(18)7036 yards/***/E

Seedy Mill G.C
(0543) 417333
Elmshurst, north of Litchfield
(18)6247 yards/***/F

Stafford Castle G.C.
(0785) 223821
Newport Rd. Stafford
(9)6347 yards/**/D

Stone G.C.
(0785) 813103
Filley Brooks, Stone
1 mile north of Stone on A34.
(9)6140 yards/**/C

Tamworth G.C.
(0827) 53850
Eagle Drive, Tamworth
(18)6083 yards/***/F

Trentham G.C.
(0782) 658109
14 Barlaston Rd. Trentham
(18)6644 yards/***/B/H

Trentham Park G.C.
(0782) 658800
Trentham Park. Trentham
4 miles south of Newcastle-under-Lyme off A34.
(18)6644 yards/**/B/H

Uttoxeter G.C.
(0889) 564884
Wood Lane, Uttoxeter
Next to Uttoxeter Racecourse.
(18)5695 yards/***/C

Westwood G.C.
(0538) 383060
Newcastle Rd. Walbridge, Leek
Just west of Leek on A53.
(18)6100 yards/**/D

Whittington Barracks G.C.
(0543) 432317
Tamworth Rd. Lichfield
3 miles from Lichfield on A51.
(8)6457 yards/**/B/H/L

Wolstanton G.C.
(0782) 622413
Dimsdale Old Hall, Hassam Parade

(18)5807 yards/**/F/H

Shropshire

Bridgnorth G.C.
(0746) 763315
Stanley Lane, Bridgnorth
1 mile from Bridgnorth
(18)6668 yards/***/B

Church Stretton G.C.
(0694) 722281
Hunters Moon, Trevor Hill,
Church Stretton
(18)5008 yards/***/C

Hawkstone Park Hotel G.C.
(093924) 611
Weston under Redcastle,
Shrewsbury
(18)6203 yards/***/C/H
(18)5063 yards(restricted
play)/***/E/H

Hill Valley G. and C.C.
(0948) 3584
Terrick Rd. Whitchurch,
Salop
1 mile north of Whitchurch.
(18)6050 yards/***/B/H
(9)2553 yards/***/D

Lilleshall Hall G.C.
(0952) 603840
Lilleshall, Newport, Salop
(18)5906 yards/**/C/H

Llanymynech G.C.
(0691) 830983
Pant, Oswestry
6 miles south of Oswestry.
(18)6114 yards/***/C/H

Ludlow G.C.
(058477) 285
Bromfield, Ludlow
(18)6239 yards/***/F/H

Market Drayton G.C.
(0630) 652266
Sutton, Market Drayton
(18)6214 yards/**/C

Meole Brace G.C.
(0743) 64050
Meole Brace, Shrewesbury
(12)5830 yards/***/E

Oswestry G.C.
(069188) 535
Aston Park, Oswestry

2 miles south of Oswestry.
(18)6046 yards/***/C/H/M

Shifnal G.C.
(0952) 460330
Decker Hill, Shifnal
(18)6422 yards/**/C/H

Shrewsbury G.C.
(074372) 2976
Condover
9 miles south of
Shrewsbury.
(18)6212 yards/***/C/H

Telford Hotel G. and C.C.
(0952) 585642
Great Hay, Telford
4 miles south of Telford.
(18)6274 yards/***/B/H

Wrekin G.C.
(0952) 244032
Ercall Woods, Wellington,
Telford
(18)5657 yards/**/C

Cheshire

Alderley Edge G.C.
(0625) 585583
Brook Lane, Alderley Edge
(9)5839 yards/***/C/H

Alsager G. & C.C.
(0270) 875700
Audley Road, Alsager
(18)6200 yards/**/F

Astbury G.C.
(0260) 272772
Peel Lane, Astbury,
Congleton
(18)6277 yards/**/C/H/M

Avro G.C.
(061) 4392709
British Aerospace,
Woodford
(9)5735 yards/E/G/H

Birchwood G.C.
(0925) 818819
Kelvin Close, Risley,
Warrington
(18)6808 yards/**/C/H

Chapel-en-le-Frith G.C.
(0298) 813943
The Cockyard, Manchester
Rd.

Chapel-en-le Frith
(18)6065 yards/***/C/H

Chester G.C.
(0244) 677760
Curzon Park North, Chester
1 mile from Chester.
(18)6487 yards/***/C/H

Congleton G.C.
(0260) 273540
Biddulph Rd. Congleton
(18)5704 yards/***/F

Crewe G.C.
(0270) 584099
Fields Rd. Haslington,
Crewe
1 mile south of Haslington
on B5077.
(18)6181 yards/**/C/H

Davenport G.C.
(0625) 876951
Worth Hall, Middlewood
Rd. Higher
Poynton
(18)6066 yards/***/B/H
Delamere Forest G.C.
(0606) 882807
Station Rd. Delamere,
Northwich
(18)6287 yards/***/F

Disley G.C
(0663) 62071
Jackson's Edge, off A6
(18)6051 yards/**/F

Dukinfield G.C.
(061) 3382340
Yew Tree Lane, Dukinfield
(16)5544 yards/***/F/H

Eaton G.C.
(0244) 680474
Eaton Park, Ecclesford
2 miles south of Chester on
A483.
(18)6446 yards/***/B/H

Ellesmere Port G.C.
(051) 3397689
Chester Rd. Hooton,
S.Wirral
9 miles north of Chester on
A41.
(18)6432 yards/***/E

Hazel Grove G.C.
(061)4833978

Buxton Rd. Hazel Grove,
Stockport
(18)6300 yards/**/F

Helsby G.C.
(0928) 722021
Towers Lane, Helsby,
Warrington
(18)6262 yards/***/C

Knights Grange G.C.
(06065) 52780
Grange Lane, Winsford
(9)6210 yards/***/E

Knutsford G.C.
(0565) 3355
Mereheath Lane, Knutsford
(9)6288 yards/**/F

Leigh G.C.
(092576) 2943
Kenyon Hall, Broseley
Lane, Culcheth
(18)6861 yards/***/C/H

Lymn G.C.
(092575) 5020
Whitbarrow Rd., Lymn
5 miles south of
Warrington.
(18)6319 yards/***/C/H

Macclesfield G.C.
(0625) 23227
The Hollins, Macclesfield
(9)5974 yards/**/C/H

Malkins Bank G.C.
(0270) 765931
Betchton Rd. Sandbach
(18)6071 yards/***/E

Mere G. and C.C.
(0565) 830155
Chester Rd. Mere,
Knutsford
(18)6849
yards/**(Wed,Fri)/A/H/L

Mottram Hall Hotel & G.C
(0625) 828135
Mottram St. Andrews
(18)6900 yards/***/B

New Mils G.C.
(0663) 43485
Shaw Marsh, New Mills,
Stockport
(9)5707 yards/***(Sun)/F

Oaklands G. & C.C.
(0829) 733884
Tarporley
(18)6169 yards/**/B

Onneley G.C.
(0782)750577
Onneley, Crewe
1 mile from Woore.
(9)5584 yards/**(Tue)/C

Portal G.C.
(0829) 733933
Tarporley
(18)7145 yards/***/B
Poulton Park G.C.
(0925) 812034
Dig Lane, Cinnamon Brow,
Warrington
3 miles from Warrington
(9)5512 yards/***/D

Prestbury G.C.
(0625) 829388
Macclesfield Rd. Prestbury
(18)6359 yards/**/B/H

Queens Park G.C.
(0270) 666724
Queens Park Gardens,
Crewe
2 miles from Crewe
(9)5370 yards/***/E

Runcorn G.C.
(09285) 72093
Clifton Rd. Runcorn
(18)6035 yards/**/C/H

St. Michael Jubilee G.C.
(051) 4246230
Dundark Rd. Widnes
(18)5612 yards/***/E

Sandbach G.C.
(0270) 21177
117 Middlewich Rd.
Sandbach
(9)5614 yards/**/C/H

Sandiway G.C.
(0606) 883247
Chester Rd. Sandiway,
Northwich
4 miles from Northwich.
(18)6435 yards/***/F/H/L

Shrigley Hall G.C.
(0625)575757
Shrigley Park, Pott Shrigley
(18)6305 yards/***/B

Tytherington G.C.
(0625) 434562
Near Macclesfield.
(18)6737 yards/***/B/H

Upton-by-Chester G.C.
(0244) 381183
Upton Lane, Upton-by-
Chester
2 miles north of Chester.
(18)5875 yards/***/C/H

Vicars Cross G.C.
(0244) 335174
Tarvin Rd. Littleton
2 miles east of Chetster off
A51.
(18)5876 yards/***/C

Walton Hall G.C.
(0925) 63061
Warrington Rd. Higher
Walton
(18)6801 yards/***/F

Warrington G.C.
(0925) 65431
London Rd. Appleton,
Warrington
(18)6217 yards/***/B/H
(18)5890 yards/***/B/H

Widnes G.C.
(051) 4242440
Highfield Rd. Widnes
(18)5688 yards/**/F/H

Wilmslow G.C.
(056587) 2148
Great Warford, Mobberley,
Knutsford
2 miles from Wilmslow.
(18)6611 yards/**/F

Lancashire & the Isle of Man

'Caddies are not allowed on the greens when wearing clogs'—recorded in the Minutes of a Lancashire Golf Club, 1894.

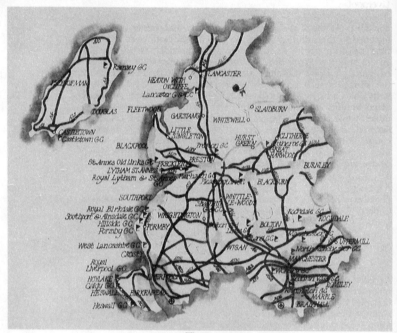

The 'Lancashire' Coast

I don't suppose they appreciate it in the slightest but the many horses
that race across the sands near Southport early each morning (and
the donkeys that do their best to race across the same sands) are per-
forming within a few yards of one of the greatest stretches of golfing
country in the world. On the Lancashire coast between Liverpool and
Blackpool lie a magnificent collection of natural golfing links. Being
more specific, between Hoylake on the Wirral Peninsula and Lytham
St Annes (a distance of less than 40 miles) are to be found the likes of
**Royal Liverpool, Wallasey, West Lancashire, Formby, Southport and
Ainsdale, Royal Birkdale, Hillside, Royal Lytham, Fairhaven and St
Annes Old Links.** A truly formidable list. Hoylake, Birkdale and
Lytham have, of course, each staged the Open Championship on a
number of occasions, while the Amateur Championship has been
played at both Hillside and Formby, and Southport and Ainsdale has
twice hosted the Ryder Cup. When the wind hammers across from

the Irish Sea any of the links mentioned can become treacherously difficult and the famous Lancashire sandhills rarely provide shelter from the elements. A visit to **Hoylake, Birkdale, Hillside, Formby** or **Lytham** will certainly not meet with disappointment (though it may result in a little damaged pride!)

The nearest of the great links courses is West Lancashire, although Formby- note also the **Formby Ladies'** Club here—and the Southport courses are also within easy reach. The A565 is the road to take out of Liverpool.

For the purposes of this piece **Liverpool** and **Manchester** have been included in Lancashire, a county to which they both once belonged (and still do in spirit). As the whole of **Merseyside** has been included—it's here that Royal Birkdale and Royal Liverpool are now situated—parts of former **Cheshire** are also included. Confused? Lets visit the Wirral. For such a relatively small area the peninsula is fairly thick with Golf Clubs. In addition to the famous links at Hoylake, **Wallasey** offers another tremendous seaside test amid some impressive sand dunes while **Heswall** offers a quite outstanding parkland challenge. Situated alongside the River Dee off the A540, it's a medium length course, beautifully maintained with views towards the distant Welsh hills. A mention also for **Caldy** which is a parkland-cum-clifftop course, and for the **Wirral Ladies'** Golf Club near Birkenhead.

Inland Golf in Lancashire
Looking to play more centrally in Lancashire, The **Shaw Hill** Golf and Country Club is most definitely one to note if travelling along the M6. Located just north of Chorley, despite its proximity to the motorway, it enjoys a very peaceful setting and is a particular favourite of golfing societies.

On the other side of the M6, **Pleasington** Golf Club enjoys similarly secluded and picturesque surroundings. The course is situated three miles west of Blackburn along the A59 and is undoubtedly one of the best parkland courses in the North of England. Still moving 'up' the country, **Preston** has a pleasantly undulating course, just north of the town, it too can easily be reached from the M6 (junction 32).

Another of the better inland courses in the county is **Clitheroe** Golf Club which is situated on the edge of the Forest of Bowland. The course lies approximately two miles south of the town with views across to Pendle Hill.

Lancashire wouldn't be complete without mentioning its county town. There are a number of Clubs at hand, perhaps the best being the **Lancaster** Golf and Country Club located three miles south of the city on the A588 at Stodday. An attractive parkland course, it is laid out close to the River Lune estuary (and can be breezy!)

Greater Manchester
And so to Manchester. The city itself is famed the world over for the liberal amount of rain that falls. Mancunians will tell you that this is

pure poppy-cock (or something like that). Of course, the only time that rain can be guaranteed these days is during the five days of an Old Trafford Test Match.

It is probably a fair assessment to say that for golf courses, Manchester, rather like London, gets top marks for quantity but is a little shaky on the quality score. Certainly it compares unfavourably with Liverpool and Leeds; it is a shame because historically Manchester was the scene of some of the earliest golf outside Scotland: The **Old Manchester** Club was founded back in 1818. Its current status is 'temporarily without a course'—one can only hope that its Members have found somewhere else to play—North Manchester perhaps? Only four miles from the city centre this is one of the best in the county. A close neighbour of North Manchester is the excellent **Manchester** Golf Club. Elsewhere in Greater Manchester, **Stand** (Whitefield) and **Worsley** (Eccles) are fine courses while to the north, **Rochdale** is well worth travelling to. There is a cluster of courses close to the River Mersey in the Didsbury—Sale area; the best is perhaps **Withington**, and there are about 10 public courses in and around the city centre. Over towards Stockport, there is a very enjoyable course at **Reddish Vale** and the area around Bolton again boasts a number of courses of which **Bolton Old Links** is probably the finest. It is a tough and interesting moorland course at which visitors are always made welcome. As for the title 'Links' it may sound a bit quaint—but there again, what are we to make of Wigan Pier?

The Isle of Man
There are five 18 hole courses on the island, with the links courses at **Castletown** and **Ramsey** particularly standing out. With fairly modest green fees and numerous relaxing places to stay the island would appear to be an ideal place for a golf holiday—ask Nigel Mansell who brought Greg Norman here!

Back in 1889 your average J.P. was possibly not the most popular man in town. However, in a certain Mr. J.C. Barrett, Birkdale possessed a man of rare insight and one clearly cognisant of the finer things in life. Mr. Barrett was a golfer. On the 30th July, 1889, he invited eight fellow addicts to his home and together they resolved to form a Golf Club.

Golfers wishing to play at Birkdale must belong to a recognised Golf Club and produce a current handicap certificate. Visitors must make prior arrangements with the **Secretary, Norman Crewe**. This applies to individual visitors as well as those hoping to organise a Society game. Mr. Crewe can be contacted by telephone on **(0704) 67920** and fax: (0704) 62327. Golf clubs may be hired from the **professional, Richard Bradbeer, (0704) 68857** and it may also be possible to obtain the services of a caddy. Individual visitors may play from Monday to Friday, green fees in 1992 being £50 per round or £70 per day. The 1993 green fees are not quoted as special rates were in operation due to a 'greens rebuilding' programme—more of which in our next edition! Societies are welcome on Wednesdays and Thursdays.

The Club is situated approximately 2 miles from the centre of Southport close to the main A565 road. From the North this road can be reached via the A59, leaving the M6 at Preston and from the South via the M62 and M57 or alternatively, as when travelling from Manchester and the East, by taking the A580 and then following the A570 into Southport.

Whilst the course possesses many of the towering sand hills so familiar with good links golf, the holes tend to wind their way between and beneath the dunes along fairly flat and narrow valleys.

From the fairways the awkward stance and blind shot are the product of poor golf, not poor fortune. Fair it may be, but easy it certainly is not! .

The course has thrown up more than its fair share of drama. Perhaps most notably in 1969 when Jack Nicklaus, ever the sportsman, conceded Tony Jacklin's very missable putt on the 18th green, so tying the Ryder Cup. In 1961, Palmer's Open, an almighty gale threatened to blow the tented village and all inside far out into the sea. In stark contrast was the 1976 Open when fire engines were close at hand as Birkdale (and all of Britain come to that) suffered in the drought. That 1976 Championship saw the mercurial Miller at his brilliant best as he shook off first the challenge of Nicklaus and then of an inexperienced and unknown 19 year old who had a name no one at the time could pronounce... Severiano Ballesteros

The Royal Birkdale Golf Club,
Waterloo Road,
Birkdale, Southport,
Merseyside PR8 2LX.

Hole	Yards	Par	Hole	Yards	Par
1	448	4	10	395	4
2	417	4	11	409	4
3	409	4	12	184	3
4	203	3	13	475	4
5	346	4	14	199	3
6	474	4	15	543	5
7	156	3	16	414	4
8	458	4	17	525	5
9	414	4	18	472	4
Out	3,324	34	In	3,616	36
			Out	3,324	34
			Totals	6,940	70

Greater Manchester

Acre Gate G.C
061-748 1226
Pennybridge Lane, Flixton
from Urmston take
the Flixton Road
(18) 4395 yards/***/E

Altrincham G.C
061-928 0761
Stockport Road, Timperley,
Altrincham, Cheshire
1 mile E. of Altrincham
on the A560
(18) 6162 yards/***/D

Ashton-In-Makerfield G.C
(09420 724229
Garswodd Park, Liverpool
Road, Ashton-In-Makerfield
On A58, off the M6 at junc-
tion 24
(18) 6169 yards/**(not
Wed)/F/M

Ashton On Mersey G.C
061-973 3220
Church Lane, Sale, Cheshire
2 miles from Sale Station
(9) 6202 yards/**(not Tues
pm)/F/H

Ashton-Under-Lyne G.C
061-330 1537
Gorsey Way, Ashton-
Under-Lyne
From Ashton take the
Mossley Road to Queens
Road
(18) 6209 yards/**/D

Blackley G.C
061-643 2980
Victoria Ave East, Blackley
Take A64 from Middleton
towards Blackley
(18) 6237 yards/**/F

Bolton G.C
(0204) 43067
Lostock Park, Chorley New
Road, Bolton
Leave M6 at junction 6
(18) 6215 yards/***/D/M

Bolton Municipal G.C
(0204) 42336
Links Road, Bolton
3 miles W. of Bolton on the
A673
(18) 6012 yards/***/E

Brackley G.C
061-790 6076
Bullows Road, Little Hutton,
Worsley
9 miles out of Manchester
on the A6
(9) 3003 yards/***/E

Bramhall G.C
061-439 4057
Ladythorn Road, Bramhall,
Stockport, Cheshire
8 miles S. of Manchester
on the A5102
(18) 6293 yards/***/C/M

Bramall Park G.C
061-485 3119
20 Manor Road, Bramall,
Stockport
8 miles S. of Manchester
leave A6 for A5102
(18) 6214 yards/***/C

Breightmet G.C
(0204) 27381
Red Bridge, Ainsworth,
Bolton
3 miles out of Bolton
on Bury road
(9) 6448 yards/**(not
Wed)/E

Brookdale G.C
061-681 4534
Ashbridge, Woodhouse,
Failsworth
5 miles N.E of Manchester
(18) 5878 yards/***/D/M

Bury G.C
061-766 4897
Unsworth Hall,
Blackford Bridge, Bury
7 miles N. of Manchester
on the A56
(18) 5953 yards/***/D

Castle Hawk G.C
(0706) 40841
Heywood Road, Castleton,
Rochdale
Leave Rochdale via

Castleton Road for
Heywood Road
(18) 3158 yards/***/F

Cheadle G.C
061-428 2160
Shiers Drive, Cheadle,
Cheshire
1 mile S. of Cheadle village
(9) 5006 yards/***(not
Tues/Sat)D/M/H

Chorlton-Cum-Hardy G.C
061-881 3139
Barlow Hall Road, Chorlton
3 miles from the city centre,
near cemetry
(18) 6003 yards/***/D

Crompton & Royton G.C
061-642 2154
Highbarn, Royton, Oldham
N. of Oldham off the A627
(18) 6212 yards/***/D

Davyhulme Park G.C
061-748 2260
Gleneagles Road,
Davyhulme, Urmston
8 miles S. of Manchester
near hospital
(18) 6237 yards/***/D/M

Deane G.C
(0204) 61944
off Juction Road, Deane,
Bolton
2 miles from junction 5
of the M61
(18) 5511 yards/***/D//H

Denton G.C
061-336 3218
Manchester Road, Denton
5 miles from city centre
on the A57
(18) 6290 yards/***/D/H

Didsbury G.C
061-998 9278
For Lane, Northendon
Signposted off the M3
at junction 9
(18) 6273 yards/**/D/H

Disley G.C
(0663) 63266
Stanley Hall Lane, Jacksons
Edge, Disley, Stockport
6 miles S. of Stockport on
the A6

(18) 6015 yards/***/F/H/M

Dunkinfield G.C
061 338 2340
Lyne Edge, Ashton under
Lyne
(18) 5585 yards/**/D

Dunham Forest G.C
061-928 2605
Oldfield Lane, Altrincham,
Cheshire
2 miles N. from junction 7
off M56
(18) 6800 yards/***/F/H

Dunscar G.C
(0204) 51090
Longworth Lane, Bromley
Cross, Bolton
3 miles N. of Bolton off the
A666
(18) 5957 yards/**/F

Ellesmere G.C
061-790 2122
Old Clough Lane, Worsley
5 miles W. of Manchester
on the A580
(18) 5957 yards/(by
arrangement)/E/H/M

Fairfield Golf And Sailing
Club
061-370 2292
Booth Road, Audenshaw
4 miles from city centre
off the A635
(18) 5654 yards/***/(not
Wed pm or weekend
am)/F

Flixton G.C
061-748 2116
Church Road, Flixton
6 miles S. of Manchester
(9) 6441 yards/**/D

Gathurst G.C
(02575) 2861
Miles Lane, Shevington,
Wigan
1 miles S. of junction 27 of
the M6
(9) 6308 yards/**(not
Wed)/D/M

Gatley G.C
061-437 2091
Waterfall Farm, Styal Road,
Heald Green, Gatley

3 miles from Manchester
airport
(9) 5934 yards/**(not
Tues)/F

Great Lever & Farnworth
G.C
(0204) 62582
Lever Edge Lane, Bolton
2 miles from Bolton town
centre
(18) 5958 yards/**/D

Haigh Hall G.C
(0924) 831107
Haigh Country Park, Haigh,
Wigan
Take B5106 from M6 for
country park
(18) 6400 yards/***/D

Hale G.C
061-980 4225
Rappax Road, Hale,
Altringham, Cheshire
2 miles S.E of Altringham
(9) 5780 yards/**(not
Thurs)/F

Heaton Manor G.C
061-432 2134
Heaton Mersey, Stockport,
Cheshire
2 miles N.W of Stockport
(18) 5876 yards/***(not
Tues/Wed)/D

Heaton Park G.C
061-798 0295
Prestwich
Leave M66 southbound by
A576 roundabout
(18) 5849 yards/***/E

Hindley Hall G.C
(0942) 55131
Hall Lane, Hindley, Wigan
Leave M61 at junction 6 for
for A6
(18) 5875 yards/***/F/M

Horwich G.C
(0204) 696980
Victoria Road, Horwich,
Bolton
2 miles from junction 6 of
the M61
(9) 5404 yards/*/F

Houldsworth G.C
061-224 5055
Wingate House, Higher

Levenshulme
Leave M6 at junction 12 for
A6
(18) 6078 yards/**/E

Lobden G.C
(0706) 343228
Lobden Moor, Whitworth,
Rochdale
Half mile from village centre on A671
(9) 5750 yards/***(not Sat)/F

Lowes Park G.C
061-764 1231
Hill Top, Bury
Take A56 N. from Bury
(9) 6035 yards/**(not
Wed)/D/M

Manchester G.C
061-643 3202
Hopwood Cottage,
Rochdale Road, Middleton
7 miles N. of the city on the
A665
(18) 6540 yards/**/C/H

Marple G.C
061-427 2311
Hawk Green, Marple,
Stockport, Cheshire
Leave A6 at High Lane for
Hawk Green
(18) 5700 yards/***/D/M

Mellor & Townscliffe G.C
061-427 2208
Tarden, Gibb Lane, Mellor,
Stockport
Leave A626 7 miles S.E of
Stockport
(18) 5925 yards/***(not
Sat)/D

North Manchester G.C
061-643 9033
Rhodes House, Manchester
Old Road, Middleton
Head for Middleton from
exit 18 of the M62
(18) 6527 yards/**/F/H

Northenden G.C
061-998 4738
Palatine Road, Northenden
1 mile through Northenden
(18) 6469 yards/***(not
Sat)/F/H

Oldham G.C
061-624 4986
Lees New Road, Oldham
Turn S. at Lees from the
A669
(18) 5045 yards/***/E

Old Links G.C
(0204) 43089
Chorley Old Road, Bolton
N. of the A58 on the B6226
(18) 6406 yards/***/D

Pike Folds G.C
061-740 1136
Cooper Lane, Victoria
Avenue, Blackley
4 miles N. of city centre off
Rochdale Road
(9) 5789 yards/**/E

Prestwich G.C
061-773 4578
Hilton Lane, Prestwich
On A6044 1 mile from junction with A56
(18) 4712 yards/***/F/H

Reddish Vale G.C
061-480 2359
Southcliffe Road, Reddish,
Stockport, Cheshire
1 mile N. of Stockport
(18) 6086 yards/**/F/H

Regent Park G.C
061 485 3199
Manor Rd, Bramhall
(18) 6293 yards/***/F

Ringway G.C
061-980 2630
Hale Mount, Hale Barns,
Altrincham, Cheshire
Leave M6 at junction 6, follow signs for Hale
(18) 6494 yards/***/C/H

Romiley G.C
061-430 2392
Goosehouse Green,
Romiley, Stockport
Signposted from village on
the B6101

(18) 6335 yards/***(not
Thurs)/F

Saddleworth G.C
(0457) 7872059
Mountain Ash, Ladcastle
Road, Uppermill, Oldham
5 miles from Oldham, off
the A670
(18) 5976 yards/***/D//H

Sale G.C
061-973 3404
Sale Lodge, Golf Road, Sale,
Cheshire
1 mile from Sale station
(18) 6346 yards/***/F/M

Stamford G.C
(04575) 2126
Oakfield House,
Huddersfield Road,
Heyheads, Stalybridge
On the B6175, off the A6018
(18) 5619 yards/**/D

Stand G.C
061-766 2388
The Dales, Ashbourne
Grove, Whitefield
1 mile N. of exit 17 of the
M62
(18) 6425 yards/**/D/H

Stockport G.C
061-427 2001
Offerton Road,
Offerton, Stockport
Take A627 from the A262
(18) 6319 yards/***D/M

Swinton Park G.C
061-794 1785
East Lancashire Road,
Swinton
5 miles from city centre on
A580
(18) 6675 yards/**/D/M

Turton G.C
(0204) 852235
Wood End Farm,
Chapeltown Road, Bromley
3 miles N. of Bolton on the
A666/676
(9) 5805 yards/***(not
Wed/Sat)/E

Walmersley G.C
061-764 0018
Garretts Close, Walmersley,

Bury
3 miles N. of Bury on the
A56
(9) 3057 yards/**(not
Mon/Tues)//E

Werneth (Oldham) G.C
061-624 1190
Green Lane,
Garden Suburb, Oldham
5 miles from Manchester
off the A6104
(18) 5363 yards/**/D

Werneth Low G.C
061-368 2503
Werneth Low Road, Hyde,
Cheshire
2 miles from Hyde town
centre
(9) 5734 yards/***(not
Sun)/D

Westhoughton G.C
(0942) 811085
Long Island, Westhoughton,
Bolton
4 miles S.W of Bolton on
the A58
(9) 5834 yards/**/F

Whitefield G.C
061-766 2904
81/83 Higher Lane,
Whitefield
Leave M62 at exit 17 for
Radcliffe
(18) 2580 yards/***/F/H

Whittaker G.C
(0706) 78310
Whittaker Lane,
Littleborough
1 mile from the town cen-
tre
(9) 5576 yards/***(not
Tues/Sun pm)/D/M

William Wroe G.C
061-748 8680
Penny Bridge Lane, Flixton
Take B5124 from exit 4 of
the M63
(18) 4395 yards/***/E

Withington G.C
061-445 9544
Palatine Road, West
Didsbury
3 miles from Manchester

city centre
(18) 6411 yards/***/F/H

Worsley G.C
061-789 4202
Stableford Avenue,
Monton, Eccles
Signposted 1 mile E.
of junction 13 of M62
(18) 6217 yards/***/D/H/M

Lancashire

Accrington and District G.C
(0254) 32734
New Barn Farm, Devon
Avenue, West End,
Oswaldthistle
5 miles from Blackburn
on the A679
(18) 5954 yards/***/D

Alt G.C
(0704) 530435
Park Road, West Southport
N. of the Marine Lake
(18) 5939 yards/***/E

Ashton and Lea G.C
(0772) 72480
Tudor Avenue, off
Blackpool Road, Lea,
Preston
3 miles from Preston off
A583
(18) 6289 yards/**/D

Bacup G.C
(0706) 873170
Maden Road,Bacup
Half mile from Bacup cen-
tre on the A671
(9) 5652 yards/**(not
Tues)/F

Baxenden and District G.C
(0254) 34555
Top o thMeadow,
Baxenden
2 miles S.E of Accrington
off the A680
(9) 5740 yards/***/E

Beacon Park G.C
(0695) 622700
Beacon Hill, Dalton,
Up Holland, Wigan
Signposted from the centre
of Up Holland
(18) 5996 yards/***/E

Bentham G.C
(0468) 61018
Robin Lane, Bentham
13 miles E. of M6 (junction
34) on B6480
(9) 5752 yards/***/E

Blackburn G.C
(0254) 51122
Beardwood Brow,
Blackburn
W. side of town off
Revidge Road
(18) 6100 yards/**/D/H

Blackpool North Shore G.C
(0253) 51017
Devonshire Road,
Blackpool
N. of the town centre
on the A587
(18) 6442 yards/***/D

Blackpool-Stanley Park G.C
(0253) 33960
North Park Drive,
Blackpool
2 miles E. of the town centre
(18) 6060 yards/***/E

Burnley G.C
(0282) 21045
Glen View, Burnley
Just past junction
of A56 and A646
(18) 5891 yards/***(not
Sat)/D

Chorley G.C
(0257) 480263
Hall othHill, Heath
Charnock, Chorley
On the A673, near junction
with A6
(18) 6277 yards/***/D/H

Colne G.C
(0282) 863391
Law Farm, Skipton Old
Road
2 miles E. of Colne
(9) 5961 yards/***/D

Darwen G.C
(0254) 701287
Winter Hill, Darwen
2 miles from Darwen
centre, off the A666
(18) 5752 yards/**/E

Dean Wood G.C
(0695) 622219
Lafford Lane, Up Holland,
Skelmersdale
Leave M6 at exit 26, take
A577 to Up Holland
(18) 6129 yards/**/D

Duxbury Park G.C
(02572) 65380
Wyreside, Knott End,
Blackpool
Leave M55 at exit 3, take
A585 then B2588
(18) 6390 yards/***/E

Fairhaven G.C
(0253)736741
2 miles from St Annes
(18) 6883 yards/**/D

Fishwick Hall G.C
(0772) 798300
1 mile east of Preston
(18) 6028 yards/**/D

Fleetwood G.C
(03917) 3114
1 mile west of Fleetwood
(18) 6723 yards/***/D

Heysham G.C
(0524) 51011
3 miles from Morecambe
(18) 6224 yards/***/D

Hindley Hall G.C
(0942) 55131
Hindley, Wigan
(18) 5840 yards/**/D/I

Ingol Golf and Squash Club
(0772) 734556
Tanterton Hall Rd, Ingol
(18) 6345 yards/***/E

Knott End G.C
(0253) 810254
Knott End on Sea
(18) 6010 yards/**/D

Lancaster G. & C. C
(0524) 751247
Ashton Hall, Ashton-with-
Stodday, Lancaster
3 miles S.W of Lancaster on
A588
(18) 6422 yards/**/F/H

Lansil G. C
(0524) 39269

Caton Road, Lancaster
1 mile E. of Lancaster centre
on A683
(18) 5608 yards/***(not Sun
am)/E/H

Leyland G.C
(0772) 421359
Wigan Road, Leyland
Off A49 from M6 exit 28
(18) 6105 yards/**/D

Longridge G.C
(077478) 3291
Fell Barn, Jeffrey Hill,
Longridge, Preston
Take B6243 from Preston to
Longridge
(18) 5800 yards/***/D

Lytham Green Drive G.C
(0253) 737390
Ballam Road, Lytham
1 mile from Lytham centre
(18) 6159 yards/**/C/H

Marsden Park G.C
(0282) 67525
Townhouse Road, Nelson
4 miles N. of Burnley, just
off A56
(18) 5806 yards/***/E

Morecambe G.C
(0524) 412841
Bare, Morecambe
Leave M6 at junctions 34 or
35 for Morecambe
(18) 5766 yards/***/F/M

Nelson G.C
(0282) 64583
Kings Causeway, Briefield,
Nelson
2 miles N. of Burnley on
the A682
(18) 5967 yards/**
(not Thurs pm)/D

Ormskirk G.
(0695) 72112
Cranes Lane, Lathom,
Ormskirk
2 miles E. of Ormskirk
(18) 6333 yards/***/C/H

Penwortham G.C
(0772) 744630
Blundell Lane,
Penwortham, Preston
1 mile W. of Preston off the

A59
(18) 5915 yards/**(not
Tues)/D

Pleasington G.C
(0254) 22177
Pleasington, Blackburn
Leave Blackburn S.W on
A674 for Pleasington
(18) 6417 yards/**/C

Poulton-Le-Fylde G.C
(0253) 892444
Myrtle Farm, Breck Roa,
Poulton-Le Fylde
3 miles E. of Blackpool
via Breck Road
(9) 958 yards/***/E

Preston GC
(0772) 700011
Fulwood Lane, Fulwood,
Preston
N. of Preston,
off Watling Street Road
(18) 6233 yards/**(by
arrangement)/C/H

Rishton G.C
(0254) 884442
Eachill Links, Blackburn
3 miles E. of Blackburn off
A679
(9) 6094 yards/**/F

Rochdale G.C
(0706) 43818
Edenfield Road, Bagslate,
Rochdale
Take A680 for 3 miles
from M62 exit 20
(18) 5981 yards/***/F

Rossendale G.C
(0706) 213056
Edwood Lane, Haslingden,
Rossendale
16 miles N. of Manchester
off A56
(18) 6267 yards/***(not
Sat)/D

Royal Lytham & St Annes
G.C
(0253) 724206
Linksgate, St Annes on Sea,
Lytham St Annes
1 mile from the centre of St
Annes on Sea
(18) 6673 yards/**/A/H/L

St Annes Old Links G.C
(0253) 723597
Highbury Road, St Annes,
Lytham St Annes
On the A584 coastal road
towards St Annes
(18) 6616 yards/**(not
Tues)/C/H

Shaw Hill Golf And
Country Club
(02572) 69221
Whittle-le-Woods, Chorley
2 miles N. of Chorley on
the A6
(18) 6467 yards/***/C/H

Silverdale G.C
(0524) 701300
Red Bridge Lane, Silverdale,
Carnforth
Leave the M6 at junction 35
for Silverdale
(9) 5262 yards/***/E

Springfield G.C
(0706) 49801
Springfield Park, Bolton
Road, Rochdale
(18) 5209 yards/***/E

Todmorden G.C
(0706) 812986
Rive Rocks, Cross Stone
Road, Todmorden
1 mile from town centre
(18) 5818 yards/***(not
Sat)/F

Towneley G.C
(0282) 38473
Todmorden Road, Burnley
1 mile from Burnley
Football Ground
(18) 5862 yards/***/E

Tunshill G.C
(0706) 342095
Kiln Lane, Milnrow
Alongside the M62 near
junction 21
(9) 2902 yards/**(not Tues
pm)/F
Whalley G.C
(025482) 2236
Portfield Road, Whalley,
Blackburn
Take A59 to Whalley, turn
S. of the town
(9) 5953 yards/***/F

Wigan G.C
(0257) 421360
Arley Hall, Haigh, Wigan
4 miles N. of Wigan on the
B5239
(9) 6058 yards/**(not
Tues)/F

Wilpshire G.C
(0254) 48260
72 Whalley Road,
Wilpshire, Blackburn
4 miles E. of Blackburn on
A666
(18) 5911 yards/**/D/H

Merseyside

Allerton Municipal G.C
051 428 4074
Allerton, Liverpool
Take the Allerton road
from city centre
(18) 5494 yards/***/E
(9) 1845 yards/***/E

Arrowe Park G.C
051-677 1527
Arrowe Park, Woodchurch,
Birkenhead
3 miles from the town centre
(18) 6377 yards/***/E

Bidston G.C
051 638 3412
Scoresby Road, Leasowe,
Wirral
1 mile from Leasowe on the
A551
(18) 6207 yards/***/E

Bootle G.C
051-928 6196
Dunnings Bridge Road,
Bootle
5 miles N. of Liverpool
on the A565
(18) 6362 yards/***/E

Bowring G.C
051 489 1910
Bowring Park, Roby Road,
Huyton, Liverpool
5 miles E. of the city centre
(9) 2500 yards/***/E

Brackenwood G.C
051 608 3093
Bracken Lane, Bebington,
Wirral

Signposted from junction 4
off M56
(18) 6285 yards/***/D

Bromborough G.C
051 334 2155
Raby Hall Road,
Bromborough, Wirral
Half mile from
Bromborough station
(18) 6650 yards/**/D

Caldy G.C
051 625 5660
Links Hey Road, Caldy,
Wirral
Take A540 from Chester to
Caldy
(18) 6665 yards/**/C

Childwall G.C
051 487 0654
Naylors Road, Liverpool
Take Childwall Valley Road
to the Bridge Inn
(18) 6425 yards/***(not
Tues)/D

Eastham Lodge G.C
051 327 3003
117 Ferry Road, Eastham,
Wirral
6 miles from Birkenhead
off the A41
(15) 6444 yards/**/D/H

Formby G.C
(07048) 72164
Golf Road, Formby,
Liverpool
6 miles S. of Southport
off the A565
918) 6781 yards/**/A/H

Formby Ladies G.C
(07048) 73493
Golf Road, Formby,
Liverpool
6 miles S. of Southport
of the A565
(18) 5374 yards/C/H

Grange Park G.C
(0744) 26318
Prescot Road, St Helens
1 mile from St Helens on
the A58
(18) 6429 yards/**/C

Haydock Park G.C
(09252) 224389

Golbourne Park,
Newton-Le-Willows
1 mile E. of junction 23 of
the M6
(18) 6043 yards/**(not
Tues)/D

Hesketh G.C
(0704) 36897
Cockle Dicks Lane,
Southport
1 mile N. of Southport centre on the A565
(18) 6193 yards/**/C/H

Heswall G.C
051 342 1237
Cottage Lane, Gayton
Heswall, The Wirral
Leave M53 at junction 4 and
to Well Lane
(18) 6472 yards/***/C/H

Hillside G.C
(0704) 67169
Hastings Road, Hillside,
Southport
At the end of Hastings
Road
off A565
(18) 6850 yards/**/F/H

Hoylake G.C
051 632 2956
Carr Lane, Hoylake
100 yards from Hoylake station
(18) 6330 yards/***/D

Huyton and Prescot G.C
051 489 3948
Hurst Park, Huyton Lane,
Huyton
Off the B5199
(18) 5738 yards/**/D/M

Kirkby (Liverpool
Municipal)
051 546 5435
Ingoe Lane, Kirkby
Leave M57 at junction 6
(18) 6571 yards/***/E/H

Leasowe G.C
051 677 5852
Leasowe Road, Moreton,
Wirral
1 mile W. of Wallasey village
(18) 6204 yards/**/D/H

Lee Park G.C
051 487 3882
Chidwall Valley Road,
Gateacre
Take A562 from Liverpool
onto B5171
(18) 6411 yards/***/D

Royal Birkdale G.C
(0604) 67920
Waterloo Road, Birkdale,
Southport
2 miles S. of Southport on
A565
(18) 6703 yards/**/A/H/L

Royal Liverpool G.C
051 632 3101
Meols Drive, Hoylake,
Wirral
10 miles W. of Liverpool
off the A553
(18) 6737 yards/***/A/H/L

Sherdley Park G.C
(0744) 813149
Elton Head Road, St Helens
2 miles from town centre
on the A570
(18) 5941 yards/***F

Southport and Ainsdale G.C
(0704) 78000
Bradshaws Lane, Ainsdale,
Southport
3 miles S. of Southport
on the A565
(18) 6612 yards/**/B/M

Southport Municipal G.C
(0704) 35286
Park Road West, Southport
At N. end of Promenade
near Marine Lake
(18) 6139 yards/***/E

Southport Old Links G.C
(0704) 28207
Moss Lane, Southport
Past the Law courts for
Manchester Road
(9) 6486 yards/**(not
Wed)/E

Wallasey G.C
051 691 1024
Bayswater Road, Wallasey
Take Wallasey Tunnel
from Liverpool centre
(18) 6607 yards/**/C/H

Warren G.C
051 639 5730
The Grage, Grove Road,
Wallasey
500 yards up Grange Road,
past station
(9) 2945/**/E

West Derby G.C
051 254 1034
Yew Tree Lane, Liverpool
4 miles E. of Liverpool centre
off A57
(18) 6333 yards/**/C

West Lancashire G.C
051 924 1076
Hall Road West,
Blundellsands, Liverpool
Follow signs from
A565 from Crosby
(18) 6756 yards/***/C/H

Wirral Ladies G.C
051 652 1255
93 Bidston Road, Oxton,
Birkenhead
Leave M53 at junction
3 for the A41
(18) 6966 yards(ladies)***(by
arrangement)/D/H
(18) 5170 yards/(men)***(by
arrangement)D/H

Woolton G.C
051 486 2298
Doe Park, Speke Road,
Woolton, Liverpool
6 miles from the city centre
(18) 5706 yards/***/D

Isle of Man

Castletown G.C
(0625) 822201
Fort Island, Castletown
Towards the airport
on Dreswick Point
(18) 6804 yards/***/F

Douglas G.C
(0624) 75952
Pulrose Road, Douglas
1 mile S. of Douglas on the
A5
(18) 6080 yards/***/F

Howstrake G.
(0624) 20430
Groudle Road, Onchan

Take A11 from Douglas to
Onchan Head
(18) 5367 yards/**/E

Ramsey G.C
(0624) 812244
Brookfield, Ramsey
5 minute from town centre
(18) 6019 yards/***/D/H

Rowany G.C
(0624) 834108
Rowany Drive, Port Erin
Course is just off the
Promenade
(18) 5840 yards/***/D

Peel G.C
(0624) 834932
Rheast Lane, Peel
Inland on the A1 towards
Douglas
(18) 5914 yards/**/D

Port St Mary G.C
(0624) 834932
Callow Road, Port St Mary
S. from Castletown on the
A7
(9) 2711 yards/***/E

Yorkshire & Humberside

While many consider the delights of Yorkshire to be exclusive to its northernmost area this is totally wrong. The small villages that nestle amid the southern Pennines or the Dales are delightful and the river Wharfe carves its way through south Yorkshire revealing extraordinary beauty along its trail. From the haunting howls of Haworth and the Bronte country to the jovial singing in a pub on Ilkley Moor, there is a rich tradition; Yorkshire folk are a proud breed—better reserve your best golf for the eighteenth fairway.

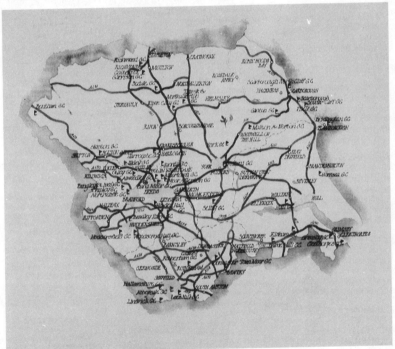

South Yorkshire

Perhaps the pick of the courses in the Sheffield area are the moorland course at **Hallamshire,** three miles west of the city off the A57, **Abbeydale,** a fine wooded parkland test to the south west and **Lees Hall,** a mix of parkland and meadowland, located south of the town centre, and occupying a lofty situation with marvellous views over the city.

Before noting some of the other courses in South Yorkshire, a word on **Lindrick**. Althought the Postman has it in Nottinghamshire the Club's administrative ties are with Yorkshire and a great number of members liveiy in the Sheffield area. Anyway, whichever side of the fence it's on (and the larger part lies in Yorkshire) it is quite superb, and well worth a double mention.

Rotherham's excellent course is located at Thrybergh Park, two miles north of the town on the A630 and is well worth inspecting. Crossing the A1 we arrive at Doncaster. The **Doncaster Town Moor** Golf Club is situated very close to the famous racetrack. Like Rotherham, it's a parkland type course though not as testing. In Doncaster,

West Yorkshire

West Yorkshire has a greater number of golf courses. Quantity is certainly matched by quality with the area just to the north of Leeds being particularly outstanding. Within a short distance of one another are **Moortown, Alwoodley, Sand Moor** and **Moor Allerton** all of which are of Championship standard.

Whilst Alwoodley, Moortown and Sand Moor are predominantly moorland in character, Moor Allerton, where there are 27 holes, is more strictly parkland. When travelling to any of the four Clubs, the A61 should be taken out of Leeds itself. Moortown and Moor Allerton are probably the most widely known courses in southern Yorkshire (if one excludes Lindrick). However, many consider Alwoodley and Sand Moor to be at least their equal. Play all four if you can! Other good courses to note around Leeds are **Roundhay, Leeds, Howley Hall** and **Temple Newsham.**

A second concentration of good golf courses is to be found to the north of Bradford, more particularly, **Northcliffe, Keighley** and **Shipley.** Northcliffe is probably the pick with some outstanding views of the nearby moors, but each is well worth a game. Yet another trio encircles Huddersfield, with **Bradley Park** to the north, **Woodsome Hall** to the south and **Huddersfield** Golf Club to the west. It was on the latter course that Sandy Herd learnt his game. The Open Champion of 1902, Herd finished in the first five in the Championship on no fewer than twelve occasions; he would have doubtless won on several of those but for a fellow called Vardon from Ganton across the way.

Two more courses in West Yorkshire demand to be visited, the first is **Ilkley** and the second is **Otley.** They are without question two of the county's most attractive courses. Our friend, the River Wharfe, winds its way through much of the Ilkley course and is a major hazard on several of the early holes. The equally charming course at Otley nestles majestically in the Wharfe Valley.

North Yorkshire
To the south and west the Yorkshire Dales; to the north and east the Yorkshire Moors. North Yorkshire is England's largest county and quite possibly England's most beautiful.

The Dales and the Moors may not sound like great golfing country and indeed by far the greater number of Yorkshire's golf courses lie in the more populated and industrial regions of South and West Yorkshire. However, golfing visitors to North Yorkshire will not be disappointed; not only does the county boast the likes of Ganton and Fulford, two of England's greatest inland courses, but there are twenty-five or so others, the majority of which are set in quite glorious surroundings.

York, they say, is a city everyone should visit at least once. I recommend at least twice for there are two outstanding golf courses within 3 miles of York Minster: **Fulford** to the south and York Golf Club at **Strensall** to the north. Fulford is the better known, but York is also a Championship course and has many admirers. It is a fine woodland type course, laid out to the edge of Strensall Common.

Next to York, Harrogate probably offers most to both sightseer and golfer. **Pannal** and **Harrogate** are the pick of the courses in the area, the former being a fairly lengthy championship challenge. It is moorland in nature and heavily wooded. Harrogate is possibly the more attractive with its lovely setting at Starbeck near Knaresborough.

Before heading towards the Dales and Moors it is worth noting **Selby** in the south of the county. Laid out over fairly sandy sub-soil the course could be described as part links, part parkland.

Two of North Yorkshire's most beautiful courses are situated fairly close to one another in the centre of the county: **Thirsk & Northallerton** and **Bedale**. The former lies very close to Thirsk racetrack. The views here are towards the Cleveland Hills on one side and the Hambleton Hills on another. Bedale Golf Club can be found off the A684 and is known for its beautiful spread of trees.

In the north of the county, **Richmond** Golf Club enjoys glorious surroundings. The town itself has a strange mixture of medieval, Georgian and Victorian architecture and is dominated of course by the famous Castle. Just south of Richmond, **Catterick Garrison's** Golf Club is worth noting.

Dropping back down in the county, **Malton and Norton** shouldn't be overlooked. It is also particularly convenient for those heading towards Ganton on the A64. **Ganton**, thought by many to be the finest inland course in the North of England, boasts a superb setting on the edge of the Vale of Pickering. It is explored fully on a later page.

Yorkshire's coast contrasts greatly with that of Lancashire, with spectacular cliffs rather than dunes dominating the shoreline. Not surprisingly, there are no true links courses to be found here. However, visitors to the resorts of Filey and **Scarborough** will be able to enjoy a game with views over sea and sand—three in total courses here—and near Flamborough Head there is a testing layout at **Bridlington.**

Humberside

To Yorkshire we must tag on Humberside, much of which once belonged to Yorkshire anyway. It has been a much maligned county and it's not fair to compare Scunthorpe and Grimsby with the likes of Harrogate and York. It has its treasures like any other county: a forty mile stretch of sand; pretty villages nestling in the Wolds and the Holderness countryside; it would be difficult to imagine a more pleasant market town than Beverley and then there's the spectacular Humber Bridge and dramatic Flamborough Head.

Unfortunately, try as I may, I cannot trot off a list of wonderful golf courses. There are enough of them about but there's no Ganton or Fulford here, alas. The best in the county is arguably at **Hornsea,** famed, of course for its pottery. It is a beautiful heathland course with particularly outstanding greens. One tip—try not to kill the ducks on the 11th!

If one has crossed all 1,542 yards of the Humber Bridge to reach the county's largest town then the **Hull** Golf Club at Kirk Ella is probably the best choice for a game, although **Hessle** is now a very good course too. Across the Humber, **Elsham** is well thought of (an old haunt of Tony Jacklin's this) and slightly nearer to Scunthorpe, **Holme Hall** at Bottesford is a championship length parkland course. Finally over to the Humberside coast, both **Grimsby** and **Cleethorpes** are also worth a game. Both towns are full of character (characters as well) and if you do play at Grimsby, don't miss out on the local fish and chips—they're reckoned to be the best in Britain!

North Yorkshire

Aldwark manor G.C.
(03473) 353
Aldwark Manor,
Aldwark Alne, York
5 miles SE of
Boroughbridge off A1
(9)2569 yards/***/E

Bedale G.C.
(0677) 422451
Leyburn Rd, Bedale
S of toen on A684
(18)5599 yards/***/D

Catterick Garrison G.C.
(0748) 833268
Leyburn Lane, Catterick Garrison
3 miles from Catterick Bridge off
the A1
(18)6291 yards/***/D

Crimple Valley G.C.
(0423) 883485
Hookstone Wood Rd, Harrogate
1 mile S of town centre
(9)2500 yards/***(pm only)/E

Easingwold G.C.
(0347) 21964
Stllington Rd, Easingwold
12 miles from Ork, off A19
(18)6262 yards/***/D

Filey G.C.
(0723) 513293
West Ave, Filey
1 mile S of town centre
(18)6030 yards/***/D/M

Forest Park G.C.
(0904) 400425
Stockton On The Forest
(18)6211 yards/***/D

Fulford G.C.
(0904) 413579
Heslington Lane, Heslington,
York
Out of York on A19
(18)6779 yards/**/F/H

Ganton G.C.
(0944) 70329
Ganton, Scarborough
11 miles W of town on A64
(18)6693 yards/***/F/H

Ghyll G.C.
(0282) 842466
Thornton-in-Craven
1 mile from Barnoldswick,
off A56
(9)5708 yards/***(not Sun)/E
Harrogate G. C.
(0423) 862999
Forest Lane Head, Starbeck,
Harrogate
1 mile from Knaresborough

on A59
(18)6204 yards/***/C/M

Hewith G.C.
(0904) 424618
aMuncaster House,
Muncastergate, York
2 miles from city centre on
A1036/A64
(11)6078 yards/**/E

Kirbymoorside G.C.
(0751) 31525
Manor Vale, Kirbymoorside
On A710 Thirsk-Scarborough Rd
(18)5958 yards/***/D

Knaresborough G.C.
(0423) 862690
Butterhills, Boroughbridge Rd
Knaresborough
2 miles from town centre off
Boroughbridge Rd
(18)6083 yards/***/D/H

Malton and Norton G.C.
(0653) 693882
Welham Park, Malton
Off A64 York-Scarborough Rd
(18)6411 yards/***/F/H
(18)6141 yards/***/F/H

Masham G.C.
(0765) 689379
Swinton Rd, Masham, Ripon
8 miles NW of Ripon on A6108
(9)5244 yards/***/D

Oakdale G.C.
(0423) 5671620
Oakdale, Harrogate
1 mile from town centre
(18)***/C/M

Pannal G.C.
(0423) 872628
Follifoot Rd, Pannal, Harrogate
Off the A61 Leeds-Harrogate Rd
(18)6659 yards/**/M/H

Pike Hills G.C.
(0904) 706566
Tadcaster Rd, Copmanthorpe,
York
4 miles from York on Tadcaster
Rd
(18)6048 yards/**/E

Raven Hall Hotel & Golf Course
(0723) 870353
Ravenscar
Half way between
Scarborough and Whitby
(9)1938 yards/***/D

Richmond G.C.
(0748) 825319
Band Hagg, Richmond
Off A6108 from Scotch Corner
(18)5704 yards/***/D

Ripon City G.C.
(0765) 6033640
Palace Rd, Ripon
1 mile W of town on A6108
(9)5645 yards/***/F/M

Scarborough North Cliff G.C
(0723) 360786
North Cliff Ave, Burniston Rd
a2 miles N of town on coast
road
(18)6425 yards/***/D/M

Scarborough South Cliff G.C.
(0723) 374737
Deepdale Ave, Scarborough
1 mile S of town on main Filey
Rd
(18)6085 yards/***/D/H

Selby G.C.
(0757) 228622
Mill Lane, Brayton Bariff, Selby
Off A63 Leeds road
(18)6246 yards/**/D/M/H

Settle G.C.
(072982) 3912
Buckhaw Brow, Settle
1 mile N of Settle on A65
(9)4600 yards/***(not Sun)/D

Skipton G.C.
(0756) 793922
Skipton
1 mile from tiown centre on N
bypass
(18)6191 yards/***(not Mon)/D/M

Thirsk & Northallerton G.C.
(0845) 522170
Thornton-Le-Street, Thirsk
2 miles N of Thirsk
(9)6257 yards/***/F/M/H

Whitby G.C.
(0947) 602768
Low Straggpeton, Whitby
On main coast road between
Whitby and Sandsend
(18)5706 yards/***/D

York G.C.
(0904) 491840
Lords Moor Lane, Strensall, York
6 miles N of York
(18)6275 yards/***/C
South Yorkshire

Abbeydale G.C.
(0742) 360763
Twentywell Lane, Dore,
Sheffield
5 miles S. of Sheffield
off the A621
(18)6419 yards/**/C

Austerfield Park G.C.
(0302) 710841
Cross Lane, Austerfield, N
Bawtry, Doncaster
4 miles N. of Bawtry
off the A614
(18)6828 yards/***/D

Barnsley G.C.
(0226) 382856
Wakefield Rd, Staincross, N
Barnsley
3 miles N. of Barnsley
on the A61
(18)6048 yards/***/D

Beauchief G.C.
(0742) 367274
Abbey Lane, Sheffield
S. of Sheffield off the A621
(18)5423 yards/***/F

aBirley Wood G.C.
(0742) 647262
Birley Lane, Sheffield
4 miles S. of Sheffield off A616
(9)5200 yards/***/E

Concord Park G.C.
(0742) 456806
Shiregreen Lane, Sheffield
4 miles N. of Sheffield off the
A6135
(18)4302 yards/***/E

Crookhill Park G.C.
(0709) 862979
Carr Lane, Conisborough, Nr
Doncaster
Leave the A1 at Doncaster
at the A630 to
Sheffield
(18)5846 yards/***/E

Doncaster G.C.
(0302) 868316
278 Bawtry Road, Bessacarr,
Doncaster
Between Doncaster
and Bawtry on the A638
(18)6220 yards/**/D/M

Doncaster Town Moor G.C.
(0302) 535286
Neatherds House,
Belle Vue, Doncaster
Near racecourse roundabout
(18)5923 yards/***/(not Sun
a.m)/D

Dore and Totley G.C.
(0742) 360492
Broadway Rd, Sheffield
S. of Sheffield offf the A61
(18)6301 yards/*(prior arrangement)/D/H

Grange Park G.C.
(0709) 558884
Upper Wortley Road, Rotherham

2 miles W. of the town
on the A629
(18)6461 yards/***/D

Hallamshire G.C.
(0742) 302153
Sandygate, Sheffield
4 miles from city centre off A57
(18)6396 yards/**/C/M

Hallowes G.C.
(0246) 413734
Hallowes Lane, Dronfield,
Sheffield
Signposted off the A61
(18)6134 yards/***/F

Hickleton G.C.
(0709) 896081
Hickleton, Doncaster
7 miles from Doncaster on the
A635
(18)6361 yards/***/F/M

Hillsborough G.C.
(0742) 343608
Worall Road, Sheffield
3 miles from city centre via
Middlewood Road
(18)5518 yards/**/C/M

Lees Hall G.C.
(0742) 554402
aHemsworth Road, Norton,
Sheffield
3 miles S. of Sheffield
(18)5518 yards/***/D

Phoenix G.C.
(0709) 363864
Pavilion Lane, Brinsworth,
Rotherham
1 mile from Rinsley roundabout
(18)6145 yards/***/D/M

Renshaw Park G.C.
(0246) 432044
Station Road, Renshaw, Sheffield
Leave M1 at junction
30 and follow signs
(18)6253 yards/**/D/H/M

Rotherham G.C.
(0709) 850812
Thrybergh Park,
Thrybergh, Rotherham
7 miles from M1 junction 35
(18)6323 yards/**/C/M

Roundwood G.C.
(0709) 523471
off Green Lane, Rawmarsh,
Rotherham
2 miles N. of Rotherham on the
A633
(9)5646 yards/***/D

Sickleholme G.C.
(0433) 51306
Saltergate Lane, Bamford,

Sheffield
14 miles W. of Sheffield
on the A625
(18)6064 yards/***(not Wed
am)/D

Silkstone G.C.
(0226) 790328
Field Head, Silkstone, Barnsley
Just beyond Dodworth village
off the A628
(18)6045 yards/**/D/H

Sitwell Park G.C.
(0709) 541046
Shrogswood Road, Rotherham
2 miles S.E. of Rotherham off the
A631
(18)6203 yards/***/D/M

Stocksbridge and District G.C.
(0742) 882003
30 Royd Lane, Townend,
Deepcar, Sheffield
9 miles from Sheffield
on the A616
(15)5055 yards/***/D/H

Tankersley Park G.C.
(0742) 468247
High Green, Sheffield
1 mile off A6135 north of
Chapeltown
(18)3204 yards/**/D

Tinsley Park G.C.
(0742) 44237
High Hazel Park, Darnall,
Sheffield
Take A57 off M1 junction 33
(18)6045 yards/***/E

Wath G.C.
(0709) 872149
Abdy, Blackamoor, Rotherham
Take A633 to B6090, then B6089
and follow signs
a(18)5776 yards/**/D

Wheatley G.C.
(0302) 831655
Armthorpe Rd, Doncaster
Leave Doncaster on A18
(18)6345 yards/***/D/M

Wortley G.C.
(0742) 885294
Hermit Hill, Wortley, Sheffield
Leave M1 at Junction
35 take A629
(18)5983 yards/***/C/M
West Yorkshire

Alwoodley G.C.
(0532) 681680
Wigton Lane, Alwoodley, Leeds
5 miles N of Leeds, via A61
(18)6301 yards/**/F/M

Baildon G.C.
(0274) 595162
Moorgate, Baildon, Shipley
5 miles N of Bradford
(18)6178 yards/**/F

Ben Rhydding G.C.
(0943) 608759
High Wood,
Benrhydding, Ilkley
On SE of town
(9)3711 yards/***(not Sat/Sun
am)/E

Bingley St Ives G.C.
(0274) 562506
The Mansion, St Ives Estate,
Bingley
Off A650 towards
Bingley centre
(18)6480 yards/**/E

Bradford G.C.
(0943) 875570
Hawksworth Lane, Guisle, Leeds
Take Ilkley road from Shipley
for Hawksworth
(18)6259 yards/***(not Sat/Sun
am)/C

Bradford Moor G.C.
(0274) 638313
Scarr Hall, Pollard Lane, Bradford
2 miles NE of city centre off
A658
(9)5854 yards/***/F

Bradley Park G.C.
(0484) 539988
Bradley Rd, Huddersfield
Leave M62 at exit 25 for
Huddersfield
(18)6202 yards/***/D

Branshaw G.C.
(0535) 643235
Branshaw Moor, Keighley
2 miles SW of Keighley
on B6143
(18)5121 yards/**/E

Calverley G.C.
(0532) 569244
Woodhall Lane, Pudsey
4 miles NE of Bradford
(18)5516 yards/***(not Sat/Sun
am)/E

City of Wakefield G.C.
a(0924) 374316
Lupset Park, Howbury Rd,
Wakefield
1 mile fromm city centre
(18)6405 yards/***/E
Clayton G.C.
(0274) 880047
Thornton View Rd,
Clayton, Bradford
2 miles SW of Bradford
off A647

(9)5518 yards/***(not Sun)/E

Cleckheaton and District G.C.
(0274) 851266
Bradford Rd, Cleckheaton
4 miles S of Bradford on A638
(18)5847 yards/***/D

Crosland Heath G.C.
(0484) 653216
Felk Stile Rd, Crosland Heath,
Huddersfield
Take A62 from Huddersfield
for 3 miles
(18)5962 yards/***(by arrangement)/D

Dewsbury District G.C.
(0924) 492399
The Pinnacle, Sands Lane,
Mirfield
3 miles from Dewsbury
(18)6256 yards/**/F/H

East Bierley G.C.
(0274) 681023
South View Rd, Bierley,
Bradford
3 miles SE of Bradford
(9)4692 yards/***(not Sun)/E

Elland G.C.
(0422) 72505
Hammerstones, Leach Lane,
Elland
Off the Blackley road, 1 mile
from junction 24
(9)5526 yards/**/F

Garforth G.C.
(0532) 863308
Long Lane, Garforth, Leeds
6 miles E of Leeds of A642
(18)6296 yards/**/D/M

Gott's Park G.C.
(0532) 638232
Armley Bridge Rd, Leeds
3 miles W of city
(18)4449 yards/***/E

Halifax G.C.
(0422) 244171
Union Lane, Ogden, Halifax
4 miles from town
centre on A629
(18)6030 yards/**/D

Halifax Bradley Hall G.C.
(0422) 74108
Stainland Rd. Holywell
Green, Halifax
Between Halifax and
Huddersfield on B6112
(18)6213 yards/***/F

Halifax West End G.C.
(0422) 363293
Highroad Well, Halifax
2 miles N.W of Halifax off A646

a(18)6003 yards/***/F

Hanging Heaton G.C.
(0924) 461606
White Cross Rd. Bennett
Lane, Dewsbury
1 mile from town centre
on A653
(9)5874 yards/**/F/M

Headingley G.C.
(0532) 679573
Back Church Lane, Adel, Leeds
5 miles from city off A660
(18)6238 yards/***/D

Headley G.C.
(0274) 833481
Headley Lane, Thornton,
Bradford
4 miles west of Bradford
on B6145
(9)4914 yards/**/E

Horsforth G.C.
(0532) 586819
Layton Rd, Horsforth, Leeds
After Rawdon off the A6120
(18)6243 yards/**/C

Howley Hall G.C.
(0924) 472432
Scotchman Lane, Morley, Leeds
Leave A650 for B6123
from Morley
(18)6420 yards/***(not Sat)/D

Ilkley G.C.
(0943) 600214
Myddleton, Ilkley
18 miles NW of Leeds of A65
(18)6256 yards/**/B/M

Keighley G.C.
(0535) 604778
Howden Park, Utley, Keighley
1 mile N of Keighley on A650
(18)6139 yards/**/D/H

Leeds G.C.
(0532) 659203
Elmete Lane, Leeds
Off Leeds ring road to A58
(18)6097 yards/**/C/M

Lightcliffe G.C.
(0422) 202459
Knowle Top Road,
Lightcliffe, Halifax
On A58 Leeds to Halifax road
(9)5388 yards/***(not
Wed/Sat)/E/M

Longley Park G.C.
(0484) 4522304
Maple Street off Somerset Rd,
Huddersfield
Half a mile from town centre
(9)5269 yards/**(not Thurs)/E

Low Laithes G.C.
(0924) 273275
Parkmill Flushdyke, Ossett
Nr Exit 40 off M1
(18)6448 yards/***/D

Marsden G.C.
(0484) 844253
aMount Road, Hemplow,
Marsden
8 miles from Huddersfield
off A62
(9)5702 yards/**/E

Meltham G.C.
(0484) 850227
Thick Hollins, Melton
Half a mile east of Melton off
B6107
(18)6145 yards/***(not
Wed/Sat)/D

Middleton Park G.C.
(0532) 700449
Middleton Park, Leeds
3 miles south of city centre
(18)5233 yards/***/E

Moor Allerton G.C.
(0532) 661154
Coal Rd, Wike, Leeds
Off A61 Harrogate Rd
(27)6045 yards/**/B/H
6222 yards/**/B/H
6930 yards/**/B/H

Moortown G.C.
(0532) 686521
Alwoodley, Leeds
(18)7020 yards/***/A

Mount Skip G.C.
(0422) 892896
1 mile east of Hebden Bridge
(9)5114 yards/***/F

Normanton G.C.
(0924) 892943
Snydale Rd, Normanton,
Wakefield
Half a mile from
Normanton on B6133
(9)5184 yards/***(not Sun)/E

Northcliffe G.C.
(0274) 596731
High Bank Lane, Shipley
Off A650 Bradford road
(18)6065 yards/***(not
Sat/Tues)/C/H

Otley G.C.
(0943) 465329
West Busk Lane, Otley
2 miles from Otley off A640
(18)6225 yards/***/C

Outlane G.C.
(0422) 74762
Slack Lane, Outlane,

Huddersfield
Off A640
(18)5590 yards/***/E

Painthorpe House G.C.
(0924) 255083
Painthorpe Lane,
Crigglestone, Wakefield
2 miles S of city off A636
(9)4100 yards/***(not Sun)/E

Phoenix Park G.C.
(0274) 667178
Phoenix Park, Dick Lane,
Thornbury
Off Thornbury roundabout,
on A647
(9)4774 yards/**/F

aPontefract & District G.C.
(0977) 792241
Park Lane, Pontefract
On the B6134 off A1
(18)6227 yards/**/E

Pontefract Park G.C.
(0977) 702799
Park Rd, Pontefract
Between town and
M62 roundabout
(9)4068 yards/***/E

Queensbury G.C.
(0274) 882155
Brighouse Rd, Queensbury,
Bradford
4 miles from Bradford on A647
(9)5102 yards/***/E/M

Rawdon G.C.
(0532) 506040
Buckstone Drive,
Rawdon, Leeds
6 miles from Leeds on A65
(9)5964 yards/**/F

Riddlesden G.C.
(0535) 602148
Howden Rough, Elam Wood Rd,
Riddlesden
Off A650, Keighley road
(18)4185 yards/***/E

Roundhay G.C.
(0532) 662695
Park Lane, Leeds
4 miles north of Leeds
(9)5166 yards/***/E

Ryburn G.C.
(0422) 831355
Norland, Sowerby Bridge,
Halifax
Off Station road from Halifax
(9)5002 yards/***/E/H

Sand Moor G.C.
(0532) 685180
Alwoodley Lane, Leeds
6 miles from Leeds on A61

(18)6429 yards/**/F/M

Scarcroft G.C.
(0532) 892263
Syke Lane, Leeds
NE of Leeds on A58
(18)6426 yards/***/C/H

Shipley G.C.
(0274) 568652
Beckfoot Lane,
Cottingley Bridge, Bingley
On A650 at Cottingley Bridge
(18)6203 yards/***(not
Tues/Sat)/F

Silsden G.C.
(0535) 52998
High Brunthwaite,
Silsden, Keighley
Off A6034 to Silsden centre
(14)4870 yards/***/E

South Bradford G.C.
(0274) 679195
Pearson Rd, Odsal, Bradford
aOff A606 to Odsal
(9)6004 yards/**/D

South Leeds G.C.
(0532) 700479
Gipsy Lane, Beeston Ringroad
Off Leeds - Dewsbury road
(18)5890 yards/***/D/M

Temple Newsam G.C.
(0532) 645624
Temple Newsam Rd, Leeds
5 miles from Leeds on A63
(18)6448 yards/***/F
(18)6029 yards/***/F

Wakefield G.C.
(0924) 258778
Woodthorpe Lane, Sandal,
Wakefield
3 miles S of Wakefield on A61
(18)6626 yards/***/D

West Bowling G.C.
(0274) 724449
Newall Hall, Rooley Lane,
Bradford
2 miles from town centre
(18)5770 yards/**/D

West Bradford G.C.
(0274) 542767
Chellow Grange, Bradford
3 miles from Bradford on B6144
(18)5752 yards/**/E

West End G.C.
(0422) 53608
The Racecourse, Paddock Lane,
Highroad Well
Take A61 Burnley road from
town centre
(18)6003 yards/***/E

Wetherby G.C.
(0937) 63375
Linton Lane, Wetherby
Off A1 at Wetherby
(18)6235 yards/***/C

Whitwood G & CC
(0977) 512835
Atofts Lane, Whitwood,
Castleford
1 mile along A655 from junction
31 of M62
(9)6282 yards/***/D

Woodhall Hills G.C.
(0532) 554594
Woodhall Rd, Calverley, Pudsey
6 miles from Leeds on A647
(18)6102 yards/***/D

Woodsome Hall G.C.
(0484) 602971
Fenay Bridge, Huddersfield
5 miles SE of Huddersfield on
A629
(18)6068 yards/***(not Tues)/D
Humberside

Beverley & East Riding G.C.
(0482) 868757
Anti Mill, The Westwood,
Beverley
1 mile from town centre on
A1230
a(18)6164 yards/**/D

Boothferry G.C.
(0430) 430364
Spaldington, Howden, Goole
3 miles from junction 12 of M62
on B1228
(18)6651 yards/***/D

Bridlington G.C.
(0662) 672092
Belvedere Rd, Bridlington
2 miles S of Bridlington Station
off A165
(18)6320 yards/***/D

Brough G.C.
(0472) 667291
Cave Rd, Brough
W of village off A63
(18)6035 yards/**(not Wed
am)/C/H

Cleethorpes G.C.
(0472) 812059
Kings Road, Cleethorpes
1 miles S of Cleethorpes off
A1031
(18)6015 yards/***/D

Driffield G.C.
Sunderlandwick, Driffield
1 mile from town centre on A164
(9)6227 yards/***/D

Flamborough Head G.C.
(0262) 850333
Lighthouse Rd, Flamborough,
Bridlington
5 miles NE of Bridlington on
B1255
(18)5438 yards/***(not Sun
am)/D/M

Ganstead Park G.C.
(0482) 811280
Longdales Lane, Coniston, Hull
2 miles E of Hull on A165
(18)6495 yards/***(not Wed/Sun
am)/D/H

Grimsby G.C.
(0472) 42630
Littlecoates Rd, Grimsby
Off A46 in Grimsby
(18)6058 yards/***/D/M

Hainsworth Park G.C.
(0964) 542362
Brandesburton, Driffield
8 miles N of Beverley on A165
(9)5360 yards/***/E

Hessle G.C.
(0482) 650171
Westfield Rd, Cottingham, Hull
4 miles W of Hull off A1105
(18)6638 yards/***(not Tues
am)/C/H

Holme Hall G.C.
(0724) 862078
Holme Hall, Bottesford,
Scunthorpe
Take A159 S from Scunthorpe
(18)6475 yards/**/D/M

Hornsea G.C.
(0964) 532020
Rolston Rd, Hornsea
On the road to Withernsea
(18)6450 yards/***(not Tues)/D

Hull G.C.
(0482) 658919
The Hall, 27 Packman Lane, Kirk
Ella
5 miles W of Kingston-Upon-
Hull, off A164
(18)6242 yards/**/C/H

Immingham G.C.
(0469) 75298
Church Lane, Immingham,
Grimsby
Turn N to Immingham off A180
(18)5809 yards/**/D

Kingsway G.C.
(0724) 840945
Kingsway, Scunthorpe
W of town centre on A18
(9)1915 yards/***/E

Normanby Hall G.C.
(0724) 720226
Normanby Park, Normanby,
Scunthorpe
Leave B1430 5 miles N of
Scunthorpe
(18)6548 yards/***/F

Scunthorpe G.C.
(0724) 866561
Burringham Rd, Scunthorpe
On B1450
(18)6281 yards/**/D/M/H

Springhead Park G.C.
(0482) 656309
Willerby Rd, Hull
From Hull, take A1105 to
Willerby
(18)6439 yards/***/F

Sutton Park G.C.
(0482) 74242
Salthouse Rd, Sutton, Hull
4 miles E of city on A165
(18)6251 yards/***/F

Withernsea G.C.
(0964) 612258
Chestnut Ave, Withernsea
17 miles E of Kingston-Upon-
Hull
(9)5150 yards/***/D

Cumbria & the North East

Just as Devon is often viewed by holiday-makers as a mere stepping stone to Cornwall (which as a Devonian pleases me greatly!) so the far north of England is often viewed by golfers as a mere pretty pathway to the delights of Scotland—Turnberry, Gleneagles etc. Indeed some even believe that north of Lytham there's nothing much in the way of golfing challenges until the Bonnie Land is reached. To those I simply say, 'shame on you!

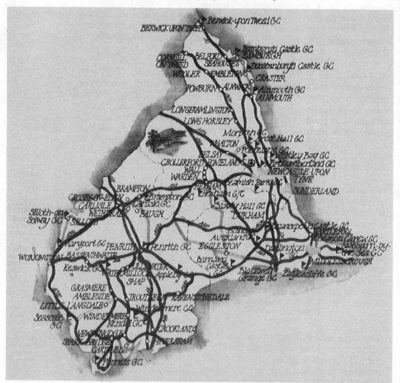

Our region covers Cumbria as well as the North East. Now admittedly Cumbria is hardly perfect golfing territory. A Sunningdale in the middle of the Lake District is hard to imagine (although some spectacular holes are clearly possible!) But there are a number of golf courses in between the fells and the lakes, and furthermore Cumbria comprises more than just the Lake District. Before the counties were rearranged and renamed in the early seventies, Cumberland was the most northerly county in the West of England,

and home not only to the famous sausage but to the **Silloth-on-Solway** Golf Club, which is, dare I say it, almost as good a links as you'll find anywhere in England. The course certainly deserves more than a fleeting visit. As for the North East, **Seaton Carew** near Hartlepool offers championship golf of a very high calibre and **Slaley Hall** is full of Northumbrian promise, while even further north along the Northumberland coast lie a string of golfing pearls—**Alnmouth, Dunstanburgh, Bamburgh** and **Goswick**—good courses with breathtaking scenery.

Cumbria

Let us make a start in the Lake District with the hope that in addition to the picnic hamper and the climbing boots, we've left room in the back of the car for the golf clubs. The Lake District is the land of poets, 'Where breezes are soft and skies are fair' (W.C. Bryant), and 'Where nature reveals herself in all her wildness, all her majesty' (S. Roger).

At Keswick the golfer can meet the poet. **Keswick** Golf Club lies 4 miles east of the lakeland town via the A66. Whilst the course now measures well over 6,000 yards, it recently held a rather dubious claim to being the shortest course in Britain—in 1976 there was a splendid Clubhouse but only five holes—no doubt some remarkable scores were returned! These days scoring is a little more difficult with several streams and some dense woodland to be avoided. As one might imagine the views are quite something and a visit will never disappoint.

Still in the Lakes, we find **Kendal**, a fine parkland course, just three-quarters of a mile from the town centre and only 2 miles from the M6 link road. Although a fair bit shorter than Keswick its first hole is often considered to be the toughest opener in Britain—231 yards, uphill all the way, out of bounds to the left and woods to the right! Should one make it to the 2nd the holes get much easier; however there is an infamous quarry on the right of the 15th fairway which has been known to receive more than golf balls. One frustrated chap after firing ball after ball into its murky depths decided to throw in his bag for good measure. Fortunately he didn't throw himself in as well but word is he never played golf again. Who said it was only a game!

The Golf Club at **Windermere** has recently celebrated its centenary and the course has improved considerably in the last few years. An ideal place for a game of golf while on holiday in the Lakes. Another first class course, still within the National Park boundary is at **Penrith**; close to the A6 but a lovely setting near Ullswater and several very challenging holes.

To the south of Cumbria the highly rated **Furness** Golf Club lays claim to being the oldest in the county. A true links and being quite exposed, scoring well is often more difficult than the card suggests.

Travelling along Cumbria's coast, **Seascale** is soon reached. Another links, and somewhat underrated. One shouldn't be put off by the

Screes and the Scafell Range. North of Workington (en route to Silloth) there is a fair course at **Maryport.**

Before leaving Cumbria, a quick mention for the somewhat isolated **Appleby** Golf Club. If you are in the vicinity it's well worth a visit. A splendid combination of moorland and heathland—very colourful.

The North East

And so to the North East—and what a mixture: Durham, Cleveland, Tyne & Wear and Northumberland. An area encompassing Tyneside, Teeside and Wearside, it also includes the Cleveland Hills, the Cheviots and the wild spectacular coast of ancient Northumbria. The four modern-day counties stretch from the far end of the Yorkshire Pennines and intrude into the Scottish Borders, the greater part of Northumberland lying north of Hadrian's Wall.

The appeal of any golf course can be affected greatly by its surroundings; nowhere in Britain does the accompanying landscape seem to dictate the enjoyment of a game as much as in this part of the world. The contrast between the industrial and rural North East is dramatic to put it mildly. The golf courses in the former tend towards the uninspiring—Seaton Carew being one great exception—whilst the likes of Bamburgh Castle and Hexham offer such magnificent scenery that the quality of the golf can often be relegated to a secondary consideration.

Cleveland

Beginning in the south of the region, Cleveland is one of the smallest counties in England and not surprisingly has very few courses. **Seaton Carew**, is far and away the best in the county. In fact, it is almost certainly the best links course on the East Coast of England, north of Norfolk. It is located approximately 3 miles south of Hartlepool and has a skyline dominated by far-off chimneys which at night appear like giant torches. Golf here is played amidst the dunes with gorse and devilishly thick rough lining the fairways. In recent years several important Championships have been held here, including the British Boys Championship in 1978 and 1986.

South of the Tees, despite its name, the golf course at **Saltburn** isn't right by the sea, it's about a mile west of the town and is a well-wooded meadowland course. Quite a contrast to Seaton Carew: a trifle easier, but certainly worth a visit. Around Teeside itself there are courses at Redcar (**Cleveland**), **Middlesborough** and **Billingham** but perhaps the best in the area is found at **Eaglescliffe**, a hilly course where there are some marvellous views of the Cleveland Hills.

Durham

Crossing into Durham, people often talk of (some even whistle about) Old Durham Town, but of course it's very much a city with a cathedral that has been adjudged the most beautiful building in the world. Without doubt the course to visit here is **Brancepeth Castle**, four miles south west of the city and set in very beautiful surroundings. Rather like St Pierre at Chepstow the course occupies land that was formerly a deer park and a 13th Century church and castle provide a magnificent backcloth.

Further north, **Beamish Park** near Stanley is another laid out in a former deer park (belonging to Beamish Hall) and is well worth a detour if heading along the A1. **Bishop Auckland** in the centre of the county is a pleasant parkland course. The land here belongs to the Church of England and one of the terms of the Club's lease is that the course has to close on Good Friday and Christmas Day. Play then at your peril!

To the south west of Bishop Auckland, **Barnard Castle** enjoys yet another delightful setting. More of a moorland course than anything else, it has a stream that must be crossed seventeen times during a round! There are some fine establishments nearby in which to celebrate (or perhaps even dry out?) Midway between Bishop Auckland and Darlington at Newton Aycliffe is the **Woodham** Golf and Country Club which has a growing reputation.

Darlington is the largest town in the county. It may not have the appeal of Durham but for golfers there's a twin attraction: to the north, **Haughton Grange** with its great selection of MacKenzie greens and to the south, **Blackwell Grange** with its fine variety of trees. Both courses are parkland and always superbly maintained.

Tyne and Wear

Tyneside is essentially a tale of two cities, Newcastle and Sunderland—the land of the Geordies where the welcome is second to none. There are plenty of golf courses in the area but the really attractive golf lies further north along the coast. The **Northumberland** (Gosforth Park) Golf Club and **Ponteland** probably have the best two courses in Tyne & Wear. The former is situated alongside Gosforth Park Racecourse and like Seaton Carew has staged several national championships. However the visitor may find it easier to arrange a game at Ponteland (at least during the week)—a particularly well-kept course this and very convenient if you happen to be flying to or from Newcastle Airport. **Whitley Bay** is another alternative. It is quite a long, windswept course with very large greens and a wide stream that can make scoring pretty difficult.

If there's one large town in England that could really do with a good golf challenge it's Sunderland, a place of great character—golf architects please note! Though closeby, **Whitburn** and **Boldon** are recommended.

Northumberland

Finally then, a look at Northumberland, a county with a splendid, almost mythical history. The first golf course on the way up, as it were, is **Arcot Hall**, 6 miles north of Newcastle and a most tranquil setting. A James Braid creation, Arcot Hall is a heathland course with a wealth of trees. The 9th with its small lake is a particularly good hole. The club has a sumptuous Clubhouse but beware of The Grey Lady who ghosts in and out from time to time! Trekking northwards again, **Morpeth** is next on the agenda. Another pleasant course designed this time by one of James Braid's old rivals—Mr. Vardon no less.

Along the rugged coast some tremendous golf lies ahead. **Alnmouth** is very pleasing. Just a little beyond are the magnificent Castle courses of **Dunstanburgh** (at Embleton) and **Bamburgh**. The golf is glorious—the scenery spectacularly superb. Dunstanburgh Castle, the ruins of which were immortalised in watercolour by Turner, occupies a wondrously remote setting. The course is a genuine links, hugging close to the shore and staring out across miles of deserted beach. Bamburgh Castle is perhaps even more special, often referred to as England's most beautiful course. Not long by any means—but the setting! Holy Island and Lindisfarne, the Cheviot Hills and a majestic castle; furthermore, the fairways are bordered by a blaze of colour, with gorse, purple heather and numerous wild orchids.. Not far from here the fairly short but underrated course at **Seahouses** should not be overlooked.

For centuries the town of Berwick-upon-Tweed didn't know whether it was coming or going, passing between England and Scotland like the proverbial shuttlecock. However, disorientated, it has a fine links course at **Goswick**, 3 miles south of the town.

Having sent the golfer north of Newcastle I am aware of having neglected **Hexham**, and the county's newest golfing gem, **Slaley Hall**. both are only a short drive west of Newcastle, along either the A69 or the A695. The journey is well worth making, on both counts and not just to enjoy the glorious scenery. A golfing holiday I believe is in order—and who needs Scotland!

Cumbria

Alston Moor G.C
(0498) 81675
The Hermitage, Alston
2 miles S. of Alston
(9) 6450 yards/***/E

Appleby G.C
(07683) 51432
Brackenber Moor, Appleby-in-Westmorland
2 miles S. of Apppleby on the A66
(18) 5895 yards/***/E

Barrow G.C
(0229) 25444
Blakesmoor Lane, Hawcoat, Barrow-in-Furness
Take A590 to Hawcoat
(18) 6209 yards/***/F/M

Brampton G.C
(069 77) 2255
Brampton
2 miles S. off the B6413
Castle Carrock road
(18) 6420 yards/***/F/H

Carlisle G.C
(0228) 513303
Aglionby, Carlisle
3 miles E. of Carlisle
(18) 6278 yards/***/F

Cockermouth G.C
(059681) 223
Embleton, Cockermouth
4 miles out of Cockermouth
(18) 5496 yards/***/E

Dunnerholme G.C
(0229) 62675
Duddon Road, Askam-in-Furness
Leave A590 for A595 for Askam-in-Furness
(10) 6101 yards/***(not Sun)/E

Furness G.C
(0229) 41232
Central drive, walney Island, Barrow-in-Furness
Follow signs for Walney Island from town
(18) 6418 yards/***/F

Grange Fell G.C
(05395) 32536
Fell Road, Grange-Over-Sands
On the main road to Cartmel
(9) 4826 yards/***/E'

Grange-Over-Sands G.C
(05395) 33180
Meathop Road, Grange-over-Sands On left as you enter Grange itself
(18) 5660 yards/***/F

Kendal G.C
(0539) 724079
The Heights, Kendal
Leave A6 for Kendal for the B5284
(18) 5483 yards/***/D

Keswick G.C
(07687) 83324
Threlkeld Hall, Keswick
4 miles along A66 from Keswick
(18) 6175 yards/***/E

Kirkby Lonsdale G.C
(0468) 71429
Casterton Road, Kirkby Lonsdale
-1 mile from town on A683
(9) 4058 yards/***(not Sun am)/E

Maryport G.C
(0900) 812605
Bank End, Maryport
On the B5300 from A596 to Workington
(18) 6272 yards/***/E

Penrith G.C
(0768) 62217
Salkeld Road, Penrith
Half mile out of Penrith on A6
(18) 6026 yards/***/D/M/H

Seascale G.C
(09467) 28202
The Banks, Seascale
N. of village, on the coast
(18) 6416 yards/***/D

Sedbergh G.C
(0587) 20993
The Riggs, Millthrop, Sedbergh

1 mile from Sedbergh on the Dent Road
(9) 4134 yards/***/E

Silecroft G.C
(0657) 4250
Silecroft, Millom
3 miles N. of Millom
(9) 5712 yards/**/E

Silloth On Solway G.C
(0965) 31304
Silloth On Solway
18 miles W. of Carlisle'
(18) 6343 yards/***/F/H

St Bees School G.C
(0946) 82295
Rhoda Grove, Rheda, Frizington
4 miles S. of Whiehaven on the B5345
(9) 5082 yards/***/F

Stonyholme Municipal G.C
(0228) 34856
St Aidans Road, Carlisle
1 mile N. of Carlisle
(18) 5600 yards/***/E

Ulverston G.C
(0229) 52824
Bardsea Park, Ulverston
On the B5087 to Bardsea
(18) 6142 yards/***/D/M/H

Windermere G.C
(09662) 3123
Cleaharrow, Windermere
9 miles from Kendal off A591
(18) 5006 yards/***/F/H

Workington G.C
(0900) 603460
Branthwaite Road, Workington
2 miles S.E. of Workington off A595
(18) 6100 yards/***/E/M/H

Co Durham

Aycliffe G.C
(0325) 310820
School Aycliffe Lane, Newton Aycliffe
Part of Sports complex off A6072
(9) 6054 yards/***/E

Barnard Castle G.C
(0833) 38355
Harmire Road, Barnard
Castle
N. of town on the B6278
5838 yards/***/F

Beamish Park G.C
091-3701133
Beamish, Stanley
Follow signs for Open Air
Museum
(18) 6000 yards/***(not
Sun)/F/H

Birtley G.C
091-4102207
Portobello Road, Birtley
Between Birtley and
Whitelands
(9) 5154 yards/**/E'

Bishop Auckland G.C
(0388) 602198
High Plains, Durham Road,
Bishop Auckland
Just N. of town, on left
(18) 6420 yards/***/D

Blackwell Grange G.C
(0325) 464464
Briar Close, Blackwell,
Darlington
On the A66 S. from
Darlington
(18) 5587 yards/***(not Wed
pm)/D

Brancepeth Castle G.C
091-3780075
Brancepeth, Durham
5 mile S.W of Durham on
A690
(18) 6300 yards/**/DH

Chester-le-Street G.C
091-3883218
Lumley Park, Chester-le-
Street
leave A1 for the A167 for
Durham
918) 6054 yards/**/F/L

Consett and District G.C
(0207) 502186
Elmfield Road, Consett
Off the A691 from Durham
(18) 6001 yards/weekends
only/E/H

Crook G.C
(0388) 762429
Low Jobs Hill, Crook
6 miles W. of Durham city
off A690
(18) 6016 yards/***/E

Darlington G.C
(0325) 463936
Haughton Grange,
Darlington
N.E of the town on the
A1150
918) 6032 yards/**/D/M

Dinsdale Spa G.C
90325) 332297
Middleton St George,
Darlington
2 miles from town
on Neasham Road
(18) 6078 yards/**/D

Durham City G.C
091-3780069
Littleburn Farm, Langley
Moor
2 miles S.W. of Durham
off the A690
(18) 6211 yards/**/D

Hobson Municipal G.C
(0207) 71605
Hobson, Nr Burnopfield,
Newcastle-Upon-Tyne
(18) 6582 yards/***/E'

Houghton-Le-Spring G.C
091-5841198
Copt Hill, Houghton-Le-
Spring
On the B1404
(18) 6450 yards/*/D/M

Mount Oswald G.C
091-3867527
South Road, Durham
S.W of Durham on the
A1050
(18) 6101 yards/***/E

Roseberry Grange G.C
091-3700670
Grange Villa, Chester-Le-
Street
3 miles W. of Chester-Le-
Street
on A693
(18) 5628 yards***/E

Seaham G.C
091-5812354
Dawdon, Seaham
6 miles S. of Sunderland off
A19
(18) 5972 yards/***/E

South Moor G.C
(0207) 232848
The Middles, Craghead,
Stanley
2 miles from Stanley off
B6313
(18) 6445 yards/***/F/M

Stressholme G.C
(0325) 461002
Snipe Lane, Darlington
8 miles N. of Scotch Corner
(18) 6511 yards/***/E

Woodham G. & C.C.
(0325) 320574
Burnhill Way, Newton
Aycliffe
1 mile N. of Newton
Aycliffe
(18) 6727 yards/***/D

Tyne & Wear

Boldon G.C
(0783) 364182
Dipe Lane, East Boldon
3 miles N.W of Sunderland
(18) 6348 yards/**/F

City of Newcastle G.C
091-285 1775
Three Mile Bridge,
Gosforth, Newcastle-Upon-
Tyne
3 miles N. of
Newcastle city centre
(18) 6508 yards/***/D

Garesfield G.C'
(0207) 561278
Chopwell
Leave the A694 for the
B6315
(18) 6603 yards/***/E

George Washington G.C
091-417 2626
Near Washington
Moat House Hotel
Signposted from the A1
(18) 6000 yards/***/E

Gosforth G.C
091-285 3495
Broadway East, Gosforth
3 miles N. of Newcastle on
A6127
(18) 6043 yards/**/D/H

Newcastle United G.C
091-286 4693
Ponteland Road, Cowgate
1 mile W. of city centre
(18) 6498 yards/**/E

Northumberland G.C
091©236 2009
High Gosforth Park
Newcastle Upon Tyne
(18)6640 yards/**/F

Ravensworth G.C
091-487 2843
Moss Heaps, Wrekenton,
Gateshead
2 miles S.E. of Gateshead
(18) 5872 yards/**/E/H

Ryton G.C
091-413 3737
Stanners Drive, Clara Vale,
Ryton
8 miles W. of Newcastle,
off A695
(18) 6034 yards/**/E

South Shields G.C
091-456 0475
Cleadon Hills, South Shields
Take A1018 N. from
Sunderland
(18) 6264 yards/***/D

Tynemouth G.C
091-257 4578
Spital Dene, Tynemouth,
North Shields
W. of town off A1058 or
A193
(18) 6403 yards/**/E/M

Tyneside G.C
091-413 2742
Westfield Lane, Ryton
W. of Newcastle off A695
(18) 6055 yards/***/D/H'

Wallsend G.C
091-262 4231
Bigges Main, Wallsend on
Tyne
Take A1058 from Newcastle
(18) 6459 yards/***/E

Wearside G.C
091-534 2518
Coxgreen, Sunderland
On S. bank of Wear
(18) 6323 yards/***/D/M/H

Westerhope G.C
091-286 9125
Whorlton Grange,
Westerhope
Take A696 W. of Newcastle
(18) 6407 yards/**/E

Whickham G.C
Hollinside Park, Whickham
5 miles W. of Newcastle
(18) 6129 yards/**/E

Whitburn G.C
091-529 2144
Lizard Lane, South Shields
Between Sunderland and
South Shields off A183
(18) 6035 yards/**/E

Whitley Bay G.C
091-252 0180
Claremont Road, Whitley
Bay
(18) 6617 yards/**/F

Northumberland

Allendale G.C
(091) 267 5875
Thornley Gate,
Allendale, Hexham
Near town off B6295
(9) 4410 yards/***/E

Alnmouth G.C
(0665) 830231
Foxton Hall, Alnmouth,
Alnwick
In town, off the A1068
(18) 6414 yards/***/D/H

Alnmouth Village G.C
(0665) 830370
Marine Road, Alnmouth
Leave A1 for A1068 for
Alnmouth
(9) 6078 yards/***/E

Alnwick G.C
(0665) 602632
Swansfield Park,
Alnwick'Leave A1 at
Alnwick
(9) 5379 yards/***/F

Arcot Hall G.C
091-2362794
Dudley, Cramlington
Leave A1 for A1068 for
Ashington
(18) 6389 yards/***/D

Bamburgh Castle G.C
(06684) 321
The Wynding, Bamburgh
Leave A1 for B1341 to
Bamburgh
(18) 5465 yards/***/D/M

Bedlingtonshire G.C
(0670) 822457
Acorn Bank, Bedlington
Half mile W. of town
(18) 6224 yards/***/E

Bellingham G.C
(0660) 20530
Boggle Hole, Bellingham,
Hexham
16 miles N. of Hexham, off
B5245
(9) 5245 yards/***/F

Berwick-Upon-Tweed G.C
(0289) 87256
Goswick, Berwick-Upon-
Tweed
4 miles S. of town off the
A1
(18) 6399 yards/**/F

Blyth G.C
(0670) 367728
New Delaval, Blyth
14 miles N. of Newcastle off
A193
(18) 6533 yards/**/E

Dustanburgh Castle G.C
(0665) 562
Embleton, Alnwick
8 miles N.E of Alnwick, off
A1
(18) 6038 yards/***/F

Hexham G.C
(0434) 603072
Spital Park, Hexham
1 mile W. of Hexham, off
the A69
(18) 6026 yards/***/D/H

Magdalene Fields G.C
(0289) 306384
Berwick-Upon-Tweed
5 minutes walk from town

centre
(18) 6551 yards/***/E

Morpeth G.C'
The Common, Morpeth
1 mile S. of Morpeth on
A197
(18) 6215 yards/***/D/H

Newbiggin-By-The-Sea G.C
(0670) 817344
Newbiggin-by-the-Sea
9 miles E. of Morpeth on
the A197
(18) 6423 yards/***/E

Ponteland G.C
(0661) 22689
53 Bell Villas, Ponteland
2 miles N. of airport on
A696
(18) 6512 yards/**/B

Prudhoe G.C
(0661) 32466
Eastwood Park, Prudhoe
12 miles W. of Newcastle
on the A695
(18) 5812 yards/**/E

Rothbury G.C
(0669) 20718
Old Racecourse, Rothbury,
Morpeth
Leave A697 for B6344 to
Rothbury
(9) 5146 yards/***(not Sat)/F

Seahouses G.C
(0665) 720794
Beadnell Road, Seahouses
Take B1340 from
Bamburgh for Seahouses
(18) 5336 yards/***/F

Slaley Hall G.& C.C
(0434) 673691
Slaley, Hexham
7 miles south of Corbridge
off A68
(18) 6995 yards/***/F

Stocksfield G.C
(0661) 843041
New Ridley, Stocksfield
On A695 between
Corbridge and Prudhoe
(18) 5594 yards/**/F/M

Warkworth G.C
(0665) 711596

Warkworth
Take A1068 from Felton to
Warkworth
(9) 5856 yards/***/E

Wooler G.C
Dodd Law, Doddington,
Wooler
2 miles N.E of town on the
Berwick Rd
(9) 6353 yards/***/E

Cleveland

Billingham G.C
(0642) 554494
Sandy Lane, Billingham
Near the town centre
(18) 6034 yards/***/D

Castle Eden & Peterlee G.C
(0429) 836220
Castle Eden, Hartlepool
At junction of A19 and A181
(18) 6293 yards/***/D

Cleveland G.C
(0642) 471798
Queen Street, Redcar
Through Coatham off the
A1042
(18) 6707 yards/***/D/H

Eaglescliffe G.C
(0642) 780098
Yarm Road, Eaglescliffe,
Stockton on Tees
On the A135 from Stockton
(18) 6045 yards/**/D

Hartlepool G.CC
(0429) 274398
Hart Warren, Hartleool
At N. end of Hartlepool, off
King Osway Drive
(18) 6215 yards/***(not
Sun)/D/H

Middlesbrough G.C
(0642) 311515/316430
Brass Castle Lane, Marton,
Middlesbrough
5 miles S. of the town
(18) 6106 yards/**(not
Tues)/D/M

Middlesbrough Municipal
G.C
(0642) 315361
Ladgate Lane,
Middlesbrough

Take A19 via A174 to
Ackham
(18) 6314 yards/***/E

Saltburn-By-Sea G.C
(0287) 22812
Guisborough Road, Hobb
Hill, Saltburn-by-Sea
1 mile from centre of town
on the B1268
(18) 5803 yards/***/F/M

Seaton Carew G.C
(0429) 266249
Tees Road, Seaton Carew,
Hartlepool
3 miles S. of the town off
the A178
(18) 6802 yards/***/F/M

Teesside G.C
(0642) 616516'
Acklam Road, Thornaby
1 mile from the A19 on the
A1130
(18) 6472 yards/**(pm
only)/E

Wilton G.C(0642) 465265
Wilton Castle, Redcar
4 miles W. of Redcar off
the A174
(18) 6019 yards/***(not
Sat)/D

Wales

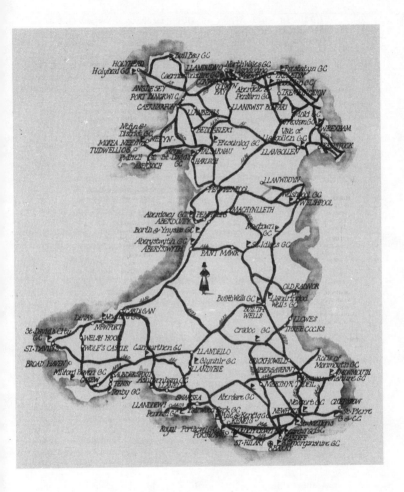

Balls in South Wales are often large, oval-shaped and made of leather. However, those belonging to the much smaller dimpled breed—usually white, though these days sometimes shocking yellow—are to be found in some particularly pleasant spots, and in a great variety of places between the Wye Valley and the Gower Peninsula. In addition to 'The Glamorgans' and Gwent our region takes in Mid Wales as well, that is the larger, less inhabited counties of Dyfed and Powys—'the real Wales', they'll tell you there.

Gwent

For many travellers their first sample of golf in South Wales will be the impressive **St Pierre** Golf and Country Club at Chepstow. Unfortunately, far too great a number make St Pierre their one and only stop. Further up the Wye Valley both **Monmouthshire** and **The Rolls of Monmouth** offer an outstanding game in delightful surroundings. Bounded by the River Usk, the Monmouthshire Golf Club lies half a mile west of Abergavenny at Llanfoist. In 1992 the Club celebrated its centenary—quite an achievement when one considers its unusual beginnings. Laid out on ground formerly used for polo and later for horseracing, golf was started here in 1892, as the Club handbook tells you, 'the result of a bet as to whether such a venture could be run successfully at Abergavenny!' Clearly the golfers backed a winner.

One other golf course in Gwent which is well worth a visit is **Newport** at Rogerstone. It is a very fine downland course and decidedly handy when travelling along the M4 (junction 27)—en route to Porthcawl perhaps?

'The Glamorgans'

Golfers in Cardiff (or Caerdydd) are quite fortunate having a number of well-established courses close at hand. Not surprisingly they tend to be busier than the majority of Welsh courses and therefore before setting off it is especially important to contact the particular Club in question. The **Cardiff** Golf Club is a superior parkland course situated some 3 miles from the city centre at Cyncoed. **St Mellons,** north east of the city, within easy access of the M4, is another popular parkland course—quite challenging, with several interesting holes. To the south west of Cardiff, **Wenvoe Castle**, one of the more hilly courses in South Glamorgan can be recommended as can the **Glamorganshire** course, located to the west of Penarth.

A short distance to the north of Cardiff, the town of Caerphilly is more famous for its castle and its cheese than for its golf; however there is some good golf in the area, **Mountain Lakes** Golf and Country Club being particularly noteworthy. Before heading off to the glorious coastal strip around Porthcawl a course certainly deserving a mention is **Aberdare**—and not merely because the professional goes by the impressive name of Mr A Palmer! (Incidentally, I heard recently that Mr Palmer once had an assistant called Mr

Nicholas!) Aberdare is an excellent woodland course, undoubtedly the finest in 'the Valleys'.

One would have to travel many a mile to find a course the equal of **Royal Porthcawl** but its near neighbour to the east, **Southerndown** gets closer than most. Situated on high ground it is an outstandingly scenic downland type course measuring a little over 6600 yards (par 70). Even closer to Porthcawl is the fine links of **Pyle and Kenfig**, on more than one occasion the venue for the Welsh Amateur Stroke Play Championship. It is a very tough challenge, being open to the elements, and boasts some very large sand dunes.

Beyond Pyle and Kenfig the M4 heads into West Glamorgan passing through Port Talbot towards Swansea, and beyond Swansea is the beautifully secluded Gower Peninsula. If you are fortunate enough to be visiting these parts, three courses that can be strongly recommended are **Fairwood Park, Clyne** and **Pennard**. Fairwood park, situated close to Swansea Airport, is a second course over which race-horses once galloped. It is a much improved course and has several long par fours. Clyne offers a moorland challenge while from Pennard's cliff-top course there are some splendid views out across the Bristol Channel.

Dyfed

For every person in New Zealand there are twenty sheep. Regrettably, I don't have the figures for Dyfed and Powys but I suspect they're fairly similar. The bad news is that the lack of human beings is unfortunately reflected by a low number of top class golf courses (unlike in New Zealand it should be said). However, the good news is that even during the summer months most of the courses remain relatively uncrowded, visitors are made very welcome and the green fees tend to be a lot cheaper than in most parts of Britain.

The two Championship courses in this region lie on Dyfed's southern coast, some 30 miles apart. Both **Ashburnham** and **Tenby** were founded before the turn of the century and each has staged more than one Welsh Amateur Championship, Ashburnham in fact being a regular venue.

Located one mile west of Burry Port, Ashburnham's links is fairly close to industrial South Wales which, I suppose, extends as far as Llanelli, or at least to where the M4 from London fizzles out. The course measures 7,000 yards from the Championship tees and 6,686 yards from the medal tees—certainly not a course for the inexperienced! Connoisseurs of the game, however, should find it an excellent challenge. There are more glorious sandy beaches around Tenby than one could care to count. As well as being a haven for the bucket and spade it is also a wonderful place for a round of golf. Tenby is a true links course with natural sand hazards and fast greens.

Moving westwards along the Dyfed coast, the next 18 holes are to be found at **Milford Haven**, a medium-length parkland course to the west of the town. In days of old the former whaling town may well have been a haven but the present day 'landscape in oils' isn't everyone's cup of tea. More attractive is **St Davids** with its beautiful Cathedral making it the smallest city in Britain. Unfortunately for golfing visitors there is only a modest 9 hole golf course. Another fine hole can be found 20 miles away at Newport offering some tremendous sea views.

Leaving 'Little England beyond Wales' and heading still further up the coast, the University town of **Aberystwyth** has an 18 hole course that looks out over Cardigan Bay. A more impressive golf course though is **Borth and Ynyslas,** one of the oldest Clubs in Wales. Borth is a superbly-maintained seaside links. The B4353 road runs right alongside much of the course and is often peppered by golf balls. Taking out insurance before playing Borth is recommended.

Inland, there is precious little golf to speak of in Dyfed, though there is a fairly testing hilltop course at **Carmarthen**—one which is decidedly better in summer than in winter and an attractive parkland course, **Glynhir,** near the foothills of the Black Mountain Range. The latter is a particularly friendly club situated close to the Glynhir Mansion where the first news of Wellington's victory at Waterloo is reputed to have been received by carrier pigeon. (Must have been a pretty sharp pigeon!)

Powy

The golf courses in Powys are few and far between, but those that there are tend to be set amidst some splendid scenery. There is an 18 hole course at **Welshpool** up in the hills near the English border (do try to visit Powis Castle and its superb gardens if you're in the area) and two interesting 9 hole courses at Newton (**St Giles**) and at Llanidloes (**St Idloes**) in the quiet of the Cambrian Mountains. Two of the region's best courses are situated right in the centre of Wales, **Llandrindod Wells** and **Builth Wells**. Both are attractive courses, Llandrindod in particular offers spectacular views. One final course to mention, and one good enough to have held the Welsh Amateur Stroke Play Championship is **Cradoc** near Brecon. A lovely course this, and again, very scenic being within the Brecon Beacons National park.

North Wales

One's first thoughts of North Wales are often of lakes, great castles and even greater mountains, or as a fine fellow by the name of Hywell ap Owain, 12th Century Prince of Gwynedd, put it (I offer it in translation):

> I love its sea-marsh and its mountains,
> And its fortress by its forest and its bright lands,
> And its meadows and its water and its valleys,
> And its white seagulls and its lovely women.

A man who had obviously seen much of the world! Of course in the 12th Century the Welsh didn't play golf, or at least if they did they kept it pretty quiet and in any case you can be pretty confident that Hywell ap Owain would have told us about it. Well, what about the golf in North Wales then? In a word, marvellous. Inland it tends to get hilly to put it mildly, and should you wish to venture up into 'them thar hills' as well as the climbing gear, don't forget to bring the waterproofs! But there again, leave room for the camera (hope you've got a large golf bag).

In the main though, it is to the coast that the travelling golfer will wish to head. Between Flint to the east of Clwyd and Aberdovey in southern Gwynedd are the impressive Championship links of Prestatyn, Maesdu, North Wales, Conwy, Royal St Davids and of course Aberdovey itself. In addition, there are several with spectacular locations, Nefyn on the Lleyn Peninsula being an outstanding example.

Clwyd

Before journeying around the coast though, a brief mention for some of the inland courses, with a few thoughts as to where one might stop off in order to eat, drink, be merry or simply rest the weary golf clubs. Away from the sea and sand probably the best two challenges are to be found at **Wrexham** and Llangollen. Wrexham, located just off the A53, is fairly close to the English border and indeed the views here are across the Cheshire Plain. Two good holes to look out for are the 4th and 14th. Llangollen's splendid course, **The Vale of Llangollen**, is set out alongside the banks of the River Dee. There are some truly excellent holes, notably the 9th. Appropriately named the River Hole it is a really tough par four of 425 yards. The golfer who likes a spot of fishing (or perhaps even the golfing fisherman) would be in his element here and on a good day should see a few of the famous Dee Salmon being landed— probably easier than netting a birdie. One name to watch in the future is the spectacular new **Chirk Golf and Country Club**, south of Wrexham on the A483. Over seven thousand yards of manicured fairways are to be complemented by a much less taxing par three course and driving range.

Remaining in Clwyd and the unfortunately named town of **Mold**. A pleasant parkland challenge here, while still further north and getting nearer the coast is the **Rhuddlan** Golf Club. They say you should never rush a round at Rhuddlan. If you are heading for the tougher links courses on the coast then this is the ideal place to groove the swing. The course is laid out close to one of North Wales' famous massive fortresses in the grounds of Bodrhydden estate and overlooks the Vale of Clwyd.

Golfwise there is not a great deal more in the deeper realms of North Wales. **Ffestiniog,** (in Gwynedd) famed for its mountain railway, has a short nine holes of the moorland variety but the scenery in these parts may prove a little too distracting. Ffestiniog nestles in the heart of Snowdonia and the encircling mountains are quite awe-inspiring.

Prestatyn warrants attention. Close to Pontin's holiday camp (or is it village nowadays?) it is a genuine links and when the prevailing westerly blows, can play very long (the Championship tees stretch the course to 6714 yards).

The A55 is the coastal road that should be followed to find our next port of call, the **Abergele and Pensarn** Golf Club, just west of Abergele. This course is a fairly new parkland layout (the bulldozer having removed the former) and it lies beneath the walls of fairy-tale Gwyrch Castle. Games are often won or lost on the last three holes at Abergele. The round is supposed to finish five, three, five— but not many scorecards seem to!

Gwynedd

A trio of Championship courses are to be found a little further along the coast and just over the county border in Gwynedd. Golfers in Llandudno are more fortunate than most, having two fine courses to choose from: **North Wales** and **Llandudno (Maesdu)**. The latter is perhaps the better known of the two but both are of a high standard and each offers superb views across the Conwy estuary towards Anglesey.

The **Caernarvonshire** Golf Club lies the other side of the estuary— yet another spectacular siting between the sea and mountains and another course where the wind can blow fiercely. A regular venue for the important Welsh Championships, Conwy is a long course and is generally considered second only to Royal St Davids in terms of golfing challenges in North Wales. It possesses everything that makes links golf so difficult—gorse, rushes, sandhills and more gorse, rushes and sandhills—quite frightening!

Heading for the golf courses of the Lleyn Peninsular, many may wish to break their journey at Caernarfon. The castle is splendid and well worth inspecting. I suppose every golfer has at one time or another drawn up a mental listing of favourite golf courses. Anyone who has made the trip to **Nefyn** is almost certain to have the course high on such a list. A sheer delight to play on, Nefyn was a regular haunt of Lloyd-George, as was neighbouring **Pwllheli**, which was in fact opened by him in 1909 when he was the Chancellor of the Exchequer. Not far from Pwllheli there is a good nine hole course at **Aberscoch,** soon to be extended to the full 18.

The subject of favourite courses has been raised and **Aberdovey** was the choice of the celebrated golf writer Bernard Darwin, 'the course that my soul loves best of all the courses in the world.' It has an interesting layout, sandwiched between the sand dunes on the one side and a railway line on the other, (the railway line in fact links Aberdovey to Harlech and is a pretty good service).

Isle of Anglesey
The Isle of Anglesey is linked by a road bridge to the mainland across the Menai Straits. There is a choice of four golf courses with plans in the pipeline for extending this number. Perhaps the best two games to be found are at Bull Bay, near Amlwch, and at Holyhead on Holy Island. Both courses are very scenic with Holyhead (Trearddur Bay) offering the greatest variety of challenge. Bull Bay enjoys a fairly remote, certainly spectacular setting on the island's northern coast. It is a hilly course with much gorse and several rocks to confront and when the wind blows it can be very tricky. The Club handbook relates how, in an exhibition match to mark the opening of the course, featuring John H. Taylor and James Braid, the latter tangled with the gorse on the short third hole and finished up with an eight! There's hope for us all.

South and Mid Wales

Gwent

Caerleon G.C
(0633) 420342
Broadway, Caerleon
Leave M4 at junction 25 for
Caerleon
(9) 3092 yards/***/E

Greenmeadow G.C
(06333) 62626
Treherbert Road,
Croesyceiloig, Cwmbran
Leave M4 at junction 26,
take A4042 N. for Cwmbran
(18) 5587 yards/***/E

Llanwern G.C
(0633) 412029
Golf House, Tennyson
Avenue, Llanwern
Leave M4 at junction 24,
take A455 to Llanwern
(18) 6206 yards/**/F/M

Monmouth G.C
(0600) 712212
Leesebrook Lane,
Monmouth ‑
N. of town on A40
(9) 5454 yards/***/D

Monmouthshire G.C
(0873) 2606
Llanfoist, Abergavenny
S. of Abergavenny on
B4269
(18) 6054 yards/***/C/H

Newport G.C
(0633) 892643
Great Oak, Rogerstone,
Newport
Leave M4 at junction 27,
take B451 towards
Highcross
(18) 6370 yards/**/C/M

Pontnewydd G.C
(06333) 2170
West Pontnewydd, Upper
Cwmbran
Leave M4 at junction 26,
take A4042 then A4057 to
Cwmbran
(18) 5340 yards/**/E

Pontypool G.C
(0495) 5763655

Trevethyn, Pontypool
Leave M4 at junction 26,
take A4042 to Pontypool
(18) 6058 yards/***/D/H

The Rolls of
Monmouth G.C
(0600) 715353
The Hendre, Monmouth
Take B4233 E. from
Abergavenny
(18) 6733 yards/***/B

St. Mellons G.C
(0633) 680401
St. Mellons, Cardiff
On A48 between Newport
and Cardiff
(18) 6275 yards/**/D/H

St. Pierre G & C C
(0291) 625261
St. Pierre Park, Chepstow
On A48 near Severn Bridge
(18) 6700 yards/***/F/H
(18) 5762 yards/***/F/H

Tredegar Park G.C
(0633) 894433
Bassaleg Road, Newport
Leave M4 at junction 28,
from A48 take A4072 N.
(18) 5575 yards/***/D/H

West Monmouthshire G.C
(0495) 310233
Pond Road, Nantyglo
Leave M4 at junction 28,
take A467 to Nantyglo
(18) 6097 yards/***/F

The Glamorgans

Aberdare G.C
(0685) 871188
Abernant, Aberdare, Mid
N.E of Aberdare off A4059
(18) 5874 yards/**/D

Bargoed G.C
(0443) 830143
Heolddu, Bargoed, Mid
17 miles N. of Cardiff on
A469
(18) 6213 yards/**/D

Bryn Meadows G.C & Hotel
(0495) 225590
The Bryn, Hengoed, Mid
15 miles N. of Cardiff on
A469

(18)5 963 yards/**/D

Brynhill G.C
(0446) 720277
Port Road, Barry, South
Take A48 from Cardiff to
Wenvoe and Port Road
(18) 6000 yards/*** (also
Sat)/F

Caerphilly G.C
(0222) 883481
Pencapel, Mountain Road,
Caerphilly, Mid
7 miles N. of Cardiff on
A469
(18) 5819 yards/**/E

Cardiff G.C
(0222) 753320
Sherborne Avenue,
Cyncoed, South
2 miles N. of Cardiff centre
(18) 6016 yards/**/B

Castell Heights G.C
(0222) 861128
Blaengwynlais, Caerphilly,
South
4 miles N. of Cardiff on
Tongwynlais-Caerphilly
Road
(18) 7000 yards/***/D/H
(9) 2670 yards/***/E

Clyne G.C
(0792) 401989
120 Owls Lodge Lane,
Mayals, Black Pill, Swansea
Leave Swansea by A4067
(18) 6312 yards/***/D/H

Creigiau G.C
(0222) 890263 5955
Creigiau, Cardiff, South
Leave M4 at junction 34,
Take A4119 to Llantrisant
(18) 5786 yards/**/D

Dinas Powis G.C
(0222) 512727
Old Highwalls, Dinas
Powis, South
Leave Cardiff on A4055
to Dinas Powis
(18) 5377 yards/***/D

Fairwood Park G.C
(0792) 203648
Upper Killay, Swansea
Leave Swansea on A4118 to
Upper Killay
(18) 6606 yards/***/F

Glamorganshire G.C
(0222) 701185
Lavernock Road,
Penarth, South
Leave Cardiff on A4160,
take B4267 to Lavernock
(18) 6150 yards/***/D/H

Glynneath G.C
(0639) 720452
Penycraig,
Pontneathvaughan, Neath,
West
North of Neath off A465
(18) 5499 yards/***/F

Inco G.C
(0792) 844216
Clydach, Swansea, West
Situated in the Swansea
Valley
(12) 6230 yards/***/E

Langland Bay G.C
(0792) 366023
Llangland Bay, Swansea,
West
Take A4067 coast road
from Swansea to Mumbles
Head
(18) 5812 yards/***/D/H

Llanishen G.C
(0222) 752205Cwm, Lisvane,
Cardiff5 miles N. of Cardiff
via Heol Hir(18) 5296
yards/***/F/HLlantrisant
and

Ponty Clun G.C
(0443) 22148
Lanelay Road,
Talbot Green, Ponty Clun
N. of Cardiff on A4119
to Llantrisant
(12) 5712 yards/**/D/H

Maesteg G.C
(0656) 732037
Mount Pleasant, Neath
Road, Maesateg, Mid
Leave A4107 for B4282 to
Maesteg

(18) 5845 yards/***/D

Merthyr Tydfil G.C
(0685) 3308
Cilsanws Mt, Cefn Coed, Nr
Merthyr Tydfil, Mid
Take A465 N. at Cefn Coed
(9) 5794 yards/***/F

Morlais Castle G.C
(0685) 2822
Pant, Dowlais, Merthyr
Tydfil, Mid
N. of Merthyr Tydfil
toward Brecon Railway
(9) 6255 yards/***(not Sat)/F

Morriston G.C
(0792) 771079
160 Clasemont Road,
Morriston, Swansea, West
3 miles N. of Swansea on
A4067
(18) 5734 yards/***/D

Mountain Ash G.C
(0443) 472265
Cefnpennar, Mountain Ash,
Mid
From A470 take A4059 to
Mountain Ash
(18) 5485 yards/***/D

Mountain Lakes G.C
(0222) 861128
Blaengwynlais, Caerphilly
Leave M4 at junction 32. 4
miles N. of Cardiff
(18) 6851 yards/***/D/H

Neath G.C
(0639) 643615
Cadoxton, Neath, West
Take A48 to Neath, E. to
Cadoxton
(18) 6465 yards/***/D

Palleg G.C
(0639) 842193
Palleg Road, Lower
Cwmtwrch, Swansea
15 miles N. of Swansea on
A4067 Brecon road
(9) 3260 yards/***/F

Pennard G.C
(0441) 283131
2 Southgate Road,
Southgate, Swansea, West
(18) 6266 yards/***/F/H

Pontardawe G.C
(0792) 863118
Cefn Llan, Pontardawe,
Swansea
N. of Swansea on A4067 to
Pontardawe
(18) 6061 yards/E/M

Pontypridd G.C
(0443) 402539
Ty Gywn, The Common,
Pontypridd, Mid
N. of Cardiff on A470 to
Pontypridd
(18) 5650 yards/***/E

Pyle and Kenfig G.C
(065 671) 3093
Waun-y-Mer, Kenfig, Mid
W. of Cardiff on M4, take
junction 37 to Porthcawl
(18) 6640 yards/**/C/H

Raf St Athan G.C
(0446) 751043
Barry 2 miles E. of
Llanwit Major on B4265
(9) 5957 yards/***(not Sun
am)/E

Radyr G.C
(0222) 842408
Drysgolf Road, Radyr,
Cardiff
Turn off A470 N. at Taffs
Well
(18) 6031 yards/**/D/H

Rhondda G.C
(0443) 433204
Ponygwaith, Ferndale,
Rhondda
3 miles past Porth on A4058
(18) 6428 yards/**/F/M

Royal Porthcawl G.C
(065 671) 2251
Porthcawl, Mid
Leave M4 at junction 37 for
A4229 to Porthcawl
(18) 6605 yards/***/F/H

Southerdown G.C
(0656) 880476
Ewenny, Bridgend, Mid
Leave M4 at junction 36 for
A4061, then B4524 for
Ogmore
(18) 6613 yards/**/C/H

Swansea Bay G.C
(0792) 814153
Jersey Marine, Neath, West
Off A48 between Neath
and Swansea
(18) 6302 yards/***/F

Tredegar and Rhymney G.C
(0685) 840743
Cwmtysswg, Rhymney,
Gwent 2 miles from
Rhymney on B4256
(9) 2788 yards/***/E

Wenvoe Castle G.C
(0222) 594371
Wenvoe, Cardiff
2 miles from
Wenvoe on A4050
(18) 6411 yards/***/F/H

Whitchurch G.C
(0222) 620125
Pontmawr Road,
Whitchurch, Cardiff
Leave M4 at junction 32,
take A470 S.
(18) 6245 yards/**/C/H

Whitehall G.C
(0443) 740245
Nelson, Treharris, Mid
Take A470 N. of Cardiff for
Treharris
(9) 5750 yards/**/F

Dyfed

Aberystwyth G.C
(0970) 615104
Brynmor, Aberystywth
At north end of promenade
(18) 5735 yards/***/F

Ashburnham G.C
(05546) 2269
Cliffe Terrace, Burry Port
On coast side of Burry Port
off A484
(18) 6916 yards/**/C

Borth and Ynyslas G.C
(097 081) 202
Borth Off B4353 to Borth
(18) 6094 yards/***/F

Cardigan G.C
(0293) 612035
Gwbert on Sea, Cardigan
From A487 take B4548 N.W
to Gwbert

(18) 6207 yards/***/F

Carmarthen G.C
(0267) 87214
Blaen-y-coed Road,
Carmarthen
Take A40, N. to A485
then onto A484
(18) 6212 yards/***/F

Cilgwyn G.C
(0570) 45286
Llangybi, Lampeter
Take A485 N.E
for 4 miles to Llangybi
(9) 5318 yards/***/F

Glynhir G.C
(0269) 850472
Glynhir Road, Llandybie,
Ammanford
From M4 junction 49 take
A483 to Llandybie
(18) 6090 yards/***/F

Haverfordwest G.C
(0437) 764523
Arnolds Down, Narberth
Road, Haverfordwest
N. of A40, 1 mile E. of the
town
(18) 5908 yards/**/E

Milford Haven G.C
(0646) 692368
Woodbine House,
Hubberston, Milford Haven
W. of the town at
Hubberston
(18) 6071 yards/***/F

Newport (Pembs) G.C
(0239) 820244
Newport
On bayside, follow
Newport Sands signs
(9) 6179 yards/***/E

St. Davids City G.C
(0437) 720392 (tourist
office)
Whitesands Bay, St. Davids
Take A487 from
Haverfordwest to St. Davids
(9) 5693 yards/***/E

South Pembrokeshire G.C
(0646) 682817
Defensible Barracks,
Pembroke Dock
Take A477 to Pembroke

and Pembroke Docks
(9) 5804 yards/***/E

Teny G.C
(0834) 2978
The Burrows, Tenby
Through town on A4139
(18) 6232 yards/***/D
POWYS

Brecon G.C
(0874) 2004
Newton Park, Llanfaes,
Brecon
S. of town on A40 from
Abergavenny
(9) 5218 yards/***/E

Builth Wells G.C
(0982) 553296
Builth Wells
W. of town on A483
(18) 5760 yards/***/E

Cradoc G.C
(0874) 3658
Penoyre Park, Cradoc,
Brecon
Through Brecon and N. on
B4520
(18) 6318 yards/***/D

Llandrindod Wells G.C
(0597) 823873
Llandrindod Wells
Take A483 from Brecon to
Llandrindod Wells
(18) 5749 yards/***/F

Old Rectory G.C
(0873) 810373
Llangattock, Crickhowell
Take A40 W. from
Abergavenny to
Crickhowell
(9) 2878 yards/***/E

Welshpool G.C
(0938) 83249
Golfa Hill, Welshpool
W. of the town on the
A458
(18) 5708 yards/***/E

North Wales
Clwyd

Abergele & Pensarn G.C
(0745) 824034
Tan-y-Goppa Road,
Abergele
Through town on the A547
(18) 6086 yards/***/D/H

Bryn Morfydd G.C
(074 578) 280
The Princess Course, Bryn
Morfydd Hotel, Llanrhaedr
From A55 take A525 to
Llanrhaedr
(9) 1190 yards/***/E

Chirk G. & C.C
(0691) 774407
Chirk, nr Wrexham
(18)/**/F

Denbigh G.C
(074 581) 4159
Henllan Road, Denbigh
On the B5382 to Henllan
(18) 5650 yard/***/F/H

Hoywell G.C
(0352) 710040
Brynford, Holywell
Take A55 to Holywell
(9) 6484 yards/***/F

Mold G.C
(0352) 740318
Clicain Road, Pantymwyn,
Mold
Take A494 to Mold, turn
onto Denbigh Road
(18) 5545 yards/***/F

Old Colwyn G.C
(0492) 515581
Woodland Avenue, Old
Colwyn
Take A55 to Old Colwyn
(9) 5800 yards/***(not Tues,
Wed, Sat, pm)/E

Old Padeswood G.C
(0244) 547401
Station Road, Padeswood,
Mold
Take A541 E from Mold for
1 mile, then A5118
(18) 6639 yards/***/F

Padeswood and Buckley

G.C
(0244) 550537
The Cala, Station Lane,
Padeswood, Mold
Take A541 E. from Mold for
1 mile, then take A5118
(18) 5775 yards/***/D/H

Prestatyn G.C
(0745) 888353
Marine Road East, Prestatyn
Take A548 to Prestatyn and
Prestatyn Sands
(18) 6764 yards/***(not Sat
& Tues am)/D/H

Rhuddlan G.C
(0745) 590271
Meliden Road
Rhuddlan
Nr. Bodrhyddan Hall on
A5151
(18) 6045 yards/***(not
Sun)/F/H

Rhyl G.C
(0745) 35317
Coast Road, Rhyl
On A548 E. of Rhyl
(9) 6185 yards/***/E/H

Ruthin Pwllglas G.C
(082 42) 2296
Ruthin Pwllglas, Ruthin
S. of the town off the A494
(9) 5418 yards/***/E/H

Vale Of Llangollen G.C
(0978) 860040
Llangollen
1 mile E. of town off A5 to
Llangollen
(18) 6461 yards/***/D/H

Wrexham G.C
(0978) 364268
Holt Road, Wrexham
E. of the town off the A534
(18) 6078 yards/***/F/H

Gwynedd

Aberdovey G.C
(0654) 72493
Aberdovey
Take A493 from
Machynlleth to Aberdovey
(18) 6445 yards/***/D/H

Abersoch G.C
(075 881) 2622

Abersoch
Take A499 from Pwllheli to
Abersoch
(9) 5910 yards/***/F

Betws-Y-Coed G.C
(069 02) 556
Betws-y-coed
Take A470 S. from
Llandudno to Betws-y-coed
(18) 4996 yards/***/F

Caernarfon G.C
(0286) 3783
Llanfaglan, Caernarfon
Half-mile S. of Caernarfon
off A487
(18) 5860 yards/***/F

Conwy G.C
(0492) 5592423
Morfa, Conwy
Take A55 from Conwy to
Bangor
(18) 6901 yards/**/F/H

Criccieth G.C
(0776) 522154
Ednyfed Hill, Criccieth
N. of the town off B4411 or
A497
(18) 5787 yards/***/F

Dolgellau G.C
(0341) 422603
Pencefn, Golfdown,
Dolgellau
Leave A5 at A494 at Druid
for Dolgellau
(9) 4512 yards/***/E

Llandudno (Maesdu) G.C
(0492) 76450
Hospital Road, Llandudno
1 mile from town centre
(18) 6513 yards/***/D/H

Nefyn and District G.C
(0758) 720218
Morfa Nefyn, Pwlheli
Leave A499 for B4417 to
Nefyn
(18) 6335 yards/***/D

North Wales G.C
(0492) 75325
72 Brymau Road,
West Shore, Llandudno
Leave AA55 for B5115
out to
West Shore
(18) 6132 yards/***/D/H

Penmaenmawr G.C
(0492) 623330
Conwy Old Road,
Penmaenmawr
Take A55 W. from Conwy
(9) 5031 yards/***/E

Portmadog G.C
(0766) 512037
Morfa Bychau, Portmadog
Take A487 to Portmadog
(18) 5838 yards/***/F/H

Pwllheli G.C
(0758) 612520
Golf Road, Pwllheli
Take A497 from Portmadog
to Pwllheli
(18) 6110 yards/***/F

Rhos-On-Sea G.C
(0492) 49641
Penrhyn Bay, Llandudno
Take B5115 from A55
to Rhos-On-Sea
(18) 6064 yards/***/E

Royal St. Davids G.C
(0766) 780361
Harlech
Take A496 from
Portmadog to Barmouth
(18) 6427 yards/***/F/H

St Deniol G.C
(0248) 353098
Penybryn, Bangor
E. of Bangor off A55
(18) 5500 yards/***/E

Anglesey

Anglesey G.C
(0407) 810219
Station Road, Rhosneigr
Leave A5 for A4080 to
Rhosneigr
(18) 5713 yards/***/F

Baron Hills G.C
(0248) 810231
Beaumaris

(9) 5564 yards/***/E

Bull Bay G.C
(0407) 830960
Bull Bay Road, Amlwch
Through Amlwch on A5025
(18) 6160 yards/**/F/H

Holyhead G.C
(0407) 763179
Trearddur Bay, Holyhead,
Gwynedd
On A5 over Menai bridge
to Holyhead
(18) 6058 yards/***/D/H

Llangefni G.C
(0248) 722193
Llangefni
W. on A5 then onto A5114
to Llangefni
(9) 1467 yards/***/E

With a St Andrews in Scotland and a St George's in England, it seems only right that there should be a St David's in Wales. Along with Royal Porthcawl in the South, the Royal St David's Golf Club at Harlech is one of the Principality's two greatest Championship links.

Of its many attributes St David's is perhaps best known for its glorious setting: on the one side stretch the blue waters of Tremedog Bay, and on the other the imperious Snowdon and the other great mountains of Snowdonia National Park; while surveying all from its lofty perch is the almost forbidding presence of Harlech Castle.

The present 'Men of Harlech' to whom I should introduce you are the **Secretary, Mr R I Jones (tel. (0766) 780361** and the Club's **professional John Barnett** who may be contacted by telephone on **(0766) 780857.**

St David's has a reputation for being one of Britain's friendliest Clubs; subject to being Members of Golf Clubs visitors and Golfing Societies are welcome at all times although those wishing to make party bookings must do so by written application to the Secretary. The cost of a day's golf in 1993 was set at £23 during the week with £28 payable at the weekend and on Bank Holidays.

The setting is indeed superb but the journey to get there can be a lengthy one—Harlech alas isn't like the proverbial Rome and there is just one road that travellers must join, namely the A496. From the North this road approaches from Blaenau Ffestiniog via Maentwrog (east of Porthmadog) and from the South via Dolgellau and Barmouth. Those coming from further afield may find Bala (if travelling from the north) and Welshpool (if motoring from the

south) useful towns to head for. Bala links with Maentwrog by way of the A4212 and the A487, while the A458 and A470 link Welshpool to Barmouth. Finally, for those not travelling by car, the train station at Harlech may prove of assistance.

Measuring less than 6500 yards from the Championship tees, St David's may not at first glance seem overly testing. However the general consensus is that the course, to adopt golfers' terminology, 'plays long'. Par is a very tight 69 and there are only two par fives on the card. Furthermore the rough can be very punishing (not to mention frustrating) and it is very rare for there not to be a stiff westerly wind.

Perhaps the most difficult holes on the course are the 10th, a long par four into the prevailing wind, and the classic 15th which requires a lengthy, angled drive followed by a precise approach. The round finishes with, to adopt another curious golfing expression, 'a nasty long short hole.'

Royal St David's Golf Club, Harlech, Gwynedd, LL46 2UB.

Hole	Yards	Par	Hole	Yards	Par
1	436	4	10	458	4
2	373	4	11	144	3
3	463	4	12	437	4
4	188	3	13	451	4
5	393	4	14	218	3
6	371	4	15	427	4
7	481	5	16	354	4
8	499	5	17	427	4
9	173	3	18	202	3
Out	3,377	36	In	3,118	33
			Out	3,377	36
			Totals	6,495	69

The two modern counties of Dumfries & Galloway and Borders (bit of a mouthful?—try the old Dumfrieshire, Kirkudbrightshire, Wigtownshire, Berwickshire, Peebleshire, Roxburghshire and Selkirkshire) encompass most of the Scottish Lowlands. A beautiful area of Britain—as of course is most of Scotland—but surely not one terribly renowned for its golf? It may not be renowned but there is still certainly no shortage of exciting and challenging courses in the area. Indeed, the very fact that the great hordes head for the more famous venues further north means that Scotland's southerly golfing gems remain by and large marvellously uncrowded.

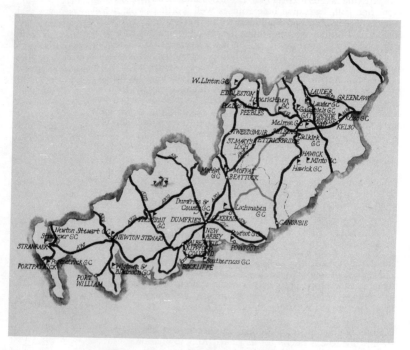

Dumfries & Galloway

The one true Championship test in this region is found at **Southerness**. Of all Scotland's great links courses this is perhaps the least widely known.

Powfoot is a fairly close neighbour of Southerness (at least as the crow flies) the course lying 5 miles west of Annan off the B724. A semi-links with plenty of heather and gorse, it offers a tremendous test of golf and is an admirable companion to Southerness. Adding to the enjoyment of a round at Powfoot is the setting—the course provides extensive views towards the Cumberland Hills to the south and the Galloway Hills to the west. The Isle of Man is also visible on a clear day.

Nearby there are two good eighteen hole courses at Dumfries, **Dumfries and County**, to the north of the town being the pick of the two, but golfers travelling north would do well to pay **Lochmaben** a visit as well. It is a very friendly Club with an interesting nine hole course designed by James Braid. The setting around the Kirk Loch is most picturesque and the course is famed for its many beautiful old trees.

Towards the western corner of Dumfries and Galloway there is more fine golf. Two nine hole courses well worth playing are at Wigtown, **Wigtown and Bladnoch** to be precise, and at **Newton Stewart**. Still further west, **Stranraer**, the ferry terminal for Larne, has a fine parkland course north of the town overlooking Loch Ryan. But the cliff top course at **Portpatrick** is surely the major golfing attraction; it is rated by many to be one of the most beautiful courses in Britain. Apparently Portpatrick for many years in the last century was Ireland's Gretna Green—couples sailing across the Irish Sea to get hitched in Portpatrick's tiny church. The golf course provides some breathtaking scenery, particularly outstanding is the view from the 13th fairway. It can often get quite breezy and although only 5,644 yards in length, the course is certainly no pushover. Guest of the **Cally Palace** in Gatehouse of Fleet can enjoy golf on the private course of this superb 18th century mansion.

Having sampled the delights of the coast of Southern Scotland one may head inland to the delights of the Border towns. En route one could slip 18 holes in at **Thornhill** or perhaps visit **Moffat**. The town has a very enjoyable moorland course with a marvellous setting in the valley of Annandale.

Borders
The Border towns offer castles aplenty, some superb woollens and some excellent rugby. Golfwise, no course here could claim to be of Championship proportions, however, the majority can boast spectacular settings, visitors are always encouraged and the green fees in these parts are just about the cheapest in Britain.

A cluster of courses are to be found in the centre of the county. The town of **Melrose** is famed for its ruined Abbey where the heart of Robert The Bruce is said to have been buried (gruesome stuff!) It has a fine nine hole course and there are others equally pleasant at **Selkirk, Hawick, Lauder, St. Boswells, Innerliethen** and **West Linton**. Kelso has an interesting layout being inside Kelso racecourse. Finally well worth noting are **Peebles** and **Galashiels**—both are public courses, well maintained and true to form set amidst magnificent countryside.

Borders

Duns G.C
(0361) 83327
Hardens Road, Duns,
Berwickshire
1 mile W. of Duns on A6105
(9) 5754 yards/***/E

Eyemouth G.C
(08907) 50551
Gunsgreen House,
Eyemouth
3 miles N. of Burnmouth on
A1107
(9) 5446 yards/***/E

Galashiels G.C
(0896) 3724
Ladhope Recreation
Ground, Galashiels,
Selkirkshire
N.E of town, off A7
(18) 5309 yards/***/E

Gatehouse G.C
(055 74) 654
Laurieston Road, Gatehouse
Quarter of a mile off A75
(9) 4796 yards/***/E

Hawick G.C
(0450) 72293
Vertish Hill, Hawick,
Roxburghshire
S. of Hawick on A7
(18) 5929 yards/***/E

Hirsel G.C
(0890) 2678
Kelso Road, Coldstream
At west end of Coldstream
on A697
(9) 2828 yards/***/E

Jedburgh G.C
(0835) 63587
Dunion Road, Jedburgh,
Roxburghshire
Half mile out of town
(9) 5522 yards/***/F

Kelso G.C
(0573) 23009
Racecourse Road, Kelso,
Roxburghshire
1 mile from town centre
within National Hunt
Racecourse
(18) 6066yards/***/F

Lauder G.C
(057) 82409
Galashiels Road, Lauder
Half mile from Lauder
off A68
(9) 6003 yards/***/F

Melrose G.C
(089682) 2855
Dingleton, Melrose,
Roxburghshire
Half mile S. of Melrose town
centre
(9) 5464 yards/**/F

Minto G.C
(0450) 87220
Minto Village, by Denholme,
Hawick, Roxburghshire
5 miles N.E. of Hawick
off A698
(18) 5460 yards/***/E

Peebles G.C
(0721) 20197
Kirkland Street, Peebles
N.W. of town off the A72
(18) 6137 yards/***/E

St. Boswells G.C
(0835) 22359
St Boswells, Roxburghshire
At junction of A68 and
B6404
(9) 2625 yards/***/E

Selkirk G.C
(0750) 20621
The Hill, Selkirk
1 mile S. of Selkirk on the
A7 to Hawick
(9) 5640 yards/***/E

Torwoodlee G.C
(0896) 2260
Edinburgh Road, Galashiels,
Selkirkshire
1 mile from Galashiels on
A7 to Edinburgh
(9) 5800 yards/***(not Sat)/F

West Linton G.C
(0968) 60256
West Linton, Peebleshire
17 miles S.W. of Edinburgh
on the A702
(18) 6024 yards/***/D

Dumfries & Galloway
Castle Douglas G.C

(0556) 2801
Abercromby Road, Castle
Douglas, Kirkcudbrightshire
In the centre of the town
(9) 5400 yards/***(not Thurs
pm)/F

Colvend G.C
(055663) 398
Sandyhills, By Dalbeattie,
Kirkcudbrightshire
6 miles from Dalbeattie on
A710
(9) 2322 yards/***/F

Dumfries & County G.C
(0387) 53585
Edinburgh Road, Dumfries
1 mile N. of Dumfries on the
A701 (18) 5928 yards/***(not
Sat)/D

Dumfries & Galloway G.C
(0387) 63582
Laurieston Avenue,
Dumfries
W. of Dumfries on the A75
(18) 5782 yards/***/D

Kircudbright G.C
(0567) 30542
Stirling Crescent,
Kirkcudbright
Near centre of town, off
B727
(18) 5598 yards/***/F

Langholm G.C
(0541) 80559
Langholm, Dumfriesshire
Between Carlisle and
Hawick on the A7
(9) 5246 yards/***/E

Lochmaben G.C
(0387) 810552
Castlehill Gate, Lochmaben,
Dumfriesshire
Leave A74 at Lockerbie for
A709 for Dumfries
(9) 5304 yards/***/F

Lockerbie
(05762) 3363
Currie Road, Lockerbie,
Dumfriesshir
Take A74 to Lockerbie
(18) 5228 yards/***(not
Sat)/F

Moffat G.C
(0683) 20020
Coatshill, Moffat
Take A701 for 1 mile off
the A74 (18) 5218
yards/***(not Wed pm)/D

New Galloway G.C
(06442) 239
Castle Douglas,
Kirkcudbrightshire
Just out of Village on the
A762
(9) 5058 yards/***/E

Newton Stewart G.C
(0671) 2172
Kirroughtree Avenue,
Minnigaff, Newton Stewart
Leave the A75 at sign for
Minnigaff Village
(9) 5500 yards/***/E

Portpatrick (Dunskey) G.C
(077681) 273
Portpatrick, Stranraer,
Wigtownshire
Signposted on the A77 to
Portpatrick (18) 5644
yards/***/D/H

Powfoot G.C
(04612) 2866
Cummertrees, Annan,
Dumfriesshire
3 miles from Annan on the
B724
(18) 6266 yards/**/F

St Medan G.C
(098 87) 358
Monreith, Port William,
Wigtownshire
3 miles S. of Port William
on the A747
(9) 4454 yards/***/E

Sanquhar G.C
(0659) 50577
Old Barr Road, Sanquhar,
Dumfriesshire
 mile from Sanquhar off
the A76
(9) 2572 yards/***/F

Southerness G.C
(038 788) 677
Southerness, Dumfries
16 miles S.W of Dumfries
off the A710
(18) 6554 yards/***/D

Stranraer G.C
(0776) 3539
Crechmore, Stranraer
Take the A718 from
Stranraer towards Leswalt
(18) 6300 yards/***/D

Thornhill G.C
(0848) 30546
Blacknest, Thornhill,
Dumfries
14 miles N. of Dumfries on
the A76 to Thornhill
(18) 6011 yards/***/F

Wigtown and Bladnoch
(098 84) 3354
Lightlands Avenue,
Wigtown, Wigtownshire
Right at town square, left at
Agnew Crescent
(9) 2732 yards/***/E

Wigtownshire County G.C
(05813)420
Mains of Park, Glenluce,
Newton Stewart,
Wigtownshire 8 miles E. of
Stranraer on the A75
(18) 5715 yards/***/D

'Hard by in the fields called the links, the citizens of Edinburgh divert themselves at a game called golf, in which they use a curious kind of bat tipt with horn and a small elastic ball of leather stuffed with feathers rather less than tennis balls, but out of a much harder consistency and this they strike with such force and dexterity that it will fly to an incredible distance.'

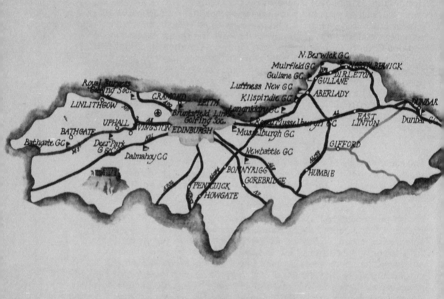

When Tobias Smollett wrote these words in 1771 golf had already been played in the 'fields' around Edinburgh for at least three hundred years. The seemingly harmless pastime wasn't always popular with the authorities. In 1593 the Town Council of Edinburgh deplored the fact that a great number of its inhabitants chose to spend the Sabbath in the town of Leith where 'in tyme of sermons' many were 'sene in the streets, drynking in taverns, or otherwise at Golf'. Shame on them! Today the east coast of Scotland is famous the world over, not only because it was here that it all began, but also because its many courses remain among the very finest the game has to offer. In a 30 mile coastal stretch between the courses of **Royal Burgess** and **Dunbar** lie the likes of **Muirfield, Gullane, North Berwick, Luffness New** and **Longniddry**—truly a magnificent seven—and there are many others.

Edinburgh

Visitors to the beautiful city of Edinburgh, the so called 'Athens of the North', should have little trouble getting a game. There are numerous first class courses in and around the capital; regrettably we only have space to mention a handful of the best. To the west of the city lie a particularly historic pair—**Bruntsfield Links** and **Royal Burgess**: between them they have witnessed nearly 500 years of golfing history. The latter Club in fact claims to be the world's oldest. (A claim hotly disputed I might add by Muirfield's 'Honourable Company'!) These more prestigious courses are of course difficult to play, but with advance preparation it is possible; another Edinburgh gem not to be missed is **Braid Hills**; in fact two fine public courses here, just south of the city. The **Dalmahoy** Hotel Golf and Country Club situated to the south west of the city nestles at the base of the Pentland Hills and has two excellent 18 hole courses. Towards the east side of Edinburgh is Musselburgh. The old Open links is not what it was, alas, although you can still play the nine holes adjacent to Musselburgh racecourse for history's sake; however, perhaps the best place for a game is at **Royal Musselburgh**, a beautiful parkland course and a little further out of the city the course at **Newbattle** can be recommended.

Links Golf

Travellers wishing to explore the delights of the East Coast should aim to pick up the A198 at Prestonpans near Musselburgh. Before it reaches Longniddry the road passes through Seton, where Mary Queen of Scots is known to have sharpened up her golf swing more than 400 years ago. 13 miles East of Edinburgh, **Longniddry** ought not to be considered as merely a stopping place en route to **Muirfield**. It is a superb course, part links part parkland with every hole having a view of the sea. **Kilspindie Golf Club** is also worth a little detour while **Luffness New** and the three neighbouring courses of **Gullane**, lie only a short distance further along the coast. Each is outstanding in its way though if you only have time to play two then Luffness New and Gullane Number One are probably the pick, although the former can be difficult to get on! The panoramic view from the top of Gullane Hill on the latter's 7th hole is one of the most famous in golf. The West Links at **North Berwick** has a wealth of charm and tradition; it is one of the most natural courses one is likely to come across and several blind shots must be encountered. Two of its holes, the 14th 'Perfection' and the 15th 'Redan' have been imitated by golf architects all over the world. As at **Dunbar** there are some splendid views across to Bass Rock.

Muirfield is of course much more *than one of the world's greatest golf links, it is also the home of the world's oldest Golf Club. —The Honourable Company of Edinburgh Golfers*

Visitors must make prior arrangements with the **Secretary, Group Captain J A Prideaux**, who may be contacted by telephone on **(0620) 842123**. For gentlemen golfers there is a requirement that they belong to a recognised Golf Club and carry a handicap of 18 or less, while for lady golfers (who may only play if accompanied by a gentleman player) the handicap limit is 24. The days on which visitors are welcome are Tuesdays and Thursdays. By tradition foursome matches are strongly favoured at Muirfield and four ball games will only be permitted in the mornings. Golfing Societies (limited to 40 players) are also received on the usual visiting days and arrangements may be made with the Secretary. The green fees for 1993 were £48 for a single round with £64 entitling the visitor to a full day's golf. All fees should be paid to the cashier in the Clubhouse Dining Room.

Travelling to Muirfield (or Gullane) will often be by way of Edinburgh. Gullane is connected to the capital city by the A198. Northbound travellers can avoid Edinburgh by approaching on the A1 which runs to Dunbar to the east of Gullane. From Dunbar the A198 can be picked up. Those coming from the north and west of Scotland will need to travel via Edinburgh. The M8 links Glasgow to Edinburgh, while the M9 should be taken from Stirling and the M90 from Perth.

One of the unique features of Muirfield (or at least unique in terms of Scottish Championship links) is its layout of two separate loops, an outer and an inner. This ensures that the golfer will not have to play successive holes into or against the same wind direction. Although quite undulating, the course doesn't require blind shots and this contributes much to Muirfield's fairness tag.

Since 1892 the Open Championship has been played at Muirfield on 14 occasions. Before the last War winners included Harry Vardon, James Braid and Walter Hagen. The first Open to be held at Muirfield after the War was in 1948, when Henry Cotton won his third title. Gary Player won in 1959 and Jack Nicklaus in 1966. Perhaps the most dramatic Open in Muirfield's history came in 1972 when Lee Trevino holed his famous chip shot from the edge of the 17th green and in the process stole the title from Tony Jacklin. In recent times British fortunes have revived dramatically however with Nick Faldo winning in 1987, and again in 1992, when he so memorably produced 'the best four holes of his life' to deny the unfortunate John Cook.

The Secretary,
The Honourable Company
of Edinburgh Golfers,
Muirfield, Gullane, East Lothian,
EH31 2EG

Hole	Yards	Par	Hole	Yards	Par
1	449	4	10	475	5
2	349	4	11	386	4
3	379	4	12	381	4
4	181	3	13	153	3
5	558	5	14	447	4
6	471	4	15	396	4
7	185	3	16	188	3
8	444	4	17	542	5
9	510	5	18	447	4
Out	3,526	36	In	3,415	36
			Out	3,526	36
			Totals	6,941	72

Baberton G.C
031 453 4911
Baberton Avenue, Juniper
Green, Edinburgh
W. of Edinburgh on the
Lanark Road
(18) 6098 yards/* (intro by
member)/F

Bathgate G.C
(0506) 630505
Edinburgh Road, Bathgate,
West Lothian
400 yards E. of George
Square
(18) 6328 yards/***/D

Braids United G.C
031 447 3327
22 Braids Hill Approach,
Edinburgh
At Braids Hill, S. of
Edinburgh
(18) 5731 yards/***/E
(18) 4832 yards/***/E

Broomieknowe G.C
031 663 9317
36 Golf Course Road,
Bonnyrigg, Midlothian
S. of Edinburgh on the
A6094 from Dalkeith
(18) 6046 yards/**/F

Bruntsfield Links G.C
031 336 1479
32 Barton Avenue,
Davidsons Mains,
Edinburgh
2-3 miles W. of Edinburgh
on A90
(18) 6407 yards/**/F/H

Carrickvale G.C
031 337 1932
Glendevon Park, Edinburgh
Opposite Post House Hotel
on Balgreen Road
(18) 6299 yards/***/F/H

Craigmillar Park G.C
031 667 2837
1 Observatory Road,
Edinburgh
3 miles from City centre
(18) 5846 yards/***/D/H or
M or L

Dalmahoy G.C
031 333 1845
Dalmahoy, Kirknewton,

Midlothian
7 miles W. of Edinburgh on
the A71
(18) 6664 yards/***/F
(18) 5121 yards/***/F

Duddingston G.C
031 661 7688 4301
Duddingston Road,
Edinburgh
E. of city centre, adjacent to
the A1
(18) 6647 yards/**/D/H

Dunbar G.C
(0368) 62317
East Links, Dunbar
Half mile from Dunbar centre on sea side
(18) 6426 yards/***/C

Gifford G.C
(062 081) 267
Gifford
5 miles S. of Haddington off
the A6137
(9) 5613 yards/***(not Tues,
Wed, weekend pm)/E

Glen G.C
(0620) 2221
Tantallon Terrace, North
Berwick, East Lothian
22 miles N.E. of Edinburgh
on the A198
(18) 6098 yards/***/E

Glencorse G.C
(0968) 77189
Milton Bridge, Penicuik,
Midlothian
9 miles S. of Edinburgh
on the A701
(18) 5205 yards/***/D/H

Greenburn G.C
(0501) 70292
Fauldhouse, West Lothian
Midway between Glasgow
and Edinburgh
(18) 6210 yards/**/E/H

Gullane G.C
(0620) 842255
Gullane, East Lothian
Off the A1 on the A198 to
Gullane
(18)6466 yards/**/F/H
(18)6127 yards/***/F/H
(18)5128 yards/***/F/H

Haddington G.C
(062 082) 3627
Amisfield Park, Haddington,
East Lothian
17 miles E. of Edinburgh
on the A1
(18) 6280 yards/**(not
pm)/E

Harburn G.C
(0506) 871256
West Calder, West Lothian
S. off the A70,
2 miles S. of West Calder
(18) 5843 yards/***/E

Honourable Company Of
Edinburgh Golfers
(0620) 842123
Muirfield, Gullane, East
Lothian
Off the A198 from Gullane
to North Berwick
(18) 6601 yards/(Tues,
Thurs, Fri am only)/A/H
(18)/M/L

Kilspindie G.C
(087 57) 358
Aberlady, East Lothian
On the South bank of the
Forth Estuary
(18) 5410 yards/***/F

Kingsknowe G.C
031 441 4030
326 Lanark Road, Edinburgh
W. of Edinburgh on the
A71
(18) 5979 yards/**/E/H

Liberton G.C
031 664 8580
297 Gilmerton Road,
Edinburgh
S. of Edinburgh on the A7
(18) 5299 yards/***/F/H

Linlithgow G.C
(0506) 842585
Braehead, Linlithgow, West
Lothian
20 miles from Edinburgh
off the M9
(18) 5858 yards/***(not Wed,
Sat)/E

Deer Park G.C
(0506) 38843
Carmondean, Livingston,
West Lothian
Signposted from
Knightsridge
from the M8
(18) 6636 yards/***/D

Longniddry G.C
(0875) 52141
Links Road, Longniddry,
East Lothian
(18) 6210 yards/***/F

Luffness New G.C
(0620) 843114
Aberlady, East Lothian
E. of Edinburgh along the
A198
(18) 6122 yards/***/F/H

Merchants of Edinburgh
G.C
031 447 219
10 Craighill Gardens,
Edinburgh
South side of Edinburgh
off the A701
(18) 4889 yards/
(intro by member)/E

Mortonhall G.C
031 447 6974
231 Braid Road, Edinburgh
2 miles S. of city centre
(18) 6557 yards/***/F/M

Murrayfield G.C
031 337 3478
43 Murrayfield Road,
Edinburgh
2 miles W. of the city centre
(18) 5727 yards/***/E/L/H

Musselburgh G.C
031 665 2005
Monktonhall, Musselburgh,
Midlothian
1 mile S. of Musselburgh
off the A1
(18) 6623 yards/***/F/H

Newbattle G.C
031 663 2123
Abbey Road, Dalkeith,
Midlothian
7 miles S.W. of Edinburgh
on the A7

(18) 6012 yards/**/D

North Berwick
(0620) 2135
West Links, Beach Road
North Berwick
(18) 6317 yards/***/D

Portobello G.C
031 669 4361
Stanley Road, Portobello,
Edinburgh
(9) 2400 yards/***/E

Prestonfield G.C
031 667 1273
6 Prestonfield Road North,
Edinburgh
Just off Dalkeith Road, nr
Commonwealth Pool
(18) 6216 yards/**(+Sat, Sun
pm)/E

Pumpherston G.C
(0506) 32869
Drumshoreland Road,
Pumpherston, Livingston
1 mile S. of Uphall, off the
A89
(9) 5154 yards/*(with member only)/F

Ratho Park G.C
031 333 1752
Ratho, Newbridge,
Midlothian
8 miles W. of Edinburgh via
A71 or A8
(18) 6028 yards/***/D

Ravelston G.C
031 315 2486
24 Ravelston Dykes Road,
Blackhall, Edinburgh
Take A90 Queensferry
Road to Blackhall
(9) 5200 yards/*(with member)/F

Royal Burgess G.C
031 339 2075
181 Whitehouse Road,
Edinburgh
Take A90 to Queensferry,
behind Barnton Thistle
Hotel
(18) 6604 yards/**/F/L

Royal Musselburgh G.C
(0875) 810276
Preston Grange House,

Prestonpans, East Lothian
(18) 6237 yards/***/D/H

Silverknowes G.C
031 336 5359
Siverknowes, Parkway,
Edinburgh
On coast overlooking
Firth of Forth
(18) 6210 yards/***/F

Swanston G.C
031 445 2239
111 Swanston Road,
Edinburgh
5 miles from Edinburgh
centre
(18) 5024 yards/**/F

Torphin Hill
031 441 1100
Torphin Road, Colinton,
Edinburgh
On S.W side of Colinton
(18) 5024 yards/***/E ·

Turnhouse G.C
031 339 1014
154 Turnhouse Road,
Edinburgh
(18) 6171 yards/**/D

Uphall G.C
(0506) 856404
Uphall, West Lothian
On outskirts of Uphall
adjacent to the A8
(18)6250 yards/***/E

West Lothian G.C
(0506) 826030
Airngarth Hill, Linlithgow,
West Lothian
On hill, marked by the
Hope Monument
(18) 6578 yards/**/D

The Ayrshire Coast

An ancient golfing rhyme from the land of Burns runs:

> *'Troon and Prestwick, old and classy,*
> *Bogside, Dundonald, Glasgow Gailes, Barassie,*
> *Prestwick St. Nicholas, Western Gailes,*
> *St. Cuthbert, Portland—memory fails,*
> *Troon Municipal (three links there)*
> *Prestwick Municipal, Irvine, Ayr,*
> *They faced the list with delighted smiles -*
> *Sixteen courses within ten miles'.*

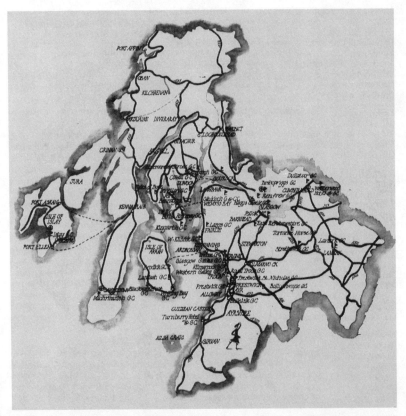

Even without Turnberry, that 'little corner of heaven on earth', some fifteen miles south of Ayr, an extraordinarily impressive list, and little wonder that this small region of Scotland's coast has become nothing short of a mecca for golfers the world over.

Prestwick, Troon and **Turnberry** have of course each staged the Open Championship. Prestwick was the birth-place of the event back in 1860 and is probably the most classical test of traditional links golf—penal the American architects would describe it, on account of the many blind shots. The Open is no longer held at Prestwick but the history of the place is overwhelming and quite magnetic. Troon and Turnberry are both firmly on the 'Open' rota. It was last played over the latter's Ailsa course in 1986 (Norman's great victory) and was last held at Troon in 1989 (Norman's near victory); in 1994 Norman will be defending at Turnberry. Understandably the golfer making a pilgrimage to the Ayrshire coast will be drawn towards this famous trio. However, if time isn't, as they say, of the essence, it would be bordering on a disgrace not to sample as many of the nearby delights as possible. As the old rhyme relates, within short distance of one another lie a number of outstanding courses and where at any of which it may be easier to arrange a game.

While not all roads lead to Ayr, as the largest town on the coast, it's probably as good a starting point as any. Here we find a belle—**Belleisle** to be precise and a most attractive parkland course. Considered by many to be the finest public course outside of St Andrews and Carnoustie and, being somewhat sheltered, it's an admirable retreat from the more windswept links nearby. Furthermore as a municipal course the green fees are very cheap.

Just north of Ayr lie a series of outstanding links courses, all within a mile or two of one another, **Prestwick St Nicholas, Barassie, Western Gailes, Glasgow (Gailes)** and **Irvine** (also known somewhat unfortunately as Bogside). Each warmly welcome visitors although telephoning in advance is strongly recommended, especially during the peak summer months. Weekdays are inevitably the best times for a visit, and the underrated municiple course at Girvan merits a place on any itinary.

To the north of the famous golfing stretch there is plenty of less testing golf to be found. This may well be necessary in order to restore battered pride! **West Kilbride** (another links type) and **Largs** (a well-wooded parkland course) should suit admirably. Both also offer some magnificent views across to Argyle and the Isle of Arran where there are no fewer than seven golf courses,. Also roughly due east of Ayr, close to the A76 there is a very good course at **Ballochmyle.**

Glasgow

Glasgow is Britain's third largest city after London and Birmingham and, being Scottish-to-boot, not surprisingly has a huge number of golf courses. Indeed some wag once said of Glasgow that there was a pub in every street with a Golf Club around each corner. One interesting statistic is that between 1880 and 1910 more than 80 golf courses were built in the Greater Glasgow area—so much for today's golf boom! Unfortunately the problem for the golfing stranger to Glasgow is that many of the city's leading Clubs only permit visitors to play if accompanied by a Member. Among the city's more traditional courses—and where arranging a game can be difficult—are **Haggs Castle**, **Pollok** and **Glasgow Killermont**. Other suggestions include **Renfrew** and **East Renfrewshire**, to the north west and south west respectively and **Bishopriggs** to the north of Glasgow. There are a number of public courses in Glasgow so the visiting golfer confined to Glasgow need not get too depressed. The pick of the municipals is probably **Lethamhill** and **Little Hill**—a game on either is remarkably inexpensive.

Gleddoch House Hotel Golf and Country Club, located at Langbank close to the Clyde Estuary offers views of the Lombard Hills. It is easily accessible from Glasgow by way of the M8 and in a nutshell could be described as a darn good hotel with a darn good restaurant and a darn good golf course! Further north, the course at **Helensburgh** is also worth a visit and on the shores of **Loch Lomond** Tom Weiskopf has designed two courses which promise to be quite outstanding—that is if the project is ever successfully financed and thus finished. (We understand that one of the courses is in fact ready to recieve a limited number of pay and play visitors).

From Glasgow, the great challenges of Troon, Turnberry and Prestwick lie to the south West (the A77 is incidentally the most convenient route), but Championship golf can also be found to the north and east; **Dullatur** is one such venue, **Lanark** another. The former is a parkland course whereas Lanark is essentially moorland.

Further Afield
Before heading for the more distant corners of Strathclyde a quick mention for two courses lying due south of Glasgow; **Torrance House** and **Strathaven** are the pair in question. Both are very easily reached by way of the A726, although Strathaven is quite a bit of a way from the city and by the time you arrive at the course you'll have climbed 700 feet above sea level.

Two great courses still remain to be charted—those magical 'M's'—**Machrie** and **Machrihanish**. Each enjoys a kind of splendid isolation and is a superb test of traditional links golf. Machrie is to be found on the distant Isle of Islay at Port Ellen.

When the golfing mind focuses on Troon it invariably thinks of the Postage Stamp, *the par three* 8th *on the* Old Course, *unquestionably the world's most celebrated short hole. During the* 1973 Open Championship, *Gene Sarazen, then at the mature age of 71, holed out with his punched five iron shot in front of the watching television cameras. Sarazen declared that he would take with him to heaven a copy of the film to show to Walter Hagen and Co. Legend has it, that on hearing of Sarazen's feat, an American flew to Britain and travelled to Troon. He strode to the 8th tee and proceeded to strike 500 balls in succession towards the green. Not surprisingly he failed to equal Sarazen's achievement whereupon he left the course and duly flew home to America. Who said it was only mad dogs and Englishmen?*

Anyone contemplating the above ought at least to consult the **Secretary** first, **Mr. J.D. Montgomerie** being the gentleman in question. The Royal Troon Club Golf possesses two 18 hole courses; **The Old** and **The Portland**. Gentlemen visitors are welcome to play both courses between Mondays and Thursdays provided prior arrangement is made with the Secretary. Lady golfers are also welcome, although they are limited to playing on the Portland Course. Visitors must be members of a recognised club and be able to produce a certificate of handicap (maximum 18). Society games may be arranged but organisers should note that their numbers must not exceed 24. In 1993 a green fee of £75 entitled the visitor to a round on each course, while a fee of £45 secured a full day's golf on the Portland Course; both fees are inclusive of lunch. There are no concessionary rates for junior golfers who, in any event, must have attained the age of eighteen before they will be permitted to play over the Old Course. Sets of clubs and trolleys may be hired from the Club's **professional, Brian Anderson (tel: 0292 313281)**. A caddy can also usually be obtained.

Troon lies just to the north of Prestwick and Ayr. The town can be reached from Glasgow and the north via the A77, which also runs from near Stranraer in the south. The A78 is the coastal road, running from Largs through Irvine to Loans just east of Troon. Travelling from Edinburgh, the A71 should be taken, whilst from the North of England the best route is probably via the A74 and the A71. Finally, Prestwick Airport is no more than two miles away.

When you leave Troon you will probably not have a video to take to heaven, but you will at least know that you have visited one of the earth's greatest golfing shrines.

*Royal Troon Golf Club,
Craigend Road, Troon,
Ayrshire KA10 6EP:
tel. (0292) 311555.
(Fax. (0292) 318204.)*

Old Course

Hole	Yards	Par	Hole	Yards	Par
1	364	4	10	438	4
2	391	4	11	481	4
3	379	4	12	431	4
4	557	5	13	465	4
5	210	3	14	179	3
6	577	5	15	457	4
7	402	4	16	542	5
8	126	3	17	223	3
9	423	4	18	452	4
Out	3,340	36	In	3,668	35
			Out	3,429	36
			Totals	7,097	71

There are two Championship courses at Turnberry; the better known Ailsa *Course, to which the Open returns for a third time in 1994, and the* Arran *Course. Both are owned and run by the Turnberry Hotel. Visitors with handicaps are welcome to play on either course although written prior arrangements must be made with the* Golf Club Manager, Mr. Ewen Bowman.

In 1993 the summer green fees were set at £75 for a day's golf consisting of one round on each course. A single round on the Arran is priced at £25. Reduced rates of £45 for a round on both courses are available to Hotel residents (they pay £15 for a single round on the Arran Course) and further reductions are available to all golfers during the winter months. Turnberry's **professional Bob Jamieson** can also be contacted on **(0655) 31000**. Caddies and hire of clubs are best arranged in advance by telephone.

The Hotel and golf courses lie approximately 17 miles south of Ayr off the A77. For those travelling from the Glasgow region, the A77 runs direct from Glasgow to Turnberry and is dual carriageway for much of the journey. Motoring from Edinburgh the A71 is the best route, picking up the A77 at Kilmarnock. Approaching from England, Carlisle is likely to be a starting point (M6 to Carlisle). The distance from Carlisle to Turnberry just under 120 miles. The quickest route is to head north on the A74, joining the A70 towards Ayr.

From its medal tees, the Ailsa Course isn't a great deal longer than the Arran, their respective distances being 6408 yards, par 70, and 6249 yards, par 69. The same from the ladies tees are 5836 yards, par 75 and 5732 yards par 73. After three holes 'inland' as it were, the Ailsa course hugs the shore tightly for a series of dra-matic holes between the 4th and the 11th. The 6th, named Tappie Toorie, is possibly the most difficult par three on the course; the shot is to a heavily guarded green across a valley (play it into the wind and you may be short with a driver). The 9th and the 10th though are the holes most likely to be remembered. The 9th 'Bruce's Castle', is played alongside the famous Turnberry lighthouse, built over the remains of Turnberry Castle, birthplace of Robert the Bruce. The Championship tee for this hole is perched on a pinnacle of rock with the sea crashing below. Stand on this tee and you can appreciate why parallels have often been drawn between Turnberry and Pebble Beach. Following the par three 11th, the holes turn inland and if the scenery is a little less spectacular the challenge in no way diminishes.

The Turnberry Hotel,
Turnberry,
Strathclyde,
KA26 9LT,
telephone (0655) 31000.

Ailsa Course

Hole	Yards	Par	Hole	Yards	Par
1	350	4	10	452	4
2	428	4	11	177	3
3	462	4	12	448	4
4	167	3	13	411	4
5	441	4	14	440	4
6	222	3	15	209	3
7	528	5	16	409	4
8	427	4	17	500	5
9	455	4	18	431	4
Out	3,480	35	In	3,477	35
			Out	3,480	35
			Totals	6,957	70

Airdrie G.C.
(0236) 62195
Rochsoles, Airdrie
1 mile N from Airdrie Cross
(town centre)
(18)6004 yards/***/F/L

Alexandra G.C.
041 556 3711
Sannox Gardens, Alexandra
Parade, Glasgow
Half mile E of city centre
(9)6004 yards/***/E

Annanhill G.C.
(0563) 21644
Irvine Rd, Kilmarnock
On the main Kilmarnock
- Irvine road
(18)6270 yards/***(not Sat)/F

Ardeer G.C.
(0294) 64542
Greenhead, Stevenston, Ayrshire
Turn into Kerelaw Road
off the A78
(18)6630 yards/***(not Sat)/E/H

Ayr Belleisle G.C.
(0292) 41258
Belleisle Park,
Doonfoot Road, Ayr
2 miles SW of the town centre
on the A719
(18)6550 yards/***/F

Ayr Dalmilling G.C.
(0292) 263893
Westwood Avenue, Ayr
2 miles from town centre,
off the A77
(18)5401 yards/***/E

Ayr Seafield G.C.
(0292) 41258
Ayr 2 miles from town centre in
Belleisle Park
on the A719
(18)5244 yards/***/F/H

Ballochmyle G.C.
(0290) 50469
Ballochmyle, Mauchline,
Ayrshire
1 mile from Mauchline village
(18)5952 yards/**/D/H

Balmore G.C.
(0360) 2120240
2 miles N of Glasgow, 7 miles
from city centre
(18)5736 yards/***/F

Barshaw G.C.
041 889 2908
Barshaw Park,
Glasgow Road, Paisley
Take A737 from Glasgow West
to Paisley
(18)5673 yards/***/E

Bearsden G.C.
041 942 2351
Thorn Road, Bearsden, Glasgow
1 mile from Bearsden Cross on
Thorn Road
(9)5569 yards/***/F/L

Beith G.C.
(05055) 3166
Bigholm Road, Beith
1 mile E of Beith
(9)5600 yards/**/E/H

Bellshill G.C.
(0698) 745124
Orbiston, Bellshill
10 miles S of Glasgow
on Bellshill to
Motherwell road
(18)6605 yards/***/D/H

Biggar G.C.
(0899) 20618
The Park, Broughton Road,
Biggar, Lanarkshire
1 mile E of Biggar on the
Broughton road
(18)5416 yards/***/E

Bishopbriggs G.C.
041 772 1810
Brackanbrae Road,
Bishopbriggs, Glasgow
Take A803 from Glasgow North
for 4 miles to Bishopbriggs
(18)6041 yards/*(intro only)/D/H

Blairbeth G.C.
041 634 3355
Burnside, Rutherglen, Glasgow
1 mile S of Rutherglen via
Stonelaw Road, off the A749
(18)5448 yards/*(with member)/F

Blairmore & Strone
(036984) 217
Strone, by Dunoon, Argyll
9 miles N of Dunoon
on the A880
(9)2112 yards/***/E

Bonnyton G.C.
(03553) 2781
Eaglesham, Glasgow
(18)6252 yards/**/E

Bothwell Castle G.C.
(0698) 853177
Blantyre Road,
Bothwell, Glasgow
Adjacent to the M74,
3 miles N of Hamilton
(18)6426 yards/***/D/H

Brodick G.C.
(0770) 2349
Brodick, Isle of Arran
By ferry from Androssan
(18)4404 yards/***/E

Calderbraes G.C.
(0698) 813425
57 Roundknowe Road,
Uddingston
At start of M74,
4 miles from Glasgow
(9)5046 yards/*(intro by member)/F

Caldwell G.C.
(050585) 616
Uplawmoor, Renfrewshire
15 miles from Glasgow
off the A736
(18)6102 yards/**/D

Cambuslang G.C.
041 641 3130
30 Westburn Drive,
Cambuslang, Glasgow
al mile from the station in
Cambuslang
(9)6072 yards/*(intro by member)/E

Campsie G.C.
(0360) 310244
Crow Road, Lennoxtown,
Glasgow
N of Lennoxtown on the B822
(18)5517 yards/**/E

Caprington G.C.
(0563) 21915
Ayr Road, Kilmarnock
S of Kilmarnock on the Ayr road
(18)5718 yards/***/F

Cardross G.C.
(0389) 841754
Main Road, Cardross, Dumbarton
Between Dumbarton and
Helensburghon the A814
(18)6466 yards/**/D

Carluke G.C.
(0555) 71070
Hallcraig, Mauldslie Road,
Carluke
2 miles from town centre
on the road to Hamilton
(18)5805 yards/**(not Tues)/E/H

Carnwath G.C.
(0555) 840251
Main Street, Carnwath
5 miles NE of Lanark
(18)5855 yards/***(not Tues,
Thurs, Sat)/D/H

Carradale G.C.
(05833) 387
Carradale, Campbeltown, Argyll
Off the B842 from
Campbeltown to Carradale
(9)2387 yards/**/E/H

Cathcart G.C.
041 638 9449
Mearns Rd, Clarkston, Glasgow
7 miles from Glasgow on A77
(18)5832 yards/*(intro by member)/F/H

Cathkin Braes G.C.
041 634 6605
Cathkin Rd, Rutherglen, Glasgow
SE of Glasgow
on road to East Kilbride
(18)6266 yards/**/D/H

Cawder G.C.
041 772 5167
Cawder Rd, Bishopbriggs,
Glasgow
Half a mile E of Bishopbriggs
of A803
(18)6229 yards/**(by prior
arrangement)/F/H
(18)5877 yards/**(by prior
arrangement)/F/H

Clober G.C.
041 956 1685
Craigton Rd, Milngavie
7 miles NW of Glasgow
(18)5068 yards/**/E

Clydebank & District G.C.
(0389) 73289
Hardgate, Clydebank
a8 miles NW of Glasgow
(18)5825 yards/**/D/H

Clydebank Overtoun G.C.
041 952 6372
Overtoun Rd, Clydebank
(18)5643 yards/***/D/B on
Sundays

Cochran Castle G.C.
(0505) 20146
Craigston Scott Avenue,
Johnstone
South of the town
(18)6226 yards/**/D/H

Colville Park G.C.
(0698) 63017
Jerviston Estate, Motherwell
1 mile N of Motherwell on A723
(18)6208 yards/**/D

Corrie G.C.
(077081) 223
Sannox, Isle of Arran
By ferry to Brodick then 7 miles
N
on A84
(9)3896 yards/***/E/H

Cowal G.C.
(0369) 5673
Ardenslate Road, Kirn, Dunoon
Half mile from A815 at Kirn
(18)6250 yards/***/D

Cowglen G.C.
041 632 0556
301 Barrhead Road, Glasgow
S side of Glasgow
(18)6006 yards/***/E/L/H

Crow Wood G.C.
041 779 1943
Garnkirk Estate, Muirhead
1 mile N of Stepps on A80
(18)6209 yards/*(with member)/D/H

Cumbernauld G.C.
(0236) 734969
Palacerigg Country Park,
Cumbernauld
Take A80 to Cumbernauld
(18)6800 yards/**/E

Douglas Park G.C.
041 942 2220
Hillfoot, Bearsden
Next to Hillfoot Station
(18)5957 yards/*(with member)/F

Douglas Water G.C.
(0555) 2295
Ayr Road, Rigside, Lanark
7 miles SW of Lanark on A70
(9)2947 yards/***/E

Douglaston G.C.
041 956 5750
Strathblane Rd, Milngavie
7 miles N of Glasgow on A81
(18)6683 yards/***/E

Drumpellier G.C.
a(0236) 724139
Drumpellier Avenue, Coatbridge
1 mile from Coatbridge, off A89
(18)6227 yards/**/D

Dullatur G.C.
(0236) 727847
Dullatur, Glasgow
12 miles E of Glasgow
on Kilsyth Road
(18)6195 yards/**/F

Dumbarton G.C.
(0389) 32830
Broadmeadows, Dumbarton
Quarter of a mile N of
Dumbarton off A814
(18)5654 yards/**/D

Dunaverty G.C.
Southend, Campbeltown, Argyll
10 miles S of Campbeltown
on B842
(18)4597 yards/***/F

Easter Moffat G.C.
(0236) 842289
Mansion House, Plains, by Airdrie
(18)6221 yards/***/D/H

East Kilbride G.C.
(03552) 20913
Chapelside, Nerston,
East Kilbride
Leave Glasgow by A7 and turn
off by Nerston
(18)6419 yards/*(with member)/F

East Renfrewshire G.C.
(03555) 206
Loganswell, Pilmuir,
Newton Mearns
1 mile from Mearns
Cross off A77
(18)6100 yards/***/C

Eastwood G.C.
(03555) 261
Muirshield Loganswell,
Newton Mearns
3 miles S of Mearns
Cross off A77
(18)5886 yards/***D

Elderslie G.C.
(0505) 22835
63 Main Road, Elderslie
Leave M8 for Linwood road
(18)6004 yards/**/D

Erskin G.C.
(0505) 863327
Bishopston, Renfrewshire

Leave M8 for B815
(18)6287 yards/*(with member)/F

Girvan G.C.
(0465) 4346
Girvan
Off A77 from Glasgow to Ayr
(18)5078 yards/***/E

Glasgow (Gailes) G.C.
(0294)311347
Gailes, By Irvine
2 miles S of
Irvine on Troon road
(18)6500 yards/***(on application)/B/H

Glasgow (Killermont) G.C.
a041 942 2340
Killermont, Bearsden
6 miles NW of Glasgow on A81
(18)5968 yards/***(on application)/C/H

Gleddoch G. & C.C.
(047554) 711
Langbank, Renfrewshire
(18)6333 yards/***(by arrangement)/C

Glencruitten G.C.
(0631) 62868
Glencruitten Rd, Oban
1 mile from town
centre off A816
(18)4452 yards/***/F/M

Gourock G.C.
(0475) 31001
Cowal View, Gourock
2 miles west of Gourock Station
via Victoria Rd
(18)6492 yards/**/E/H

Greenock G.C.
(0475) 20793
Forsyth St, Greenock
1 mile SW of town on road to
Gourock
(18)5838 yards/***(not Sat)/F/H

Haggs Castle G.C.
041 427 1157
70 Drumbreck Rd, Glasgow
SW of Glasgow near Ibrox
Stadium
(18)6464 yards/*/F

Hamilton G.C.
(0698) 282872
Riccarton, Firniegair, Hamilton
2 miles up Larkhall Rd, off M74
(18)6264 yards/*(with member)/F

Hayston G.C.
041 776 1244
Campsie Road, Kirkintilloch
10 miles NE of Glasgow off A803
(18)6042 yards/**/D

Helensburgh G.C.
(0436) 74173
15 Abercromby St, Helensburgh
Off Sinclair St on NE of town
(18)6053 yards/**/D/H

Hollandbush G.C.
(0555) 893484
Acretophead, Lesmahagow
(18)6100 yards/***/E

Innellan G.C.
(0369) 3546
Knockmillie Rd, Innellan, Argyll
4 miles from Dunoon
(9)4878 yards/***/E

Irvine G.C.
(0294) 75626
Bogside, Irvine
(18)6434 yards/***(not Sat)/F

Irvine Ravenspark G.C.
(0294) 76983
aKidsneuk, Irvine
On A78 between Irvine and
Kilwinning
(18)6429 yards/***/F

Kilbirnie Place G.C.
(0505) 683398
Largs Rd, Kilbirnie
On outskirts of Kilbirnie
(18)5411 yards/***(not Sat)/F

Kilmalcolm G.C.
(050587) 2139
Portafield Rd, Kilmalcolm
Take A740 to Linwwod
then A761 to Bridge of Weir
(18)5890 yards/**/D

Kilmarnock (Barassie) G.C.
(0292) 311077
29 Hillhouse Rd, Barassie,Troon
(18)6473 yards/**(not Wed)/B

Kilsyth Lennox G*.C.
(0236) 822190
Tak-ma-Doon Road,
Kilsyth, Glasgow
12 miles NE of Glasgow
on the A80
(9)5944 yards/***(not weekend
am)/E/H

Kirkhill G.C.
041 641 3083
Greenless Road, Cambuslang,
Glasgow
Take the East Kilbride Road
from Burnside
(18)5862 yards/***/F

Kirkintilloch G.C.
041 776 1256
Todhill, Campsie Road,
Kirkintilloch, Glasgow
1 mile from Kirkintilloch on road
to Lennoxtown
(18)5269 yards/*(with member)/F/H

Knightswood G.C.
041 959 2131
Lincoln Avenue,
Knightswood, Glasgow
Off Dumbarton Road from city
centre
(9)2717 yards/***/E

Kyles of Bute G.C.
(0700) 811355
Tighnabruaich, Argyll
Take A885 from Dunoon,
then B836 to
Tighnabruaich
(9)2389 yards/***(not Sun am)/E

Lamlash G.C.
(07706) 296
Lamlash, Brodick, Isle of Arran
On A841, 3 miles S
of ferry terminal
(18)4681 yards/***/F

Lanark G.C.
(0555) 3219
The Moor, Whitelees Road,
Lanark
Leave A73 at Lanark, take
Whitelees Road
(18)6423 yards/**/F/H

Largs G.C.
(0475) 673594
Irvine Road, Largs
1 mile S of Largs on A78
a(18)6220 yards/***/D/H

Larkhall G.C.
(0698) 88113
Burnhead Rd, Larkhall
On E of town on B7019
(9)6236 yards/***/F

Leadhills G.C.
(0659) 74222
Leadhills, Biggar
(9)2400 yards/***/E

Lenzie G.C.
041 776 1535
19 Crosshill Road, Lenzie
Take A80 to Stepps and into
Lenzie Road
(18)5982 yards/*(with member)/F

Lethamhill G.C.
041 770 6220
Cumbernauld Road, Glasgow
On A80 adjacent to Hogganfield
Loch
(18)6073 yards/***/E

Linn Park G.C.
041 637 5871
Simshill Road, Glasgow
Off B766, 5 miles S of Glasgow
(18)4848 yards/***/F/H

Littlehill G.C.
041 772 1916
Auchinairn Rd, Bishopbriggs,
Glasgow
3 miles N of city centre
(18)6228 yards/***/E

Lochranza G.C.
(077083) 273
Lochranza, Isle of Arran
(9)1815 yards/***/E

Lochwinnoch G.C.
Burnfoot Road, Lochwinnoch
On A760, 10 miles W of Paisley
(18)6202 yards/**/E/H

Loudoun G.C.
(0563) 821993
Galston, Ayrshire
From Kilmarnock take A71
towards Galston
(18)5854 yards/**/F

Machrie G.C.
(0496) 2310
Machrie Hotel, Port Ellen,
Isle of Islay
On A846, adjacent to airport
(18)6226 yards/***/D/H

Machrie Bay G.C.
(077084) 267
Machrie, By Brodick,
Isle of Arran
Take ferry to Brodick, take
String Road to Machrie
(9)2123 yards/***/E

Machrihanish G.C.
(058681) 213
Machrihansih, Campbeltown
5 miles W of Campbeltown
on B843
a(18)6228 yards/***/D/H/
(9)2395 yards/***/D/H

Millport G.C.
(0475) 530311
Golf Road, Millport, Isle of
Cumbrae
Take McBrayne ferry from Largs
to Cumbrae
(18)5831 yards/***/F/H

Milngavie G.C.
041 956 1619
Laighpark, Milngavie, Glasgow
Off A809, NW of Glasgow
(18)5818 yards/*(with member)/D

Mount Ellen G.C.
(0236) 872277
Johnston House,
Johnston Rd, Gartcosh
1 mile S of A80
(18)5526 yards/***/E

Old Ranfurly G.C.
(0505) 613612
Ranfurly Place, Bridge of Weir
7 miles W of Paisley
(18)6266 yards/**/D/L/H

Paisley G.C.
041 884 3903
Braehead, Paisley
From Glasgow,
take A737 to Paisley
(18)6424 yards/***/D/L

Pollok G.C
041 632 1080
90 Barrhead Rd, Glasgow
On A762, 4 miles S of Glasgow
(18)6257 yards/**(male
only)/C/H

Port Bannatyne G.C.
(0700) 2009
Port Bannatyne Mains Rd, Port
Bannatyne
Isle of Bute
2 miles N of Rothesay ferry terminal
(13)4654 yards/***/E

Port Glasgow G.C.
(0475) 704181
Devol Farm Indl. Estate,
Port Glasgow
(18)5712 yards/**/E

Prestwick G.C.
(0292) 77404
2 Links Rd, Prestwick
1 mile from Prestwick airport
(18)6544 yards/***/F/M/L

Prestwick St Cuthbert G.C.
(0292) 77101
East Rd, Prestwick
Off A77, near airport
(18)6470 yards/**/E

Prestwick St Nicholas G.C.
(0292) 77608
Grangemuir Rd, Prestwick
On seafront off A79
(18)5926 yards/**/D/H

Ralston G.C.
a041 882 1349
Strathmore Ave, Ralston, Paisley
To E of Paisley, off main road
(18)6100 yards/*(by arrangement)/F

Ranfurly Castle G.C.
(0505) 612609
Golf Road, Bridge of Weir
Leave M8 at junction 29, take
A240 and A761
(18)6284 yards/**/F/L

Renfrew G.C.
041 886 6692
Blythswood Estate, Inchinnan
Rd, Renfrew
Take A8 to Renfrew
(18)6818 yards/*(with member)/D/H

Rothesay G.C.
(0700) 2244
Canada Hill, Rothesay,
Isle of Bute
Take hourly steamer from
Wemyss Bay
(18)5440 yards/***/E/H

Routenburn G.C.
(0475) 673230
Largs, Ayrshire
1 mile N of Largs off A78
(18)5650 yards/**/E/H

Royal Troon G.C.
90292) 311555
Craigend Road, Troon
3 miles from Prestwick airport
on B749
(18)6641 yards/**/A/H(18 max)
(18)6274 yards/**/B/H

Sandyhills G.C.
041 778 1179
223 Sandyhills Road, Glasgow
On E of city
(18)6253 yards/***/E/H

Shiskine G.C.
(077086) 293
Blackwaterfoot, Isle of Arran
(12)3000 yards/***/E

Shotts G.C.
(0501) 20431
Blairhead, Shotts
Between Edinburgh and
Glasgow off M8
(18)6125 yards/***/E

Skelmorlie G.C.
(0475) 520152
Skelmorlie, Ayrshire
5 miles N of Largs
(13)5104 yards/***(not Sat)/E

Strathaven G.C.
(0357) 20421
Overton Avenue, Glasgow Road
On outskirts of town on A726
(18)6226 yards/**/F

Tarbert G.C.
(08802) 565
Kilberry Road, Tarbert
Leave A83 from Tarbert for
B8024
a(9)2230 yards/***/E

Torrance House G.C.
(03352) 33451
Strathaven Road, East Kilbride
(18)6640 yards/***/F/H

Troon Municipal G.C.
(0292) 312464
Harling Drive, Troon
Take A77 from Glasgow
(18)6687 yards/***/E
(18)6327 yards/***/E
(18)4784 yards/***/E

Turnberrry G.C.
(0655) 31000
Turnberry Hotel, Turnberry
Off A77 from Glasgow
(18)6950 yards/***/A/H
(18)6276 yards/***/B/H
(Less for hotel guests)

Vale of Leven G.C.
(0389) 52351
Northfield Course, Bonfield,
Alexandria
Leave A82 at Bonhill
(18)5156 yards/**/E

Vaul G.C.
(08792) 566
Scarinish, Isle of Tiree
(9)6246 yards/***/E

Westerwood Hotel and Golf
Course
(0236) 725281
St Andrews Drive, Cumbernauld
(18)6800 yards/***/F

Western Gailes G.C.
(0294) 311649
Gailes, by Irvine
5 miles N of Troon on A78
(18)6664 yards/***(not
Thurs/Sat)/F/H

West Kilbride G.C.
(0294) 823911
Fullerton Drive, Seamill,
West Kilbride
Leave A78 at Seamill
(18)6247 yards/**/F/L/H

Whitecraigs G.C.
041 639 4530
72 Ayr Road, Giffnock
7 miles S of Glasgow on A77
(18)6230 yards/*(intro only)/F

Williamwood G.C.
041 637 2715
Clarkston Road, Netherlee
5 miles S off Glasgow centre
on B767
(18)5808 yards/***/F/H

Windyhill G.C.
041 942 7157
Bal Jaffray Rd, Bearsden
Take A809 for 1 mile to A810
(18)6254 yards/**/F

Wishaw G.C.
a(0698) 372869
55 Cleland Rd, Wishaw
In town centre, 3 miles S of
Motherwell
(18)6160 yards/***(not Sat)/D

Inland Gems

While there is an inevitable temptation to head for the 'bigger Clubs', the Gleneagles and the Blairgowries, the region boasts a staggering number of smaller Clubs where golf can be equally enjoyable. **Taymouth Castle** and **Callander** are perhaps two of Scotland's lesser known courses, at least to many south of the border, yet they are two of the most scenic courses one is likely to find anywhere. At Callander in early spring the deer come down from the Perthshire hills to forage, a glorious sight, while the course at Taymouth Castle is situated in a conservation area surrounded by beautiful woods.

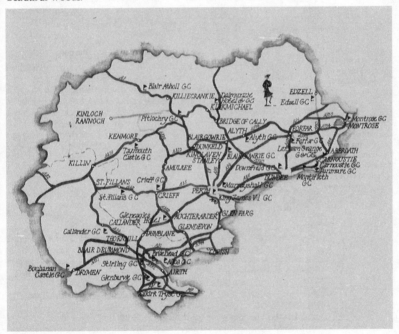

For golfers travelling northwards, before Gleneagles is reached some excellent golf is to be found at **Falkirk Tryst, Glenbervie** (Larbert), **Braehead** and **Alloa**, while over to the west of the Central region and somewhat isolated is picturesque **Buchanan Castle**. The town of **Stirling** is known as the 'Gateway to the Highlands' and Stirling's golf course has a beautiful setting beneath the Ochil Hills and in the shadows of Stirling Castle.

The world renowned **Gleneagles Hotel** near Auchterarder is a superb base, not only to secure a game on one or more of its own magnificent courses but also for exploring the many fine golf courses nearby.

After Gleneagles, **Blairgowrie** is probably the best known inland course and it too is featured on a later page. However, the golfer should undoubtedly pay a visit to the 'fair city of Perth'. The **King James VI** Golf Club on Moncrieffe Island is steeped in history while nearby at Scone—former crowning place of Kings—is the **Murrayshall** Country House Hotel and its superb golf course.

A little distance to the west of Perth there is more fine golf at **Crieff** where there are 27 holes and a very pretty nine hole course even further west at **St Fillans** . To the north of our region and tucked away amid some breathtaking scenery, **Dalmunzie House** should not be forgotten either; situated at Spittal O'Glenshee, the hotel has its own spectacular nine hole golf course where drives are said to travel further in the rarefied atmosphere!

Returning to Blairgowrie, if a game cannot be arranged on either of the Club's outstanding courses, then the heathland course at **Alyth** is very nearby and certainly won't disappoint. Perth's delights as mentioned are at hand to the south, while to the west is **Taymouth Castle** and to the north along the A9 stands **Pitlochry**. The latter is another course many will choose to play, for this is one of the most attractive in Britain—a veritable 'theatre in the hills'. Green fees at all these courses are relatively inexpensive and certainly very good value. Still further north the scenic 9 holer at **Blair Atholl** is also well worth a visit.

Closer to the Coast

Some of Scotland's greatest links courses are to be found between Dundee and Montrose on the Tayside coast. However, just to the north west of Dundee lies **Downfield** one of the country's finest inland courses. Indeed, five times Open Champion Peter Thomson rates this heavily wooded parkland course as one of the best inland courses in the world. It is said that Downfield is very popular with American visitors because it reminds them of some of their better courses 'back home'.

East of Dundee, The Medal Course at **Monifieth** has staged the Scottish Amateur Championship, while **Panmure** at Barry has in the past hosted the Seniors Championship. Both are classic links courses and fairly inexpensive to play over. **Carnoustie** is, of course, one of Scotland's greatest golfing shrines and Letham Grange may well become one in time. **Montrose,** like Monifeith, is a public links (two courses at each in fact) and when the winds blow can be extremely difficult. As earlier noted, green fees along this great coastal stretch are relatively cheap and provided some forward planning is done a game is possible at most times.

Finally, Two inland courses to the north east of Tayside which strongly merit attention are **Edzell** and **Letham Grange**. The former, just north of Brechin, and in a charming village is a beautiful heathland course where some marvellous mountain views can be enjoyed. Letham Grange is in fact a Hotel and Country Club and is situated at Colliston near Arbroath. The hotel is a splendidly restored Victorian Mansion, and with 36 holes of golf now on offer is well worth a visit.

Tayside

Aberfeldy G.C
(0887) 20535
Taybridge Road,
Aberfeldy, Perthshire
10 miles from Ballinluig
off the A827
(9) 2733 yards/***/F

Alyth G.C
(08283) 2268
Pitcrocknie, Alyth,
Perthshire
Off the B954 road, off the
A926
(18) 6226 yards/***/F

Arbroath G.C
(0241) 72666
Elliot, Arbroath, Angus
2 miles S. of
Arbroath on A92
(18) 6078 yards/***/F

Auchterarder G.C
(0764) 62804
Orchil Road,
Auchterarder, Perthshire
S.W of town, off the A9
(18) 5737 yards/***/F

Blair Atholl G.C
(079681) 274
Blair Atholl, Perthshire
6 miles N. of
Pitochry on the A9
(9) 5710 yards/***/F

Blairgowrie G.C
(0250) 873116
Rosemount, Blairgowrie,
Perthshire
Take A923 from Perth and
turn off to Rosemount
(18) 6588 yards/***/F/H
(18) 6895 yards/***/F/H

Brechin G.C
(03562) 2383
Trinity, by Brechin, Angus
In Trinity village, 1 mile N.
of Brechin on B966
(18) 5267 yards/***/D

Caird Park G.C
(0382) 453606
Mains Loan, Dundee
N. of city, just off Kingsway
(18) 6303 yards/***/F

Callander G.C
(0877) 30090
Aveland Road, Callander,
Perthshire
Signposted off the A84
(18) 5125 yards/***/D

Camperdown G.C
(0382) 623398
Camperdown Park, Dundee
In Coupar Angus Road, off
Kingsway
(18) 6561 yards/***/E

Carnoustie
(0241) 53789
Links Parade, Carnoustie,
Angus
12 miles E of Dundee,
off the A630
(18) 6020 yards/***/F/H
(18) 5732 yards/***/F/H
(18) 6931 yards/***/F/H

Comrie G.C
(0764) 70544
c/o Sec, Donald C
McGlashan
10 Polinard, Comrie,
Perthshire
6 miles W. of Crieff on the
A85
(9)5966/***/F

Craigie Hill G.C
(0783) 22644
Cherrybank, Perth
1 mile W. of Perth
(18) 5739 yards/***/E

Crieff G.C
(0764) 2397
Perth Road, Crieff,
Perthshire
18 miles along the A85,
Perth-Crieff Road
(18) 6402 yards/***/F
(9) 4772 yards/***/F

Dalmunzie Hotel & G.C
(025085) 226
Spittal of Glenshee,
Blairgowrie, Perthshire
22 miles N. of Blairgowrie
on the A93
(9) 2035/***/E

Downfield G.C
(0382) 825595
Turnberry Avenue, Dundee
Leave Dundee by
Kingsway
and take A923
(18) 6804 yards/***/F

Dunblane New G.C
(0786) 823711
Perth Road, Dunblane,
Perthshire
6 miles N. of Stirling on A9
(18) 6876 yards/**/D

Dunkeld and Birnam G.C
(035 02) 524
Fungarth, Dunkeld,
Perthshire
1 mile N. of Dunkeld off
the A9
(9) 5264 yards/***/E

Dunning G.C
(076484) 398
Rollo Park, Dunning, Perth
9 miles S.W of
Perth off the A9
(9) 4836 yards/***/F/H

Edzell G.C
(03564) 7283
High Street, Edzell,
By Brechin, Angus
Leave the A94
for the B966 at by-pass
(18) 6299 yards/***/F

Forfar G.C
(0307) 62120
Cunninghill, Arbroath Road,
By Forfar, Angus
1 mile from town
on road to Angus
(18) 6255 yards/***/C

Gleneagles Hotel & G.C
(0764) 62231
Auchterarder, Perthshire
Take A9 from Perth S.W
for 16 miles
(18) 6471 yards/*/F
(18) 5964 yards/*/F

Killin G.C
(056 72) 312
Killin, Perthshire
On outskirts of village
(9) 2508 yards/***/E/H

King James VI G.C
(0738) 32460
Moncreiffe Island, Perth
By footbridge
over River Tay
(18) 6026 yards/***(not
Sat)/D

Green Hotel G.C
(0577) 63467
Beeches Park, Kinross,
Perthshire
17 miles S. of Perth
(18) 6111 yards/***/D

Kirriemuir G.C
(0575) 72729
Kirriemuir, Angus
1 mile N. of town centre
(18) 5591 yards/**/E

Letham Grange G.C
(024 189) 373
Letham Grange, Colliston,
By Arbroath, Angus
Take the A933 for 4 miles
(18) 6789 yards/***/F/H

Milnathort G.C
(0577) 64069
South Street, Milnathort
2 miles N. of Kinross,
off the M90
(9) 5411 yards/***/E

Monifieth Links G.C
(0382) 532767
Dundee, Angus
Just outside Monifieth
on the A930
(18) 6657 yards/***(not
Sat)/D/H
(18) 5123 yards/***(not
Sat)/E/H

Montrose Links Trust
(0674)72932
Trail Drive, Montrose,
Angus
1 mile from town centre
off the A92
(18) 6451 yards/***/F/H
(18) 4815 yards/***/F/H

Murrayshall Hotel & G.C
(0738) 52784
Murrayshall, by Scone,
Perthshire
On the A94 from Perth
(18) 6416 yards/***/F/H

Muthill G.C
(0764) 81523
Peat Road, Muthill, Crieff
Signposted off the A822
(9) 2371 yards/***/E

North Inch G.C
Near centre of
Perth off the A9
(18) 4736 yards/***/E

Panmure G.C
(0241) 53120
Barry, Angus
Take A930 to Barry
(18) 6317 yards/***(not
Sat)/D/H

Pitlochry G.C
(0796) 2796
Golf Course Road, Pitlochry
Half mile from
Pitlochry on A9
(18) 5811 yards/***/F/H

St Fillans G.C
(0764) 85312
St Fillans, Perthshire
On A85 between Crieff and
Lochearnhead
(9) 5268 yards/***/E

Strathtay G.C
(08874) 367
Tighanoisinn, Grandtully,
Perthshire
4 miles W. of Ballinkrig
(9) 4980 yards/***/E

Taymouth Castle G.C
(088 73) 228
Kenmore, by Aberfeldy,
Tayside
6 miles W. of Aberfeldy
(18) 6066 yards/***/D/H

Central

Aberfoyle G.C
(08772) 441
Braeval, Aberfoyle,
Stirlingshire
1 mile from Aberfoyle on
the A81
(18) 5205 yards/***/D

Alloa G.C
(0259) 722745
Schawpark, Sauchie,
Clackmannanshire
On A908 between Alloa
and Tillicoultry
(18) 6230 yards/***/E

Alva G.C
(0259) 60431
Beauclerc Street, Alva,
Clackmannanshire
3 miles N. of Alloa
on the A91
(9) 2407 yards/***/F

Bonnybridge G.C
Larbert Road, Bonnybridge,
Stirlingshire
3 miles W. of Falkirk on the
B816
(9) 6060 yards/*(with member only)/F

Braehead G.C
(0259) 722078
Cambus, By Alloa,
Clackmannanshire
1 mile W. of
Alloa on the A907
(18) 6013 yards/***/E/H

Bridge of Allan G.C
(0786) 832332
Sunlaw, Bridge of
Allan, Stirling
Over the River Allan
off Stirling Road
(9) 4932 yards/***(not
Sat)/E

Dollar G.C
(02594) 2400
Brewlands House, Dollar,
Clackmannanshire
(18) 5144 yards/**/F

Falkirk G.C
(0324) 611061
Stirling Road, Cumlins,
Falkirk
2 miles W. of Falkirk
centre on A9
(18) 6202 yards/**/E

Falkirk Tryst G.C
(0324) 562091
Burnhead Rd, Larbert
1/4 mile from Larbert
Station
(18)6053 yards/***/D

Glenbervie G.C
(0324) 562605
Stirling Road, Larbert,
Stirlingshire
1 mile N. of Larbert
on the A9
(18) 6469 yards/*
(by intro only)/C

Grangemouth
Municipal G.C.
(0324) 714355
Polmont Hill, Polmont,
Falkirk, Stirlingshire
Leave M9 at junction 4 and
follow signs to Hill
(18) 6314 yards/***/F/H

Muckhart G.C
(025 981) 423
Drumburn Road, Muckhart,
Dollar, Clackmannanshire
Signposted off the A91 and
A823 S. of Muckhart
(18) 6115 yards/***/E

Polmont G.C
(0324) 711277
Maddiston, by Falkirk,
Stirlingshire
4 miles S. of Falkirk
(9) 3044 yards/**/E

Stirling G.C
(0786) 64098
Queens Road, Stirling
Half mile W. of town cen-
tre on A811
(18) 5976 yards/**/D

Tillicoultry G.C
(0259) 50124
Alva Road, Tiilicoultry
(9) 2528 yards/***/E

Tulliallan G.C
(0259) 30897
Alloa Road, Kincardine
on Forth, By Alloa
2 miles N. of Kincardine
Bridge on Alloa Road
(18) 5982 yards/***/F

KEY

*** Visitors welcome at all times
** Visitors on weekdays only
* No visitors at any time
(Mon, Wed) No visitors on specified
days

GREEN FEES PER ROUND
A - £30 plus
B - £20 - £30
C - £15 - £25
D - £10 - £20
E - Under £10
F - Green fees on application

RESTRICTIONS
G - Guests only
H - Handicap certificate required
H(24) - Handicap of 24 or less
required
L - Letter of introduction required
M - Visitor must be a member of
another recognised club.

W*alter Hagen—a shrewd judge you might think—once described Carnoustie as the greatest course in the British Isles. Doubtless the disciples of St. Andrews and several honourable gentlemen at Muirfield would beg to differ. Greatest or not, very few would dispute that when the winds blow—as they invariably do in these parts—Carnoustie is the toughest of all our Championship links.*

There are presently six Clubs at Carnoustie and play is over three 18 hole courses; the **Championship**, the **Burnside** and the **Buddon**. Administrative matters are in the hands of the Carnoustie Golf Links Management Committee and persons wishing to visit Carnoustie should direct correspondence to the Committee's **Secretary, Mr. E.J.C. Smith**. . Contact by telephone can be made on **(0241) 53789** and by fax on (0241) 52720. Starting times must be booked in advance.

In 1993, the green fees at Carnoustie were £34 for a single round on the Championship course with £40.50 securing a round over both the Championship and Burnside courses. Fees to play just the Burnside or Buddon courses are good value and it is also possible to obtain a three day and five day pass enabling up to three or five rounds over the Championship course. Details can be obtained by phoning the above number (caddies can also be arranged.)

The Forth Road Bridge and the M90 link the Edinburgh region with Perth; Perth in turn is linked to Dundee by the A85 and Dundee to Carnoustie by the A390. Those on golfing tours will quite likely be coming via St. Andrews: the A91 (A919) runs from St. Andrews towards Dundee; it picks up the A92 just before the Tay Road Bridge and on crossing the Bridge the A930 should immediately be joined. From the north, the A92 runs from Aberdeen to within a couple of miles of Carnoustie at Muirdrum, while the A958 links the town with Forfar.

Scotland is the land of Burns. It is also the land of burns—streams or little rivers anywhere else in the English-speaking world—and Carnoustie is famous for them. The ubiquitous Barry Burn and its wee brother Jocky's Burn traverse the fairways in the most unfriendly of places, often in front of greens and across the spot you'd ideally like to drive to. More than anything else though, Carnoustie is renowned for its incredibly tough finishing stretch. The 16th is an exceptionally long short hole and Jack Nicklaus is said to have once needed a driver followed by an 8 iron to get up! The 17th has the Barry Burn meandering across its fairway, making it a particularly difficult driving hole and at the 18th the Burn crosses in front of the green necessitating one of the most exciting (or nerve-racking) closing shots in golf.

The Carnoustie Golf Links Management Committee, Links Parade, Carnoustie, Tayside, DD7 7JE

Championship Course

Hole	Yards	Par	Hole	Yards	Par
1	407	4	10	446	4
2	425	4	11	353	4
3	342	4	12	477	5
4	375	4	13	161	3
5	387	4	14	483	5
6	524	5	15	456	4
7	390	4	16	245	3
8	168	3	17	433	4
9	420	4	18	444	4
Out	3,438	36	In	3,498	36
			Out	3,438	36
			Totals	6,936	72

Fife

As long ago as 1457 the Scottish Parliament, unimpressed by the performance of its sharp shooters, felt that too much golf and football were to blame for the lack-lustre performances on the battlefields. An Act was passed stating that because of their interference with the practice of archery, the 'fute-ball and golf be utterly cryit down and nocht usit'. History would seem to suggest that the Scots didn't take a blind bit of notice, and golf steadily grew in popularity. Juggle the figures that make up 1457 and we have 1754, per-

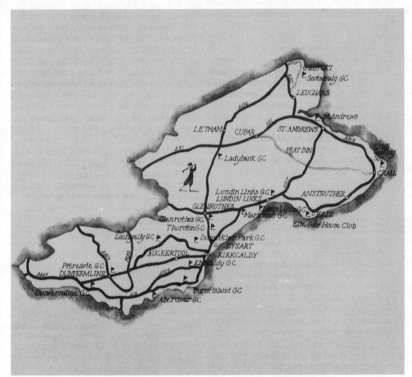

haps the most significant date in golf's history—the year the Society of St Andrews golfers drew up its written rules of golf.

Today **St Andrews**, deep in the Kingdom of Fife, is the place every golfer in the world wants to visit. Even if you have only swung a club at the local municipal you'll be itching to do the same at St Andrews. However, for those contemplating a pilgrimage to the centre of the golfing world it should be said that St Andrews has several near neighbours that warrant the most discerning attention. Between Dunfermline, to the west of Fife, and St Andrews, lie what are undoubtedly some of the finest courses in Scotland.

Travelling Around the Coast

For six hundred years Dunfermline was the country's capital and the body of its most famous king, Robert the Bruce, lies buried in Dunfermline Abbey (minus his heart, apparently, which is in Melrose Abbey). The town has two courses, **Dunfermline** and **Pitreavie.** Both are parkland courses at which visitors are welcome provided some prior arrangement is made. Neither is unduly hard on the pocket.

East of Dunfermline there is a testing links at **Burntisland** with fine views over the Firth of Forth and there are again two courses in Kirkcaldy, the **Dunnikier Park** and **Kirkcaldy** Golf Clubs, (and make sure you pronounce it Ker-coddy!) Dunnikier Park is a public course. One other good golf club to note in the area is **Aberdour.** Beyond Kirkcaldy, out along a glorious stretch of spectacular coast are Fife's famous five—**Leven Links, Lundin Links, Elie, Balcomie** and of course **St Andrews.** The first two are often considered as a pair, probably on account of there being very little land in between (an old stone wall serves as the boundary). Two proud clubs share the 6,433 yards links at Leven, the **Leven Golfing Society** and **Leven Thistle,** however, the visitor is always made to feel welcome—as indeed he, or she is at the more hilly **Lundin**—an excellent course, which although very much a links has an abundance of trees on the back nine.

Elie, or the Golf House Club, lies a short distance from the two across Largo Bay, the A917 linking the town with Leven. Elie is famed for its unique periscope by the first tee and for the fact that it was here that James Braid fashioned many of the skills that won him five Open Championships. A charming and very natural links— you won't see trees anywhere here—and not too demanding in length, several of the holes are laid out right alongside a rocky shoreline. A ballot system operates at Elie during the summer but otherwise there are no general restrictions on times visitors can play.

Following the aforementioned A917 eastwards from Elie, the town of Crail is soon reached. Just beyond the town at Fife Ness is the magnificent Balcomie links, home of the two hundred year old **Crail Golfing Society.** Together with St Andrews it is featured a few pages on. Incidentally, when visiting St. Andrews, or if just passing by, try to visit the **British Golf Museum**—it's right next to the 1st tee on the **Old Course.**

Inland Golf

Just as the leading courses of Surrey aren't all heathland and gorse neither are those of Fife all seaviews and sandhills. **Ladybank** is actually only a few miles north of Leven but is completely different in character with heathland fairways and much pine and heather—a very beautiful course and well worth a visit. North of Ladybank lies

Cupar, one of the oldest nine-hole golf courses in Scotland and a clubhouse that has to be approached through a cemetery (slightly older even than the golf course!)

In an area steeped in history, **Glenrothes** is a relative newcomer to the scene. Young, perhaps, but an excellent course nonetheless. Situated to the west of the town it is a fairly hilly parkland type, offering many superb views. A friendly welcome awaits but the names of two of the holes worry me a little—the 11th, titled 'Satan's Gateway' and the 18th, 'Hells End'! A restful 19th is clearly in order and fortunately in Glenrothes quality places abound.

Two other courses that are well worth visiting if journeying inland are at **Thornton,** where the River Ore makes for some challenging holes, and at **Lochgelly**—convenient if travelling between Dunfermline and Kirkcaldy. The final mention though goes to **Scotscraig,** an Open Championship qualifying course at Tayport. Although close to the sea it is actually a downland type course rather than a true links, and is an admirable test of golf. Following that testing game at Scotscraig one is likely to be left with a difficult decision. To the north, Carnoustie and many other great challenges await; but then no golfer who experienced the pleasures of the Kingdom of Fife ever left easily.

Organised golf came to St. Andrews in 1754 when twenty-two Noblemen and Gentlemen formed the St. Andrews Society of Golfers. In 1834 the Society became the Royal and Ancient Golf Club.

All the world can play at St. Andrews, and all the world wants to. Arranging a game on the **Old Course** can be a little difficult. The St. Andrews Links Management Committee handles all matters relating to times of play and they should be contacted well in advance. The **Secretary, Mr. D. N. James** can be contacted by telephone on **(0334) 75757** and by fax on (0334) 77036. There are no handicap limits to play over the Old Course. However a handicap certificate or letter of introduction is required. There is no Sunday golf on the Old Course. In 1993 the green fee for a round was priced at £40.

There are four other eighteen hole links at St. Andrews, the **New Course,** (1896), the **Jubilee** (1897) —recently lengthened and improved by Donald Steel—the **Eden** (1914) and the new **Strathyrum Course.** No handicap certificate is required to play over any of the above and the green fees for 1993 were £18, £16, £16 and £12 respectively. A 9 hole course, the Balgove, is also available (at a modest green fee of £5 for 18 holes, together with a driving range and extensive practice facilities.

St. Andrews is situated 57 miles north east of Edinburgh. Northbound, the most direct route to take is the M90 after crossing the Forth Road Bridge. The A91 should be joined at junction 8. Southbound travellers should head for Perth which is linked to Dundee by the A85 and to the north of Scotland by the A9. A combination of the A90 and the A913 takes one to Cupar where the A91 can be picked up.

Nature fashioned St. Andrews and over the centuries the Old Course has seen little change. Myriad tiny pot bunkers remain both a fascination and a frustration—just enough room as Bernard Darwin put it 'for an angry man and his niblick'. Laid out on a narrow strip of land ranging from 50 to 100 yards in width, St. Andrews is famed for its enormous double greens. There are seven in all, some more than an acre in size. With little definition between the fairways there tends to be no standard way of playing a particular hole. Wind direction will determine the preferred line. Individual holes are unlikely to be easily remembered the first time, especially as one will probably be walking in a semi-trance. History is everywhere. On the first hole a voice from somewhere says 'they've all walked this bridge'—and of course they have.

The St. Andrews Links Management Committee, Golf Place, St. Andrews, Fife, KY16 9JA.

Old Course

Hole	Yards	Par	Hole	Yards	Par
1	370	4	10	342	4
2	411	4	11	172	3
3	371	4	12	316	4
4	463	4	13	425	4
5	564	5	14	567	5
6	416	4	15	413	4
7	372	4	16	382	4
8	178	3	17	461	4
9	356	4	18	354	4
Out	3,501	36	In	3,432	36
			Out	3,501	36
			Totals	6,933	72

Aberdour G.C.
(0383) 860256
Seaside Place, Aberdour
(18)5469 yards/**/E

Anstruther G.C.
(0333) 312055
Marsfield, Shore Rd. Anstruther
4 miles south of St Andrews
(9)4120 yards/***/E

Auchterderran G.C.
(0592) 721579
Woodend Rd. Cardenden
On the Glenrothes to
Cardenden road
(9)5400 yards/***/F

Burntisland G.C.
(0592) 874093
Dodhead, Burntisland
1 mile north east
of town on B923
(18)5871 yards/***/F/H

Canmore G.C.
(0383) 724969
Venturefair Avenue,
Dunfermline
1 mile north of Dunfermline
on A823

(18)5474 yards/**/C·
Crail G.C.
(0333) 50960
Balcomie Club House, Fifeness,
Crail
2 miles east of Crail
(18)5270 yards/***/D/H

Cupar G.C.
(0334) 53549
Hilltarvit, Cupar
10 miles from St Andrews off
A91
(9)5300 yards/**/D

Dumfermline G.C.
(0383) 723534
Pitfirrane, Crossford,
Dunfermline
4 miles west on Kincardine
Bridge Rd.
(18) 6244 yards/**/D

Dunnikier Park G.C.
(0592) 261599
Dunnikier Way, Kircaldy
(18)6601 yards/***/D/H

Elie G.C.
(0333) 330301
Golf Club House, Elie, Leven
6 miles from Leven on A917
(18)6241 yards/***/F

Glenrothes G.C.
(0592) 754561
Golf Course Rd. Glenrothes
At West of town, 8 miles from
M90
(18)6449 yards/***/E

Kinghorn G.C.
(0592) 890345
Macduff Crescent, Kinghorn
3 miles west of Kircaldy,
off the A92
a(18)5246 yards/***/E

Kircaldy G.C.
(0592) 260370
Balwearie Road, Kircaldy
W. of the town on the A907
(18)6004 yards/***(not Sat)/D

Ladybank G.C.
(0337) 30814
Annesmuir, Ladybank
6 miles S. of Cupar on the
Edinburgh-Dunbar road
(18)6617 yards/***/C

Leslie G.C.
(0592) 741449
Balsillie, Leslie
West of Glenrothes on the A911
(9)4940 yards/***/E

Leven Thistle G.C.
(0333) 26397
Balfourst, Leven
In Links Road, off Church Road
from the Promenade
(18)6434 yards/***/D

Lochgelly G.C
(0592) 80174
Cartmore Road, Lochgelly
W. of town off A910
(18)5491 yards/***/F

Lundin Links G.C.
(0333) 320202
Golf Road, Lundin Links
3 miles east of Leven on A915
(18)6377 yards/**(+Sat pm)/F/H

Pitreavie (Dunfermline) G.C.
(0383) 722591
Queensferry Road, Dunfermline
Leave A90 for A823 to
Dunfermline
(18)6086 yards/***/D

St Andrews
(0334) 75757
St Andrews
(9)1754 yards/***/F(Balgove)
(18)5971 yards/***/F(Eden)
(18)6284 yards/***/F(Jubilee)
(18)6500 yards/***/F(Strathyrum)
(18)6604 yards/***/F(New)
(18)6933 yards/**(Not

Sun)/F/H/L(Old)

St Michaels G.C.
(0334) 83365
Leuchars, St Andrews
200 yards west
of village on A919
(9)5510 yards/***(not Sun a.m.)/E

Saline G.C.
(0383)852591
Kinneddar Hill, Saline
5 miles NW of
Dunfermline off A907
(9)5302 yards/***(not Sat)/E

Scoonie G.C.
(0333) 27057
North Links, Leven
a10 miles SW of St Andrews
(18)5500 yards/***/F

Scotscraig G.C.
(0382) 552515
Golf Road, Tayport
South of Tay Bridge off B946
(18)6496 yards/***/F/M

Thornton G.C.
(0592) 77111
Station Road, Thornton
Thornton Village
(18)6177 yards/***/F

Mist-covered mountains and bottomless lochs, bagpipes, whisky and haggis. I doubt whether there is a more romantic place in the world than the Highlands of Scotland. I doubt also that there is a place quite so shatteringly beautiful. For our purposes 'the Highlands' covers the administrative regions of Grampian and Highland. The latter extends from the Cairngorms northwards, encompassing the Great Glen and the Western Isles. Grampian covers a similarly vast area, the entirety of north eastern Scotland. The area was at one time covered by a dense forest of pine broken only by the soaring granite peaks of the Grampian mountain range. It was the home of the savage Caledonian tribe, a land where wolves hunted in packs. Nowadays very little of the forest remains. As for the wolves, most of them were killed by the Caledonians, but then unfortunately most of the Caledonians were killed by the Romans. No wonder they called life 'nasty, brutish and short'!

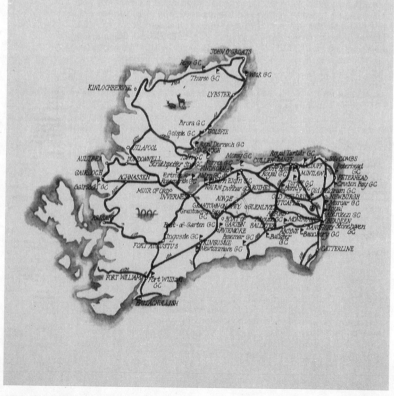

Grampian

Let us make a start in Grampian. Forgetting the wolves, the savages and the Romans, what we need is a good 18 holes—and, of course, a suitable 19th. Aberdeen is a fine place to begin. **Balgownie** and **Murcar** lie right on the town's doorstep and are unquestionably two of the finest courses in Scotland. Balgownie links is the home of the **Royal Aberdeen** Golf Club and is featured ahead but **Murcar** is certainly not overshadowed and is a true Championship test. It is a classic Scottish links with plenty of sandhills and a meandering burn and is quite a bit more undulating than Balgownie.

If the above are the best two courses around Aberdeen, (there are dozens in the area) and they are to the north of the city then perhaps the most spectacular is to the south at **Stonehaven**, laid out right alongside the lashing North Sea. And in total contrast to Stonehaven—and indeed to Aberdeen's great links layouts is the new 'American-styled' course at **Newmachar,** north west of the city.

Looking to play outside Aberdeen, the golfer is faced with two equally appealing choices—one can either head north along the coast towards Cruden Bay, or alternatively head inland along the A93. The latter choice broadly involves following the path of the River Dee and will take the traveller through some truly magnificent scenery. The 18 hole courses at **Banchory, Aboyne, Ballater** and **Braemar** all lie along this road and not surprisingly boast spectacular settings. Journeying due northwards from Aberdeen, **Cruden Bay** is clearly the first stopping point. A truly splendid golf links this, situated some 23 miles north of Aberdeen on Scotland's Buchan Coast. The old fishing and whaling town of **Peterhead** has an interesting seaside course where fierce sea winds can make scoring tricky.

From fishing port to Georgian elegance—The **Duff House Royal** Golf Club at Macduff is overlooked by an impressive baroque- style mansion. The course too has a touch of class being designed by Alister Mackenzie immediately prior to his constructing the legendary Augusta National course in America—note the many two-tiered greens. Although not far from the sea, Duff House is very much a parkland type challenge. Nearby **Royal Tarlair** at Banff is well worth a visit and like Duff House is always beautifully maintained. To the south of Banff, along the A947, **Turriff** can also be recommended while even further inland (but a marvellous drive anyway) from the Banff/ Macduff area on the A97, is the charming little course at **Huntly**.

Crossing the salmon-filled River Spey at Fochabers the City of **Elgin** is soon reached. There aren't too many cathedrals in this part of the world but Elgin, the capital of Morayshire, has a beautiful one that dates from the 13th Century. It also possesses one of the finest inland golf courses in the north of Scotland. A mile or so south of the city and some distance away from the often fierce coastal winds, the course is sheltered by many pines and silver birch trees. Inevitably, it occupies a glorious setting with distant purple hills forming a spectacular horizon.

Inland from Elgin, a drive through the Glen of Rothes will lead the golfer to **Dufftown** where there is a pleasant and not too difficult course but if a coastal challenge is sought then Lossiemouth is the place to head for. Here, the **Moray** Golf Club has two outstanding links courses, the 'Old Course' which is more than a hundred years old and the 'New Course', a little over ten years old. Whilst the fighter aircraft from nearby RAF Lossiemouth may occasionally irritate, it would be difficult to find a finer combination of superb natural golf and scenic splendour.

Highland

In Scotland where there is land there is golf and although the Highland region may be a wild and somewhat remote part of the country it nonetheless has its share of golfing gems—and more than that, in the minds of many, it has in **Royal Dornoch** the finest of them all.

As well as its gems, the region has a number of golf's genuine outposts, none more so than the **Gairloch** Golf Club situated in the far west of Scotland with views across to the Isle of Skye. There are 9 holes at Gairloch, each wonderfully named. The 6th, however, baffles me—'Westward Ho!' is its title?! The 9th though has more of a Celtic ring to it—'Mo Dhachaidh'. There is no Sunday golf at Gairloch though visitors can play at all other times. Others in the 'lonely category' include **Fort Augustus** on the edge of Loch Ness and **Fort William**, a moorland course, laid out in the shadows of Ben Nevis. In addition the very intrepid golfer will find a number of courses to play in the Western Isles and the Hebrides although the scenery may cause many to lift their heads too quickly.

In the south of Highland, the area around Aviemore has become an increasingly popular holiday retreat, particularly for winter sports enthusiasts. However, whilst the skis must go on the roof, the golf clubs can fit in the boot, and there are five or six courses at hand each of which possesses a truly glorious setting. Picking two of the best, the **Kingussie** and **Boat of Garten** Golf Clubs lie either side of Aviemore close to the A9. Both have spectacular courses at which visitors are always made welcome. Neither is particularly long, though the hills at Kingussie and the narrow fairways and small greens at Boat of Garten can make scoring extremely difficult and you are more likely to see eagles than score one! At Boat of Garten you may also catch a glimpse of one of the famous ospreys.

Inverness, as the so-called 'Capital of the Highlands', is where many may choose to spend a day or two—the Loch Ness monster lives nearby and the famous fields of destruction at Culloden Moor are only a few miles to the east. Golfers may wish to note the city's 18 hole course situated just south of the town centre. However, many are likely to be drawn towards **Nairn** (16 miles away) where in addition to the magnificent championship links there is an excellent second course, **Nairn Dunbar**.

On the Chanonry Peninsula, linked to Inverness by way of the Kessock Bridge, the A9 and the A832, is the flattish links course of

Fortrose and **Rosemarkie**—surrounded by sea and well worth a visit. **Strathpeffer Spa**, a moorland course, is the prettiest of stepping stones for those heading north of Inverness along the A9. This road passes through **Tain**, home of the famous Glenmorangie whisky, and where there are another outstanding 18 holes—but by now most will be itching to reach Dornoch, **Royal Dornoch** being regularly ranked among the top ten golf courses in Britain.

Having played Royal Dornoch, many may find it difficult to tear themselves away, but there are two excellent courses a short distance to the north, namely, **Golspie** and **Brora**. Both are testing links courses set in the most majestic surroundings with views to distant hills and along what is a truly spectacular coast. Brora (where the greens are reputed to be the equal of those at Royal Dornoch and are ringed by electric fences to keep the sheep out!) stretches alongside three miles of deserted sandy beach. Being so far north golf can be played at absurdly late hours and at both, the green fees are very inexpensive.

Beyond Brora we really are getting remote! However, the A9 makes it all the way to John O'Groats. There are 18 hole courses at **Wick** and **Reay**, but the furthest north is **Thurso**, not too far from the Dounreay Power Station. I should imagine it gets pretty cold up there, but if you do make it, and are looking for fresh challenges then there is always the golf club in the Arctic—fittingly called the 'Polar Bear Club'—and which, I suppose it goes without saying, was founded by Scotsmen!

KEY

*** Visitors welcome at all times
** Visitors on weekdays only
* No visitors at any time
(Mon, Wed) No visitors on specified days

GREEN FEES PER ROUND

A - £30 plus
B - £20 - £30
C - £15 - £25
D - £10 - £20
E - Under £10
F - Green fees on application

RESTRICTIONS

G - Guests only
H - Handicap certificate required
H(24) - Handicap of 24 or less required
L - Letter of introduction required
M - Visitor must be a member of another recognised club.

There are two words that are normally associated with Royal Dornoch; one is 'greatness' and the other is 'remoteness'. It is the course every golfer wants to play but the one that very few actually do.

So what is the charm of Dornoch? Firstly, there's the setting (this is when people forgive its remoteness!) Bordered by the Dornoch Firth and a glorious stretch of sand, distant hills fill the horizon creating a feeling that one is playing on a stage.

The **Secretary** at Royal Dornoch is **Mr. Ian Walker**, he may be contacted by telephone on **(0862) 810219** and by fax on (0862) 810729. All written correspondence should be addressed to **The Secretary**, . **William Skinner** is the Club's **professional**; he may be reached on **(0862) 810902.**

Visitors are welcome at Royal Dornoch seven days a week. However, it is probably wise to telephone the Club prior to setting off to check if any tee reservations have been made. The cost of a single round on the Championship course in 1993 was priced at £30 (£35 at the weekend). A three day (Monday,Tuesday and Wednesday) ticket is available, priced at £75 in 1993. There is now a second eighteen hole course at Dornoch, the Struie Course measuring 5242 yards, par 68. A day ticket, enabling a round over both courses was available in 1993 at a cost of £40 midweek, £45 at the weekend. A day ticket for the Struie Course alone could be purchased for £15 during the week (£10 per round) with £60 securing a full week's golf.

Travelling to Dornoch gets ever easier. The A9 runs from Perth to John O'Groats, Perth being linked to Edinburgh by the M90. There are regular flights from London and other parts of the country to Inverness Airport and the links itself has an adjacent landing strip for light aircraft. Moreover there is now a road bridge over the Dornoch Firth and this reduces the motoring time from Inverness to 40 minutes.

By today's standards Dornoch could probably be described as being of only medium length, the links measuring 6577 yards, par 70 (s.s.s. 72). However, the last thing in the world that Dornoch is, is an easy course. It Ohas been said that the prevailing wind at Dornoch comes from every direction but even when the winds don't thunder in from across the Firth or down from the hills, the links can be the proverbial 'smiler with the knife'.

Today there are signs that Dornoch is at last shedding its remoteness tag. In 1985 the Club staged the Amateur Championship for the first time in its history—this being in the minds of many alarmingly overdue. One cannot help wondering what it would be like if the hallowed links were ever visited by the greatest of all compliments.

Royal Dornoch Golf Club, Golf Road, Dornoch

Hole	Yards	Par	Hole	Yards	Par
1	336	4	10	148	3
2	179	3	11	445	4
3	414	4	12	504	5
4	418	4	13	168	3
5	361	4	14	448	4
6	165	3	15	322	4
7	465	4	16	405	4
8	437	4	17	406	4
9	499	5	18	457	4
Out	3,274	35	In	3,303	35
			Out	3,274	35
			Totals	6,577	70

Grampian

Aboyne G.C
(03398) 86328
Formaston Park, Aboyne,
Aberdeenshire
Signposted on the A93 from
Aberdeen
(18) 5330 yards/***/F

Auchenblae G.C
(05612) 407
Auchenblae, Laurencekirk
5 miles N. of Laurencekirk
(9) 2174 yards/***/E

Auchmill G.C
(0224) 642121
Auchmill, Aberdeen
(9) 2538 yards/***/E

Ballater G.C
(03397) 55567
Ballater, Aberdeenshire
40 miles W. of Aberdeen
on A93
(18) 5704 yards/***/D

Banchory G.C
(03302) 2365
Kinneskie, Banchory,
Kincardineshire
18 miles W. of Aberdeen
(18) 5305 yards/***/F

Balnagask G.C
(0224) 876407
St Fitticks Road, Aberdeen
2 miles S.E of the city centre   —
(18) 5468 yards/***/E

Bon-Accord G.C
(0224) 633464
19 Golf Course Road,
Aberdeen
Beside Pittodrie Stadium
near the beach
(18) 6384 yards/***/F

Braemar G.C
(03397) 41618
Cluniebank, Braemar,
Aberdeenshire
Half mile from the village
centre
(18) 4916 yards/***/E

Buckpool G.C
(0542) 32236
Barhill Road, Buckie,

Banffshire
At end of A98 to Buckpool
(18) 6259 yards/***/E

Caledonian G.C
(0224) 632 443
20 Golf Road, Aberdeen
Adjacent to the Pittodrie
Stadium
(18) 6384 yards/***/F

Cruden Bay G.C
(0779) 812285
Aulton Road, Cruden Bay,
Peterhead, Aberdeenshire
7 miles S. of Peterhead
(9) 4710 yards/***/E
(18) 6370 yards/***/F

Cullen G.C
(0542) 40585
The Links, Cullen, Buckie,
Banffshire
W. of Cullen off the A98
(18) 4610 yards/***/E

Deeside G.C
(0224) 867697
Bieldside, Aberdeen
3 miles W. of Aberdeen on
the A93
(18) 6332 yards/***/D/H or
M or L

Duff House Royal G.C
(02612) 2062
Barnyards, Banff,
Banffshire
2 minutes from town cen-
tre off A97 and A98
(18) 6161 yards/***/F/H

Elgin G.C
(0343) 54238
Hardhillock, Elgin,
Morayshire
Signposted off the A91
(18) 6401 yards/***/D

Forres G.C
(0309) 72949
Muiryshade, Forres
1 mile S. from town centre
(18) 5615 yards/***/E/H

Fraserburgh G.C
(0346) 28287
Philorth, Fraserburgh,
Aberdeenshire
1 mile S.E of Fraserburgh on
the A92

(18) 6217 yards/***/E

Garmouth and Kingston
G.C
(034 387) 388
Garmouth, Fochabers,
Moray
(18) 5649 yards/***/E

Hazelhead G.C
(0224) 321830
Hazelhead Park, Aberdeen
4 miles W. of the city centre
(18) 5303 yards/***/E
(18) 5673 yards/***/E

Hopeman G.C
(0343) 830578
Hopeman, Moray
(18) 5439 yards/***/E

Huntly G.C
(0466) 2643
Cooper Park, Huntly,
Aberdeenshire
Half mile from town centre
on the A96
(18) 5399 yards/***(not Wed
or Thur)/F/H

Inverallochy G.C
(03465) 2324
Inverallochy, Nr
Fraserburgh, Aberdeenshire
3 miles S. of Fraserburgh on
the B9033
(18) 5137 yards/***/E

Inverurie G.C
(0467) 24080
Blackhall Road, Inverurie,
Aberdeenshire
On the A96 Aberdeen-
Inverness Road
(18) 5096 yards/***/E

Keith G.C
(05422) 2469
Fife Park, Keith, Banffshire
Half mile off the A96
(18) 5811 yards/***/F

Kings Links G.C
(0224) 632269
Golf Road, Kings Links,
Aberdeen
E. of city, near Pittodrie
Stadium
(18) 5838 metres/***/E

Kintore G.C
(0467) 32631
Balbithan Road, Kintore,
Inverurie, Aberdeenshire
12 miles N.W. of Aberdeen
off the A96
(9) 2650 yards/***/E

Macdonald G.C
(0358) 20576
Hospital Road, Ellon,
Aberdeenshire
Leave Ellon on A948 for
Auchnagatt
(18) 5986 yards/***/E

Moray G.C
(034 381) 2018
Stotfield Road, Lossiemouth,
Moray
6 miles N. of Elgin off the
A941
6643 yards/***/F/H
6005 yards/***/F/H

Murcar G.C
(0224) 704354
Bridge of Don, Aberdeen
3 miles N.E of Aberdeen on
the A92
(18) 6240 yards/**/F

Newburgh-On-Ythan G.C
Newburgh, Aberdeenshire
14 miles N. of Aberdeen on
the Peterhead Road
(9) 6404 yards/***(not Tues
pm)/F

Nigg Bay G.C
(0224) 871286
St Fitticks Road, Balnagask,
Aberdeen
S.E of the city centre
(18) 5984 yards/***/E

Peterhead G.C
(0779) 72149
Craigewan Links, Peterhead,
Aberdeenshire
30 miles from Aberdeen,
between A92 and A975
(18) 6182 yards/***/D
(9) 2950 yards/***/E

Royal Aberdeen G.C
(0224) 702571
Balgownie, Bridge of Don,
Aberdeen
Over River Don, 2 miles N.

of Aberdeen on A92
(18) 4033 yards/**/F/H
(18) 6372 yards/**/F/H

Royal Tarlair G.C
(0261) 32897
Buchan Street, Macduff
48 miles from Aberdeen on
the A98
(18) 5866 yards/***/D

Spey Bay G.C
(0343) 820424
Spey Bay, Fochabers, Moray
Follow the B9104 Spey Bay
road to the coast
(18) 6059 yards/***/F/H

Stonehaven G.C
(0569) 62124
Cowie, Stonehaven
N. of the town on the A92
(18) 5103 yards/***(not
Sat/Sun am)/F

Strathlene G.C
(0542) 31798
Portessie, Buckie, Banffshire
Take A942 to Buckie and to
Strathlene
(18) 6180 yards/***/E

Tarland G.C
(033981) 81413
Tarland, Aboyne,
Aberdeenshire
3 miles W. of Aberdeen on
the A93
(9) 5812 yards/***/E

Torphins G.C
(033982) 493
Golf Road, Torphins,
Banchory, Aberdeenshire
6 miles W. of Banchory on
A980
(9) 2330 yards/***/E

Turriff G.C
(0888) 62745
Rosehall, Turriff,
Aberdeenshire
Signposted off the B9024
(18) 6105 yards/***/E

Westhill G.C
(0224) 740159
Westhill Heights, Westhill,
Skene, Aberdeenshire
6 miles from Aberdeen on
the A944

(18) 5866 yards/***(not
Sat/Sun pm)/E/H

Highland

Abernethy G.C
(0479 82) 637
Nethybridge, Inverness-shire
N. of Nethybridge on the
B970 (9) 2484 yards/***/F

Alness G.C
(0349) 883877
Ardross Road, Alness, Ross-
shire 10 miles N.E. of
Dingwall on the A9
(9) 4718 yards/***/E

Askernish G.C
Askernish, Lochboisdale,
South Uist, Western Isles
Take ferry from Oban to
S.Uist
(9) 5114 yards/***/F

Boat of Garten G.C
(0479 83) 282
Boat of Garten, Inverness-
shire
Take the A9 to the B970
(18) 5720 yards/***/E

Brora G.C
(0408) 21417
Golf Road, Brora, Sutherland
65 miles N. of Inverness on
the A9
(18) 6110 yards/***/F

Carrbridge G.C
(047984) 674
Carrbridge, Inverness-shire
200 yards from the village
on the A938
(9) 2623 yards/***/F

Fort Augustus G.C
(0320) 6460
Markethill, Fort Augustus,
Inverness-shire
Entrance is just off the A82
(9) 5454 yards/***/E

Fortrose and Rosemarkie
G.C
(0381) 20529
Ness Road East, Fortrose,
Ross-shire
Take A9 from Inverness
and follow signs to Fortrose
(18) 5973 yards/***/F

Fort William G.C
(0397) 4464
North Road, Turlundy, Fort
Wiiliam 2 miles N. of Fort
William off the A82
(18) 5686 yards/***/F

Gairloch G.C
(0455) 2407
Gairloch, Ross-shire
S. of the town, on the A832
(9) 2093 yards/***(not Sun)/E

Golspie G.C
(04083) 3266
Ferry Road, Golspie,
Sutherland
Take A9 from Inverness to
Golspie
(18) 5900 yards/***/F

Grantown-On-Spey G.C
(0479) 2079
Golf Course Road,
Grantown-On-Spey
N. of town off the A939
(18) 5745 yards/***/E

Invergordon G.C
(0349) 852116
Cromlet Drive, Invergordon,
Ross and Cromarty
The club house is in King
Geoge Street
(9) 6028 yards/***/E

Inverness G.C
(0463) 239882
Culcabock Road, Inverness
1 mile from town centre on
S. of River Ness
(18) 6226 yards/***/D/H

Kingussie G.C
(054 02) 600
Gynack Road, Kingussie,
Inverness-shire
Take A9 to village and follow signs
(18) 5504 yards/***/E

Lybster G.C
Main Street, Lybster,
Caithness
13 miles S. of Wick on the
A9 (9) 1898 yards/***/E

Muir of Ord G.C
(0463) 870825
Great Northern Road, Muir
of Ord, Ross and Cromarty

12 miles N. of Inverness on
the A862
(18) 5129 yards/***/E

Nairn G.C
(0667) 53208
Seabank Road, Nairn
1 mile N. of the A96, near
Nairn
(18) 6556 yards/***/F/H

Nairn Dunbar G.C
(0667) 52741
Lochloy Road, Nairn
Half mile E. of town on the
A96
(18) 6431 yards/***/D

Newtonmore G.C
(05403) 328
Golf Course Road,
Newtonmore, Inverness-
shire
Near centre of village off
the A9
(18) 5890 yards/***/E

Reay G.C
(084 781) 288
By Thurso, Caithness
11 miles W. of Thurso
towards Bettyhill
(18) 5865 yards/***/E

Royal Dornoch G.C
(0862) 810219
Golf Road, Dornoch,
Sutherland
Take A949 for Dornoch and
follow signs
(18) 6577 yards/***/F/H
(9)***/F

Sconser G.C
(0478) 2277
Sconser, Isle of Skye,
Inverness-shire Between
Broadford and Portree on
the main road
(9) 4796 yards/***/E

Stornoway G.C
(0851) 2240
Castle Grounds, Stornoway,
Isle of Lewis Near town centre, in castle grounds
(18) 5119 yards/***(not
Sun)/E/H

Strathpeffer Spa G.C
(0997) 21219

Strathpeffer, Ross-shire
5 miles W. of Dingwall on
the A834
(18) 4792 yards/***/E

Tain G.C
(0862) 2314
Tain, Ross-shire
Half mile from town
centre off A9 N.
(18) 6222 yards/***/F

Tarbat G.C
(086287) 236
Portmahomack, Ross-shire
7 miles E. of Tain on the
B9165 off A9
(9) 2329 yards***(not Sun)/E

Thurso G.C
(0847) 63807
Newlands of Geise, Thurso,
Caithness
2 miles S.W of Thurso station on B870
(18) 5818 yards/***/E

Torvean G.C
(0463) 237543
Glenurquhart Road,
Inverness, Inverness-shire
1 mile W. of city on the A82
(18) 4308 yards/***/F

Wick G.C (0955) 2726
Reiss, Wick, Caithness
3 miles N. of Wick on the A9
(18) 5976 yards/***/E

Orkney & Shetland

Orkney G.C
(0856) 2457
Grainbank, St Ola, by
Kirkwall, Orkney
Half mile W. of Kirkwall
(18) 5406 yards/***/E

Shetland G.C
(059584) 369
Dale, P.O Box 18, Lerwick,
Shetland
3 miles N. of Lerwick on the
main road
(18) 5776 yards/***/F

Stromness G.C
(0856) 850772
Ness, Stromness, Orkney
(18) 4600 yards/***/E

It is no secret that Northern Ireland has experienced a turbulent history; what is less widely known, however, is that it is a stunningly beautiful place. It is a land of forests and lakes, of mountains and glens. It boasts some of the most spectacular coastal scenery in the British Isles and where else can you view the handiwork of a giant? So much in a country no larger than Yorkshire.

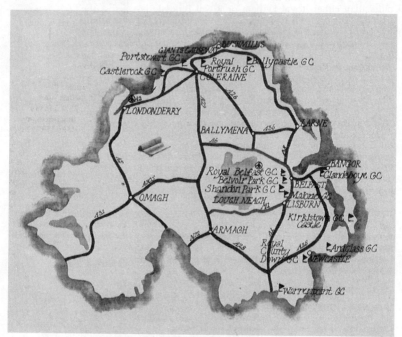

The quality of golf is equally outstanding. There are approximately sixty courses in all, a large number of which are to be found close to the aforementioned coast enjoying some quite splendid isolation. Belfast, which is about the size of Bristol, has no shortage of good courses, and not just parkland types either, and then, of course, there are the two jewels in the crown—Portrush and Newcastle, or if you prefer, **Royal Portrush** and **Royal County Down**.

Belfast and County Down

Belfast is a likely starting point and getting there should be fairly straightforward. Approaching from Dublin it is a case of following the N1 and the A1, while from Britain car ferries run regularly from

Stranraer and travelling by air is even simpler should you be thinking of hiring a car when you arrive.

Resist at all costs the temptation to zoom off northwards to Portrush or southwards to Newcastle; Belfast offers much more than you probably imagine. The best known golf course immediately at hand is the appropriately named **Royal Belfast**. It is situated just outside the city on the north coast alongside Belfast Lough and is a classic example of well-manicured parkland golf. A number of holes here are very scenic, particularly around the turn and there is considerable challenge to combine with the charm. Royal Belfast is the oldest Golf Club in Ireland having been founded in 1881. It is therefore older than either Royal Lytham or Royal Birkdale just across the Irish Sea. The course is understandably very popular but with a little forward planning the visitor should be able to arrange a game. The Clubhouse by the way is a magnificent 19th century building.

Remaining in Belfast, **Malone** Golf Club at Dunmurry is one of the leading inland courses in all Ireland—a visit is therefore strongly recommended—and two 'Parks' are also decidedly worth inspecting. The first is Belvoir (pronounce it Beever) and the second is Shandon. Belvoir **Park** lies about five miles south of the city centre, **Shandon Park** just to the north; both are Championship courses. The former is definitely the pick of the two with its magnificent tree-lined fairways, however Shandon has the advantage of offering some interesting views over historical Stormont. **Clandeboye** Golf Club, not too far from Royal Belfast along the Bangor Road offers a different test of golf. Clandeboye is more wooded and 'heathy' with a considerable splash of gorse. There are two courses; the more difficult Dufferin and the Ava. Both are attractive and on the Dufferin course some very precise shots are called for.

To the south of Newtownards, **Scrabo** Golf Club is worth an inspection—its opening hole is reckoned to be the toughest in Ireland—and circling back towards Belfast, **Lisburn** is almost in the same league as Malone and Belvoir Park.

The next golf course to play is **Kirkistown Castle**. It lies near the foot of the Ards Peninsula (once described somewhat alarmingly as the proboscis of Ulster!) Kirkistown is a real old-fashioned gem. James Braid assisted in the design of the course and is reputed to have commented wistfully 'If only I had this within 50 miles of London'.

If you're not in a rush it is worth spending some time on the Ards Peninsula. It is a remote and very beautiful corner of Ireland and Lough Strangford is one giant bird sanctuary and wild life reserve. From Portaferry, a ferry can be taken to Strangford and from here a short drive will take you to **Ardglass** on the coast. Perched on craggy rocks the layout here is reminiscent of some of the better seaside courses in Cornwall.

Beyond St John's Point and around Dundrum Bay, a journey of approximately twelve miles lies Newcastle, an attractive seaside town and where, as the famous song tells you, 'the mountains O'Mourne sweep down to the sea'. For golfers it is a paradise. **Royal County Down** Golf Club is quite simply one of the greatest courses in the world. If one is staying in the area some sight seeing is strongly advised. To the south and west the mountain scenery is quite magnificent while the southern coastal road takes in some very different but beautiful views. It is an area where smuggling was once notorious and before reaching the border we recommend that you smuggle in a quick 18 holes at **Warrenpoint**, where Ronan Rafferty learnt to play.

The Causeway Coast

Our journey now takes us back northwards, past Belfast to the Antrim coast. Here there is perhaps the most spectacular scenery of all and, equally important, yet more glorious golf

Now, what kind of being can pick thorns out of his heels whilst running and can rip up a vast chunk of rock and hurl it fifty miles into the sea? Who on earth could perform such staggering feats? The answer is Finn McCool (who, alas is not eligible for Ryder Cup selection). Finn was the great Warrior Giant who commanded the armies of the King of all Ireland. He inhabited an Antrim headland, probably not far from Portrush in fact. Having fallen madly in love with a lady giant who lived on the Hebridian Island of Staffa, Finn began building a giant bridge to bring her across the water. Either Finn grew fickle or the lady blew him out but the bridge was never completed; still the Giants Causeway remains a great monument to one Finn McCool.

Royal Portrush is a monument to the Royal and Ancient game. However, don't limit your golf to Portrush, there are three other superb eighteen hole courses nearby. To the east of Portrush, **Ballycastle** has an attractive situation overlooking an inviting stretch of sand and, if it didn't look so cold, the sea would be equally inviting. It is nothing like as tough as Portrush, more of a holiday course really, but tremendously enjoyable all the same.

Four miles west of Portrush and further along the coast is the fishing town of **Portstewart**. It has another very fine golf course.

One final course remains to be played on this splendid Causeway coast and that is **Castlerock**, just a few miles across the River Bann from Portstewart. Once again it is a classic links set amid towering sand dunes and a game here will test every department of your game!

There are many golfing delights in Northern Ireland that we have not explored, however should Castlerock be your last port of call you'll have no excuses for not leaving Ireland a very contented soul. What's more, if this has been a first visit to the country you'll probably have a very different view of the place from the one you had when you arrived. This really is a charming land.

Co Antrim

Ballycastle G.C
(02657) 62536
Cushendall Road,
Ballycastle
40 miles W. of Larne on the
A2
(18) 5882 yards/***/D/H

Ballyclare G.C
(09603) 22696
25 Springvale Road,
Ballyclare
Travel N. from Belfast to
A8
for Ballyclare
(18) 5840 yards/**(not
Thur)/E/H

Ballymena G.C
(0266) 861207
128 Raceview Road,
Broughshane, Ballymena
2 miles E. of town on the
A42
(18) 5168 yards/***/E/H

Bushfoot G.C
(02657) 31317
50 Bushfoot Road,
Portballintrae, Bushmills
Take A2 from Portrush to
Bushmills
(9) 5572 yards/***/E(D at
weekends)/H

Cairndhu G.C
(0574) 83324
192 Coast Road, Ballygally,
Larne
4 miles N. of Larne on the
A7
(18) 6112 yards/***(not
Sat)/F

Carrickfergus G.C
(09603) 62203
North Road, Carrickfergus
9 miles N. of Belfast on the
A2
(18) 5752 yards/***(not
Sat)/D/H

Cushendall G.C
(02667) 71318
Shore Road, Cushendall,
Ballymena
<25 miles N. of Larne on the
A2

(9) 4678 yards/***/E

Dunmurry G.C
(0232) 610834
91 Dunmurry Lane, Belfast
S.W from Belfast to Upper
Malone Road
(18) 5832 yards/**(not
Tues/Thurs pm)/D/H

Greenisland G.C
(0232) 862236
156 Upper Road,
Greenisland, Carrickfergus,
Belfast
9 miles N. of Belfast on the
A2
(9) 5887 yards/***(not
Sat)/E

Larne G.C
(09603) 82228
54 Ferris Bay Road,
Islandmagee, Larne
Cross to Isle of Magee at
Whitehaven off A2
(9) 6082 yards/***(not
Sat)/E/H

Lisburn G.C
(0846) 677216
68 Eglantine Road, Lisburn
3 miles S of Lisburn on the
A1
(18) 5708 yards/***/D

Masserene G.C
(08494) 28096
51 Lough Road, Antrim
1 mile S. of Antrim,
towards airport
(18) 6614 yards/***(not
Sat)/F

Royal Portrush G.C
(0265) 822314
Bushmills Road, Portrush
1 mile E. of Portrush on the
A2
(18) 6273 yards/***/C/H
(18) 6784 yards/***/C/H

Whitehead G.C
(09603) 53631
McCraes Brae, Whitehead
Leave Belfast by A2 to
Whitehead and follow
signs
(18) 6426 yards/***(not
Sat)/E

Co Armagh

Ashfield G.C.
(0693) 861315
Freeduff, Cullyhana
(18) 5645 yards/***/E

County Armagh G.C
(0861) 522501
Newry Rd, Armagh
1 mile from Armagh,
towards Newry
(18) 6184 yards/***/E

Craigavon Golf & Ski
Centre
(0762) 6606
Silverwood, Lurgan
2 miles from Belfast off M1
(18) 6496 yards/***/E

Lurgan G.C
(0762) 322087
Lurgan
Beside Lake Lurgan
(18) 6380 yards/***/B

Portadown G.C
(0762) 335356
Carrickblacker, Portadown
2 miles S of Portadown
(18) 6119
yards/***(Tues,Sat)/D

Trandragee G.C
(0762) 840727
Trandragee, Craigavon
5m from Portadown
towards Newry
(18) 6084 yards/**/F

Belfast

Balmoral G.C
(0232) 381514
Lisburn Rd, Belfast
2 mile S of Belfast
(18) 6250 yards/***(Sat)/D

Belvoir Park G.C
(0232) 646714
Newtownbreda, Belfast
3 miles outside Belfast
(18) 6476 yards/***(Sat)C

Cliftonville G.C
(0232) 744158
Westland Rd, Belfast
2 mile from Belfast
towards Antrim
(9) 6240 yards/***(Sat)/D

Fortwilliam G.C
(0232) 370770
Downview Ave, Belfast
3 miles N of Belfast
(18) 5642 yards/***(Sat)/D

The Knock G.C
(0232) 483251
Summerfield, Dundonald
4 miles E of Belfast
(18) 6292 metres/***(Sat)/D

Malone G.C
(0232) 612578
Upper Malone Rd,
Dunmurry
4 miles from Belfast
(18) 6433
yards/***(Sat)Wedpm/F

Ormeau G.C
(0232) 641069
Ravenhill Road, Belfast
2 miles SE of Belfast
(9) 5306 yards/**/F

Shandon Park G.C
(0232) 794856
Shandon Park, Belfast
3 miles from Belfast
towards Knock
(18) 6252 yards/***/C

Co Down

Ardglass G.C
(0396) 841219
Castle Place, Ardglass
7 miles S of Downpatrick
(18) 6000 yards/***/D

Banbridge G.C
(08206) 22342
Huntly Rd, Banbridge
(18) 5879 yards/***/E

Bangor G.C
(0247) 270922
Broadway, Bangor
(18) 6450 yards/**/C

Bright Castle G.C
(0396) 841319
Bright, Downpatrick
(18)7000 yards/***/E

Carnalea G.C
(0247) 270368
Carnalea
2 miles from Bangor
(18) 5513 yards/***/D

Clandeboye G.C
(0247) 271767
Conlig, Newtownards
Off A21 to Bangor
(18) 6650 yards/***(Sat)/B
(18) 5634 yards/***(Sat)/B

Donaghadee G.C
(0237) 883624
Warren Road, Donaghadee
6 miles from Bangor
(18) 6099 yards/***(Sat)/F

Downpatrick G.C
(0396) 612152
Saul Rd, DownpatrickNr A7
(18) 6196 yards/***/B

Helens Bay G.C
(0247) 852601
Helens Bay, Bangor
Off A2 E of Belfast
(9) 5638 yards/***(Sat)/F

Holywood G.C
(02317) 3135
Nuns Walk, Demense Rd,
Holywood
6 miles E of Belfast
(18) 5885 yards/***(Sat)/D

Kilkeel G.C
(069) 3762296
Mourne Park, Ballyardle
3 miles S of Kilkeel
(9) 5623
metres/***(Tues,Sat)/E

Kirkistown Castle G.C
(02477) 71233
Cloughey, Newtownards
(18) 6157 yards/***/F

Mahee Island G.C
(0238) 541234
Comber
Mahee Island
(9) 5580 yards/***/D

Royal Belfast G.C
(03967) 23314
Holywood, Craigavad
(18) 6205 yards/***/C

Royal County Down G.C
(039) 6723314
Newcastle
(18) 6968 yards/A/Winter B
(18) 4100 yards/A/Winter B

Scrabo G.C
(0247) 812355
Scrabo Road, Newtownards
(18) 6000 yards/**(Wed)/D

The Spa G.C
(0238) 562365
Grove Rd, Ballynahinch
(9) 5770 yards/***(Sun)/E

Warrenpoint G.C
(069) 3772219
Lower Dromore Rd,
Warrenpoint
5 miles S of Newry
(18) 6215
yards/***(Sun,Wed)/D

Co Fermanagh

Enniskillen G.C
(0265) 848314
Enniskillen
1 miles NE of Enniskillen
(18) 5476 yards/***/D

Co Londonderry

Castlerock G.C
(0265) 848314
Circular Rd, Castlerock
5 miles from Craigavern
Bridge
(18) 6362 yards/**/F
(9) 4708 yards/**/F

City of Derry G.C
(0504) 46369
Prehan, Londonderry
(18) 6450 yards/***/D

Moyola Park G.C
(0648) 68392
Shanemullagh,
Castledawson
(18) 6517 yards/***/D

Portstewart G.C
(0265) 832015
Strand Rd, Portstewart
5 miles W of Portrush
(18) 6800 yards
(18)+(9)***/C/***/E

Cao Tyrone

Dungannon G.C
(08687) 22098
Mullaghmore, Dungannon
1 mile outside Dungannon
(18) 5914 yards/***/D

Fintona G.C
(0662) 841480
Fintona
10 miles S of Omagh
(9) 6250 yards/***/D

Killymoon G.C
(06487) 62254
Killymoon, Cookstown
(18) 6000 yards/***(Sat)/D

Newtownstewart G.C
(06626) 61466
Golf Course Rd,
Newtownstewart
(18) 6100 yards/***/D

Omagh G.C
(0662) 3160
Dublin Rd, Omagh
(18) 5800/***/E

Strabane G.C
(0504) 882271
Ballycolman, Strabane
(18) 6100 yards/***/F

KEY

*** Visitors welcome at all times
** Visitors on weekdays only
* No visitors at any time
(Mon, Wed) No visitors on
specified days

GREEN FEES PER ROUND
A - £30 plus
B - £20 - £30
C - £15 - £25
D - £10 - £20
E - Under £10
F - Green fees on application

RESTRICTIONS
G - Guests only
H - Handicap certificate required
H(24) - Handicap of 24 or less
required
L - Letter of introduction required
M - Visitor must be a member of
another recognised club.

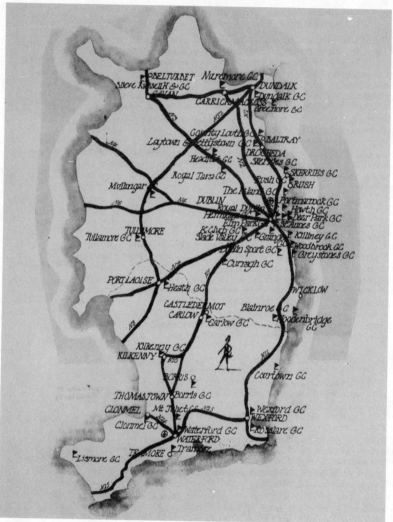

Ireland

Dublin & the North East

From the time you arrive in Ireland and crack your first drive straight down the middle, to the time you leave, having holed that tricky putt on the final green (and then drained your last drop of Guinness at the 19th), you cannot fail to be impressed by the natural charm and helpfulness of the Irish people. Nowhere is it more immediately apparent than in Dublin—what a contrast to many of the world's capital cities! Nothing seems rushed and nothing seems too much trouble. You see, the welcome from these folk is quite simply second to none.

You may have come by rail and sea, car and car ferry or you may have flown—whichever way you'll be itching to play some golf. In Dublin, as indeed throughout Ireland, the only real problem is deciding where to start.

Dublin

Within ten miles of the city centre there are two great championship links and at least twenty other courses, the majority of which are of a very high standard. **Portmarnock** is the most celebrated, and indeed is one of the great golf links of the world. **Royal Dublin** is said to be the only Championship course located within the boundaries of a capital city. It lies just to the north of Dublin's centre on Bull Island in the charmingly named area of Dollymount. It is generally considered less severe than Portmarnock, (although the winds are equally fierce) it is not as long and the rough isn't quite so punishing. It makes an ideal place for us to crack that first one straight down the middle.

The two best known holes on the course are probably the 5th and the 18th. The former is one of the most intimidating holes to be found anywhere. There is a story that when Danny Kaye visited the course he took one look at the 5th and turned to his caddy to ask for a rifle! The 18th is a shortish par five, reachable with two good hits but only if the second is carried over a dog-leg out of bounds—an all or nothing finish. The Irish Open Championship has been played here on a number of occasions. In 1966 Christy O'Connor came to the 16th needing three birdies to tie Eric Brown—he finished eagle-birdie-eagle! Another memorable finish occurred in 1985 when Seve Ballesteros defeated Bernhard Langer in a thrilling play-off to win his second Irish title.

Portmarnock lies to the north of Royal Dublin, and a short distance to the north of Portmarnock on a tiny peninsula is **The Island** golf links. Until the mid 1970s the course could only be reached by rowing boat from the village of Malahide and the fare paid was included within the green fee. It is a delightful, often spectacular, very old-fashioned type of course, not overly long but deceptively tough with a number of semi-blind holes—something of an Irish Prestwick perhaps.

Not too far from Malahide (and close to Dublin Airport) is the impressive **St Margaret's** Golf & Country Club.

If most of the celebrated golf courses are found to the north of Dublin there are many more to the south and west of the capital, indeed, the city is practically encircled by golf courses—what a marvellous prospect! Noted 18 hole courses worthy of mention here include; **Hermitage, Howth, Deer Park, The Grange** and **Slade Valley**; while a good 9 hole course not far from Dun Laoghaire is found at **Killiney**. Without question the most talked about course in the Dublin area is the new Palmer-designed course at the **Kildare Country Club** at Straffan.

The leading club to the south of Dublin is **Woodbrook**. It too has played host to the Irish Open, in addition to many other important tournaments. Woodbrook offers a mixture of semi-links and parkland golf and although not the most challenging of courses is always immaculately kept. At Brittas Bay, Pat Ruddy's dramatic new links course **The European Club** has very recently opened. A few miles further down the coast is the pleasant course at **Greystones**, from the back nine of which there are some marvellous views of the Wicklow Mountains, and a nearby new 18 hole golf and hotel complex, the attractively priced **Charlesland** Golf and Country Club Hotel —more great views. Near the town of Wicklow, **Blainroe** Golf Club has a much improved—and pretty demanding—championship length layout. Finally there is a very scenic 9 hole course at **Woodenbridge**; it's a bit of a drive from Dublin, but well worth it.

North of Dublin

Thirty miles north of Dublin in the charming village of Baltray near Drogheda is the **County Louth** Golf Club. In the opinion of many this is the most attractive links on the east coast. **Baltray**, as the course is known, enjoys a wonderfully remote setting, but while it may be a peaceful place the course will test your game to the full. The **Laytown and Bettystown** links which while not in the same class as Baltray certainly poses enough problems. It is the home club of the former Ryder Cup player Des Smyth.

Further north the course at **Dundalk** deserves inspection. Again it's not in the same league as Baltray, but then very few are. Still, it's definitely worth visiting if only for the tremendous scenery it offers. Although very much a parkland type challenge, the course is set out alongside the shores of Dundalk Bay with the Mountains of Mourne and the Cooley Mountains providing a spectacular backdrop.

Dundalk in fact provides a fine base for playing our final recommendation in the north east, the course at **Greenore** where a more dramatic location couldn't be wished for. Laid out alongside Carlingford Lough, Greenore golfers have recently built three new holes which are destined to be the envy of every golf course in Ireland. You don't believe it? Then go and visit, you'll be made most welcome!

Travelling Inland

For those who enjoy horseracing as well as golf (this must include near enough every Irishman), a good route to take out of Dublin is the N7. Given a clear road The Curragh is little more than half an hour's drive away. This is the Epsom of Ireland. Golf has been played on the great stretch of heathland since the 1850s and the Curragh Golf Club was founded in 1883 making it the oldest Golf Club in the Republic. Rather like England's senior links, Westward Ho!, the fairways are shared with the local farmer's sheep. There's also a nearby army range—one presumes golf is rarely uneventful at the Curragh! It's actually a very good course and the green fees are typically modest.

Venturing further inland, **Mullingar** in County Westmeath has long rivalled Carlow as Ireland's top inland course; and is considered a veritable paradise by those who know about these things. **Headfort** near Kells, and **Royal Tara** at Navan, both in County Meath are two more of the region's better parkland courses, and in County Offaly, **Tullamore** is of a similar nature although it perhaps has a little more variety. All three enjoy delightful locations and welcome visitors at most times.

Finally, two hotel golf courses that are not exactly close to Dublin, but decidedly worth inspecting nonetheless are at the **Nuremore** Hotell near Carrickmacross, in Co. Monaghan and one of Ireland's newest gems, the spectacular **Slieve Russell** Hotel course at Ballyconnell in Co. Cavan.

South East Ireland

Continuing to wander down through the counties of Ireland, County Laois is the next we come across. There's only one eighteen hole course, **The Heath** and no guesses as to the type of golf offered. The course is laid out on common land and rather like The Curragh, there's a fair chance that you'll spot more sheep than golfers. Stumbling into County Carlow we find probably the best inland course (aside from the new Mt. Juliet) in south east Ireland. **Carlow** is a superb course; well-bunkered and well-wooded, it presents a considerable test of golf but a very fair one nonetheless.. There are a number of convenient hotels in Carlow itself but for a real treat stay in Castledermot at **Kilkea Castle** , a splendidly converted 12th century castle. Kilkea has its own turf nursery and there are firm plans to build an 18 hole golf course in the grounds.

Kilkenny is one of those places that has to be visited. It's a town steeped in Irish history. In medieval times it housed the Irish Parliament, then there's the famous Kilkenny Castle, an impressive collection of churches and Kytelers Inn. The city's golf course is a bit of a youngster in comparison, but it's a fine parkland course, very typical of Ireland's better inland courses. Nearby, Thomastown is the setting for the magnificent new **Mt. Juliet** complex (056) 24455, featuring 18 spectacular holes designed by Jack Nicklaus, and a luxurious Country House Hotel

From Kilkenny it's a pleasant drive to **Borris** where there is an excellent 9 holer and it's certainly not a long way to Tipperary either. Visitors to the county with the famous name should slip a game in at **Clonmel**. This is a fairly isolated part of Ireland and you may just have the course to yourself on a quiet weekday. Before heading down to the Waterford area a quick recommendation for the 18 hole course at **Courtown**, close to the north Wexford coast which boasts some fabulous beaches—in fact the golden sands stretch practically all the way south to Wexford town.

Waterford is our penultimate destination. The world famous Waterford Crystal factory is reason enough for stopping a while in this part of Ireland, but there are other sound reasons too. The first is **Waterford Castle**, the kind of place you dream about: an ivy-clad 12th century castle dominating a small island which can only be reached by ferry. The course, designed by Ryder Cup golfer Des Smyth, opened in the summer of 1992. The other good reasons for visiting Waterford are **Tramore** Golf Club and **Waterford** Golf Club—both offer very good parkland golf. The former, just 15 minutes from Waterford, is a real test and is good enough to have staged the Irish Amateur Championship in 1987, the latter, however, is possibly more enjoyable having greater variety; especially on the back nine which features a magnificent downhill finishing hole: if ever there was a hole that tempted the golfer to open his shoulders and let rip, this is it—a good drive will run forever, a bad drive—well... Anyway, read on as the course is described in greater detail on a later page.

We end our journey at **Rosslare** in the far south east corner of the country. Having started on a heath, we end on a links; Rosslare may not have the glamour of a Portmarnock or a Royal Dublin but for lovers of the traditional game—rolling sand dunes and a hammering wind—it will do perfectly.

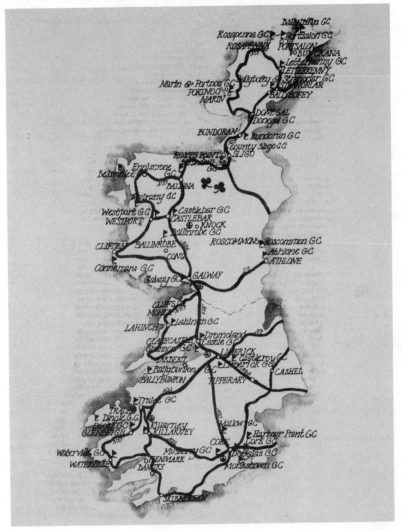

Ballyliffin GC
Rosapenna GC ▸ Portsalon GC
ROSAPENNA   PORTSALON
                    ▸ BUNCRANA
                  Letterkenny GC
                  LETTERKENNY
Ballybofey &   Stranorlar GC
Narin & Portnoo GC   STRANORLAR
POKINOO   BALLYBOFEY
NARIN
              DONEGAL
              Donegal GC

      BUNDORAN ▸ Bundoran GC
              County Sligo GC
      ROSSES POINT   SLIGO

Belmullet ▸ Enniscrone GC
              BALINA
Ballyarny   GC

Westport GC ▸ Castlebar GC
WESTPORT   CASTLEBAR
                KNOCK
              ▸ Ballinrobe GC

CLIFDEN BALLINROBE   ROSCOMMONS ▸ Roscommon GC
                              Athlone GC
Connemara GC   CONG   ▸ ATHLONE

          Galway GC GALWAY

          CLIFFS OF
          MOHER
          ▸ Lahinch GC
LAHINCH
          CLARECASTLE ▸ Dromoland
          Shannon GC   Castle GC
          GC   LIMERICK
          ▸ARDERT   Castletroy GC
          ▸ Ballybunion GC Limerick GC ▸ CASHEL
          BALLYBUNION
                    TIPPERARY

          ▸ Tralee GC
      TRALEE
    Dingle GC   Mallow GC
  Dooks GC ▸ Killarney   ▸ Harbour Point GC
  GLENBEIGH KILLARNEY   Cork GC
                    Muskerry   ▸ CORK
Waterville GC   GC   ▸ Douglas GC
WATERVILLE ▸ KENMARE   Monkstown GC
        BANTRY

          SKIBBEREEN

Without any shadow of doubt some of the greatest golf courses in the world are to be found in the south west of Ireland. But as any Irishman worth his Guinness will tell you, great golf in the west of Ireland certainly isn't confined to the south western corner—it starts from County Donegal downwards. Apart from its magnificent golf, the south west is renowned for its beautiful scenery: majestic Killarney, the glorious Ring of Kerry and the Dingle Peninsula; stunning for sure but further north can be equally spectacular. This is what W.M. Thackeray had to say of the area around Westport: 'It forms an event in one's life to have seen the place, so beautiful is it, and so unlike all other beauties that I know of'. Clearly inspired, he continued: 'But the Bay—and the Reek which sweeps down to the sea—and a hundred islands in it, were dressed up in gold and purple and crimson, with the whole cloudy West in a flame'. Marvellous! And have you ever been to Connemara?

Donegal
And have you ever been to Donegal! I don't suppose many golfers are likely to begin a tour in the very far north and head all the way downwards but we shall have a go all the same. (It is possible I suppose if one were approaching from the Causeway Coast?) Let us start at **Ballyliffin** on the very northern tip of Donegal, not far from Malin Head.

Rosapenna is our next port of call. Like Ballyliffin it is somewhat isolated, but a fine eighteen hole course nonetheless. It was laid out in 1893 by Old Tom Morris and is part-links, part-inland in nature, although I understand that 9 new 'links holes' are presently being constructed. There are said to be more rabbits on this course than on any other—not a description of the members I might add! The place has a bleak beauty and the coast is very dramatic—note the spectacular nearby Atlantic Drive. Not far from Rosapenna there is a magnificently situated course at **Portsalon** and another delightfully old fashioned links at **Nairn and Portnoo**. Further inland, 18 holes can be played at **Letterkenny** and again at **Ballybofey & Stranorlar**.

Donegal town, famed for its tweeds and woollens, has one of the longest courses in Ireland measuring 7,200 yards (try playing it in a fierce wind!) The course is actually outside of the county town at **Murvagh**. and truly great course it is page. A little south of Rossnowlagh is **Bundoran**, another tough, though fairly open links.

The West Coast Four- and more

Our next visit is a more established favourite. **County Sligo**, or **Rosses Point** as it is commonly known, is rated among the top ten courses in Ireland and is the home of the prestigious West of Ireland Amateur Championship. Laid out right alongside the Atlantic coast it is a true links and can be greatly affected by the elements. This great course is tackled ahead. County Sligo and surrounds is another charming area of Ireland; it is the country of W.B. Yeats and the landscape is dominated by the formidable Ben Bulben mountain. Rosses Point is marketed alongside Enniscrone, Westport and Connemara as one of the 'West Coast Four' but there are many other fine golfing challenges in this part of Ireland and a recommended neighbour of Rosses Point is the links at **Strandhill**, adjacent to County Sligo airport. Furthermore, at **Belmulett** in the far northwest of Co.Mayo, a magnificent links course is being constructed at Carne Beach amid Ballybunion-like sand dunes!

Perhaps the most underrated of the West Coast four is the delightful links at **Enniscrone**, laid out on the shores of Killala Bay; it is, to quote Peter Dobereiner, 'an undiscovered gem of a links.' A short drive from Ballina and we reach **Westport**, Thackeray's paradise. The town nestles in the shadows of the massive Croagh Patrick mountain. It was on its peak that St. Patrick is said to have fasted and prayed for 40 days. The golf course (from which there are many marvellous views of Croagh Patrick) is another on the grand scale—7,000 yards when fully stretched. It's a relatively new course having been designed by Fred Hawtree in 1973. Although some holes run spectacularly along the shoreline, (note particularly the superb par five 15th which curves around Clew Bay) Westport is most definitely a parkland type course and is a very friendly Club. The Irish Amateur Championship has been played here twice in recent years.

Connemara is located about thirty miles south of Westport amid very rugged country. It is a wild, remote and incredibly beautiful part of the world. The course must be one of the toughest links that one is ever likely to meet; we visit it a few pages on.

Finally, we reach Galway—a fascinating and lively city. Golfwise, there is the very established **Galway** Golf Club, at Salthill, and the very new **Galway Bay** Golf and Country Club near Oranmore, the acclaimed creation of Christy O'Connor Jnr.

We begin our brief tour of south west Ireland in County Clare where **Lahinch** The St Andrews of Ireland is found, as we;; as the true golf connoisseur who may well select Dromoland Castle as a base. This hotel has recently upgraded a 18 hole course of distinction.

Kerry's Gold

If we have crossed the Shannon via the Tarbert Ferry, **Ballybunion** is the first great Club we come across in County Kerry. Like **Lahinch, Dromoland, Killarney, Waterville** and **Tralee** it's featured ahead. **Killarney** though provides a more central base and as an enormously popular tourist destination has numerous hotels and guesthouses. **Tralee** is about 20 miles north west of Killarney. The links is actually some eight miles from the town itself; the journey takes a little longer than you expect but no golfer in the world could be disappointed when he reaches this course.

There are very reasonable 18 hole courses at **Dingle** (Ballyferiter) and **Dooks** but **Waterville** is the other great course in County Kerry. Waterville is one of the longest courses in Europe, when played from the back tees. It has its charm as well though and it has been described as 'the beautiful monster'.

Cork

Coming down from rather dizzy heights, County Cork deserves a brief inspection. In the city itself, the **Cork** Golf Club at Little Island is decidedly worth a visit. Approximately five miles east of the town centre the course overlooks Cork Harbour and is one of the top ten inland courses in Ireland. It was at Little Island that one of Ireland's legendary golfers Jimmy Bruen learnt to play. Other golfing challenges near to Ireland's second city include **Muskerry, Monkstown, Harbour Point** and **Douglas,** plus a very fine new 18 hole course, **Lee Valley,** which opened in July 1993.

Not far away at **Mallow** we reach the end of this extraordinary (not to say exhausting!) golfing tour and the order of the day is an enjoyable round of golf. As everybody knows, Ireland is the land of 40 shades of green—after such a trip I think we are in need of 40 winks, and we'll certainly get them here.

Ballybunion is a place of true pilgrimage; two of the greatest golf courses in the world lying side by side. The Old Course at Ballybunion has long been regarded as the ultimate test in links golf. It has a very wild beauty; no course could be closer to the sea and a number of the holes run right along the cliff edges. It's incredibly spectacular stuff and when the wind lashes in from the Atlantic, it is not a place for faint hearts.

What then of the New Course, constructed in the mid 1980s? Architect Robert Trent Jones had this to say: 'When I first saw the piece of land chosen for the new course at Ballybunion, I was thrilled beyond words. I said it was the finest piece of linksland I had ever seen. I feel totally confident that everyone who comes to play at Ballybunion will be as thrilled as I was by the unique majesty of this truly unforgettable course'.

Happily, Ballybunion isn't jealous of its treasures and visitors are always made to feel welcome. The **Golf Manager** at Ballybunion is **Jim Mckenna**. He can be contacted by telephone on **(068) 27146** or from the U.K. on **(01035368) 27146**. The **professional** at Ballybunion, **Brian Callaghan**, can also be reached on the above number. A full day's green fee in 1993 was priced at £25 for members of other Irish golf clubs or £40 if not. This entitles the visitor to a round over both the Old and New—not of course compulsory, but if the body can take it, and it's likely to receive a fair battering en route, it would be a tragedy not to play the pair. A single round over the Old Course was priced at £30 in 1993 with £20 payable for 18 holes on the New.

The nearest airports to Ballybunion are at Shannon, a distance of approximately sixty miles to the north east, and the new Kerry Airport at Farranfore, some thirty miles due south. Cork's airport is about eighty miles to the south east. From either Cork or Shannon the journey can take about an hour and a half but there cannot be a soul on earth who didn't enjoy a trek through the south west of Ireland. From Shannon, travel via Limerick and from Cork via Mallow and Listowel; from Ballybunion town the course is about a mile's drive along the coast.

There is certainly no shortage of land at Ballybunion and both courses can be stretched to 7,000 yards—an alarming prospect! From the medal tees the two are of fairly similar length, the Old measuring 6503 yards, par 71, the New, 6477 yards, par 72. But don't be fooled by the scorecard, each is a monster when the mood takes it.

Old Course

Hole	Yards	Par	Hole	Yards	Par
1	377	4	10	356	4
2	434	4	11	443	4
3	217	3	12	185	3
4	504	5	13	485	5
5	508	5	14	136	3
6	364	4	15	228	3
7	417	4	16	483	5
8	151	3	17	379	4
9	455	4	18	381	4
Out	3,427	36	In	3,076	35
			Out	3,427	36
			Totals	6,503	71

West Ireland
Co Clare

Dromoland Castle G.C
(061) 368444
Newmarket on Fergus
E. of Ennis on the N18
towards Shannon
(18) 6300 yards/***/D

Ennis G.C
(065) 24074
Drumbiggle, Ennis
1 mile W. of Ennis
(18) 5890 yards/***(not
Sun)/D

Kilkee G.C
(048) 341
East End, Kilkee
Just out of Kilkee
on Georges Head
(9) 6185 yards/***/D

Kilrush G.C
(065) 51138
Parknamoney, Kilrush
N.E of town on the R483
(9) 2739 yards/***/E

Lahinch G.C
(065) 81003
Lahinch
Take the R85 from Ennis
(18) 6702 yards/***/C
(18) 5265 yards/***/D
(C at weekends)

Shannon G.C
(061) 61020
Shannon airport, Shannon
N. of Limerick on the N18
(18) 6854 yards/**/D

Spanish Point G.C
(065) 84198
Spanish Point, Miltown
Malbay
2 miles from Mitown
Malbay, near power station
(9) 6171 metres/**/E/H

Co Cork

Bandon G.C
(023) 4111
Castlebernard, Bandon
Through Bandon
on the river side

(18) 5496 yards/***/E

Bantry Park G.C
(027) 50579
Donemark, Bantry
Outside Bantry near the
Reendonegan lake
(9) ***/E

Cork G.C
(021) 353451
Little Island
Take N25 E. from Cork,
then the R623
(18) 6635 yards/**(not
Thurs)/D

Charleville G.C
(063) 81257
Ardmore, Charleville
25 miles S. of Limerick on
the N20
(18) 6380 yards/**/E

Cobh G.C
(021) 812399
Ballywilliam, Cobh
15 miles from Cork on the
N25 and R625 to Cobh
(9) 4338 yards/***
(not weekends am)E

Doneraile G.C
(022) 24137
Doneraile
Take the V R522 to
Doneraile,
off the N20 from Cork
(9) 5528 yards/***/E

Douglas G.C
(021) 895297
Marylborough Hill, Douglas
Half mile from the bridge
at Douglas on the R609
(18) 6179 yards/**/D

Dunmore G.C
(023) 33352
Clonakilty
S. of the town on the headland
of Duneen Bay
(9) 4464 yards/***/E

East Cork G.C
(021) 631687
Goatacrue, Midleton
Take N25 E. out of Cork,

left at roundabout
(18) 5207 yards/**/F/H

Fermoy G.C
(025) 31472
2 miles N. of town
off the N8
(18) 5550 yards//**
(not Mon/Wed pm)/E

Glengarriff G.C
(027) 63150
Glengarriff
Take N71 S. from Kilarney
to
harbour area
(9) 4328 yards/***/E

Kanturk G.C
(029) 50534
Fairy Hill, Kanturk
On the N579 Cork-Kanturk
road
(9) 5527 yards/***/E

Kinsale G.C
(021) 772197
Ringenane, Belgooly
8 miles S. of Cork on the
R600
(9) 5332 yards/**/E

Macroom G.C
(022) 41272
Lackaduve, Macroom
W from Cork on the N22
(9) 5439 yards/***/E

Mallow G.C
(022) 21145
Ballyellis, Mallow
E. of the town
at the Mallow Bridge
(18) 6559 yards/**(not
Tues)/F

Mahon G.C
(021) 362480
Cloverhill, Blackrock
Left off the R609 Douglas
road
(18) 4818 yards/***/E

Mitchelstown G.C
(025) 24072
Mitchelstown
At junction of N8 and
N73, N. of Cork
(9) 5057 yards/***/E

Monkstown G.C
(021) 841225
Parkgariffe, Monkstown
S. of Cork on the R610
(18) 6170 yards/**(not
Tues/Wed)/D

Muskerry G.C
(021) 385104
Carrigrohane
W. out of Cork on R617 to
Blarney village
(18) 5786 yards/**(not
Wed/Thurs)/D

Skibbereen G.C
(028) 21227
Skibbereen
Out of town on R595 to
Baltimore
(9) 5774 yards/***/E

Youghal G.C
(024) 92787
Knockaverry, Youghal
Take N25 from Cork to
Youghal
(18) 6223 yards/**/D
CO DONEGAL

Ballybofey & Stranorlar G.C
(0704) 31093
Ballybofey
Signposted on the Donegal-
Strabanne road
(18) 5913 yards/***(not
Wed/Thurs/Fri)/E

Ballyliffin G.C
(077) 76119
Ballyliffin
(18) 6524 yards/***/E

Buncrana G.C
Buncrana
take the R238 N. from the
N13
(9) 2020 yards/***/F

Bundoran G.C
(072) 41302
Bundoran
Take the N15 coastal road
to Bundoran
(18) 6328 metres/***/F

Donegal G.C
(073) 345054
Murvagh
S. of Donegal, off the N15 to

Sligo
(18) 7271 yards/***/D

Dunfanaghy G.C
(074) 36208
Dunfanaghy
Quarter mile off main road,
E. of village
(18) 5066 yards/***/E

Greencastle G.C
(077) 81013
Greencastle, via Lifford
Behind the lighthouse,
just out of town
(9) 5386 yards/**/E

Gweedore G.C
(075) 31140
Derrybeg, Gweedore
Leave the N56 coast road
for R257 to Derrybeg
(18) 6230 yards/***/E

Letterkenny G.C
(074) 21150
Barnhill, Letterkenny
On the R245 outside of
town
on the lough
(18) 6299 yards/***(not
Tues/Wed)/F

Nairn and Portnoo G.C
(075) 45107
Portnoo
Take the N56 to rdara,
then R261 to Portnoo
(18) 5950 yards/***(not
Sun)/E

North West G.C
(074) 61027
Lisfannon, Fahon, Lifford
2 miles S. of Buncrana on
the R238
(18) 6203 yards/**(not
Wed)/E

Otway G.C
(074) 58319
Rathmullen
Out of town, beside the
lough
(9) 4134 yards/***/F

Portsalon G.C
(074) 59102
Portsalon
Take R245 N. to Millford,

then R246 to town
(18) 5844 yards/**/E

Rosapenna G.C
(074) 55301
Downies
On the R248 to Downies
and Rosapenna
(18) 6254 yards/***/E

Co Galway

Athenry G.C
(091) 94466
Derrydonnel, Oranmore
Leave N6 E. of Galway for
the R348 to Athenry
(18) 6000 yards/***(not
Sun)/E

Ballinasloe G.C
(0905) 42126
Ballinasloe, Rosgloss
2 miles S. of town on the
R335
(18) 5800 yards/***/E

Connemara G.C
(095) 23502
Ballyconneely
Out of town on the cliff
tops at Slyne Head
7107 yards/***/F

Galway G.C
(091) 22169
Blackrock, Salthill, Galway
2 miles W. of Galway cen-
tre
(18) 6376 yards/**(not
Tues)/D

Gort G.C
(091) 31336
Laughtry, Shaughnessy,
Gort
Take N18 S. from Galway
to Gort
(9) 4976 yards/***/E

Loughrea G.C
(091) 41049
Loughrea
N. of town on the N6
99) 5578 yards/***/E

Mountbellow G.C
(0905) 79259
Shankhill, Mountbellow
Leave N17 from Galway for
N63 for Mountbellow
(9) 5564 yards/***/E

Oughterard G.C
(091) 82131
Oughterard
15 miles W. of Galway
on the N59
(18) 6150 yards/***/E

Tuam G.C
(093) 24354
Barnacurragh, Tuam
Half mile form town
on the Athenry road
(18) 6321 yards/**/E

Portumna G.C
(0509) 41059
Portumna
Half mile W. of Portumna
on the R352
(9) 5776 yards/***/F

Co Kerry

Ballybunion G.C
(068) 27146
Sandhill Road, Ballybunion
1 mile out of town on the
dunes
18) 6542 yards/***/A/H/L
(18) 6477 yards/***/A/H/L

Ceann Sibeal G.C
(066) 56255
Ballyferriter
(18) 6222 yards/***/E

Dooks G.C
(066) 67370
Dooks, Killorglin
8 miles W. of Killorglin
(18) 6021 yards/***/E

Kenmare G.C
(064) 41291
Kenmare, Killarney
Take N71 S. from Killarney
to Kenmare
(9) 2410 yards/***/E

Killarney G.C
(064) 31034
O'Mahony's Point, Killarney
3 miles W. of the town

on the R562
7027 yards/**/B/H
6764 yards/**/B/H

Tralee G.C
(066) 36379
West Barrow, Ardfert
Take N22 N from Killarney
to N21 and Tralee
(18) 6900 yards/***
(not weekend am)/B

Waterville G.C
(0667) 4102
Waterville
1 mile out of Waterville
(18) 7184 yards/***/B

Co Leithem

Ballinamore G.C
(078) 44346
Crevy, Ballinamore
Take R209 from Carrick to
Ballinamore
(9) 5680 yards/***/F

Carrick On Shannon G.C
(078) 67015
Woodbrook, Carrick on
Shannon
Right before town on the
N4
(9) 3922 yards/***/F

Co Limerick

Adare Manor G.C
(061) 86204
Adare N. from Limerick
on the N20 to Adare
(9) 5700 yards/**/D

Castleroy G.C
(061) 335261
Castletroy, Limerick
3 miles out of town
on the N7
(18) 6340 yards/**/D

Limerick G.C
(061) 44083
Ballyclough, Limerick
S. out of Limerick on the
Cork road
(18) 5767 yards/**(not
Tues)/D

Newcastle West G.C
(069) 62015
Newcastle West
1 mile from Limerick on the

Cork road
(9) 5482 yards/***/F

Co Mayo

Achill Island G.C
(098) 45197
Keel, Achill
Follow R319 over Achill
Sound to Keel
(9) 5550 yards/***/E

Ballina G.C
(096) 21050
Mossgrove, Shanaghy,
Ballina
E of the town on the R294
(9) 5702 yards/***/E

Ballinrobe G.C
(092) 41448
Coolnaha, Ballyhaunis
Out f town on the N83
Sligo road

(9) 5790 yards/***(not
Sun)/EBelmullet G.C
(097) 81266
Belmullet, Ballina
Take N59 from Ballina to
Belmullet
(9) 2829 yards/***/E
Castlebar G.C
(094) 21649
Rocklands, Castlebar
S. of the town on the N84
(18) 6109 yards/**/F

Claremorris G.C
(094) 71527
Rushbrook, Castlemaggaret,
Claremorris
S. of town on the N17 to
Tuam
(9) 6454 yards/***/E

Mulrany G.C
(098) 36107
Mulrany, Westport
N. on the N50
from Westport to Mulrany
(9) 6380 yards/***/E

Swinford G.C
(094) 51378
Brabazon Park, Swinford
Out of town on the R320
(9) 5230 yards/***/D

Westport G.C
(098) 25113
Carrowholly, Westport
2 miles N. of town, past
Westport Quay
(18) 6950 yards/***(not
Sun)/C

C o Roscommon

Ballaghaderreen G.C
(0907) 60295
Ballaghaderreen
On the R293, left out of
town
(9) 5686 yards/***/E

Boyle G.C
(079) 62594
Roscommon Road, Boyle
On the N61 road to
Roscommon
(9) 4957 yards/***/E

Castlerea G.C
(0907) 20068
Clonallis, Castlerea
N. of the town on the N61
(9) 5466 yards/***(not
Sun)/E

Roscommon G.C
(0903) 6382
Mote Park, Roscommon
S. of the town next to the
railway
(9)6215 yards/***/F

Co Sligo

Ballymote G.C
(071) 3460
Carrigans, Ballymote
On the R293 before town
(9) 5032 yards/***/E

County Sligo G.C
(071) 77134
Rosses Point
N. of town on the R291 to
Rosses Point
(18) 6631 yards/***(not
Tues)/C

Enniscrone G.C
(096) 36297
Enniscrone (Inniscrone)
On the R297 near Bartragh
Island

(18) 6610 yards/***/D

Strandhill G.C
(071) 68188
Strandhill
Signposted on road W.
from Sligo to Strandhill
(18) 5937 yards/***/D

East Ireland
Co Carlow

Borris G.C
(0503) 73143
Deer Park, Borris
Take N9 S. from Carlow
and onto R705
(9) 6026 yards/***/E

Carlow G.C
(0503) 31695
Deerpark, Dublin Road,
Carlow
1 mile from the station on
the N9
(18) 6347 yards/***/D

Co Cavan

Belturbet G.C
(049) 22287
Erne Hill, Belturbet
5 miles N. of Cavan
on the N3
(9) 5180 yards/***/E

County Cavan G.C
(049) 31283
Arnmore House, Drumellis,
Cavan 1 mile from Cavan
on the N198
(18) 5119 metres/***(not
Sun)/E

Virginia G.C
(049) 44103
Virginia
50 miles N. of Dublin
on the N3 to Cavan
(9) 4520 yards/***/F

Co Dublin

Balbriggan G.C
(01) 412173
Blackhall, Balbriggan
On the N1 just outside
town
(18) 5717 yards/**(not

Tues)/E

Ballinascorney G.C
(01) 512516
Ballinascorney
W. of Dublin on the N81
(18) 5322 yards/***/F

Beaverstown G.C
(01) 436439
15 miles N. of Dublin
towards airport
(18) 6400 yards/***/F

Beech Park G.C
(01) 580522
Johnstown, Rathcoole
7 miles from Rathcoole on
the Kitteel road
(18) 6250 yards/***/E

Castle G.C
(01) 904207
Woodside Drive,
Rathfarnham, Dublin 14
S. of city on the N81
(18) 6240 yards/**(not
Tues)/D

Carrickmines G.C
(01) 895676
Carrickmines, Dublin
7 miles S. of Dublin
on the R117
(18) 6044 yards/**/F

Clontarf G.C
(01) 311305
Donnycarney House,
Malahide Road, Dublin 3
N.E of Dublin
on the Malahide Road
(18) 5447 yards/**(not
Mon/Wed)/D

Corballis G.C
(01) 450583
Donabate
Take N1 from Dublin, then
R126 to Donabate
(18) 4971 yards/***/E

Deer Park Hotel G.C
(01) 322624
Howth
Take Howth road for
8 miles out of Dublin
(18) 6647 yards/**/D

Donabate G.C
(01) 436346
Donabate
Leave N1 from Dublin for
R126 for Donabate
(18) 6187 yards/**(not
Wed)/D

Dun Laoghaire G.C
(01) 803916
Eglinton Park, Dun
Laoghaire
Follow railway along coast
road, take York road
(18) 5463 yards/***(not
Wed/Thurs pm or Sat)/D

Edmondstown G.C
(01) 932461
Edmondstwn, Rathfarnham,
Dublin 16
Take N18 from Dublin to
Rathfarnham
(18) 5663 yards/**/D

Elm Park G.C
(01) 693438
Nutley House,
Donnybrook, Dublin 4
Close to the University and
Hospital
(18) 5485 yards/**/D

Forest Little G.C
(01) 401183
Forest Little, Cloghran
N. of Dublin on the N1
(18) 5852 yards/**(not
Tues/Fri am)//D

Foxrock G.C
(01) 895668
Torquay Rd, Foxrock
On the right past the castle
at Dalkey Point
(9) 5699 yards/**/F

Grange G.C
(01) 932832
Grange Road,
Rathfarnham, Dublin 16
S. out of city centre, take
N81 to Rathfarnham
(18) 6200 yards/**(not
Tues/Wed pm)/F

Hermitage G.C
(01) 268491
Lucan
2 miles short of Lucan on

the N4
(18) 6034 yards/**(not
Tues/Wed)/C

Howth G.C
(01) 323055
Ten miles from Dublin, follow coast road
(18) 5573 yards/**/D

Island G.C
(01) 436462
Corballis, Donabate
N. from Dublin on N1, onto
R126 to Donabate
(18) 6320 yards/**(not
Wed/Thurs)/D

Killiney G.C
(01) 851983
Killiney
3 miles past Dun Laoghaire
on the N11
(9) 6201 yards/***/D

Kilternan Hotel G.C
(01) 955559
S.E from Dublin on the
Enniskerry Road
(18) 5413 yards/*(with
member only)/E

Malahide G.C
(01) 461642
Coast Road, Malahide
N. from Dublin on the N1,
take R106 to Malahide
(18) 6500 yards/***/C

Milltown G.C
(01) 976090
Lower Churchtown Road,
Dublin 14
3 miles S. of the city centre
(18) 5669 yards/***(not
Tues/Wed pm)/D

Lucan G.C
(01) 282106
Celbridge Road, Lucan
W. on N4 through Lucan,
onto R403
(9) 6281 yards/**(not
pm)/D

Newlands G.C
(01) 592903
Clondalkin, Dublin 22
Near junction of N7 and
R113
(18) 6184 yards/**(not

Tues/Wed)/D

Portmarnock G.C
(01) 323082
Portmarnock
leave Dublin on R107 coast
road
7079 yards/***(by arrangement)/F

Rathfarnham G.C
(01) 931201
Newtown,
Rathfarnham,
Dublin 16 2 miles S.
of Rathfarnham
on the N81
(9) 5787 yards/**(not
Tues)/E

Rush G.C
(01) 437548
Rush
N. on the N1, onto R127
and then Rush
(9) 5598 yards/**(not
Wed/Thurs)/E

Royal Dublin G.C
(01) 336346
Bull Island, Dollymount,
Dublin 3
N.E from city on coast road
towards Bull Island
(18) 6929 yards/**(not
Wed)/B/H

St Annes G.C
(01) 332979
Bull Island, Clontarf, Dublin
5
N.E from Dublin on coast
road towards Bull Island
(9) 5813 yards/*/D

Skerries G.C
(01) 491567
Hackestown, Skerries
N. on the N1, take R127
right to Skerries
(18) 5852 yards/**(not
Tues/Wed)/D

Slade Valley G.C
(01) 582207
Lynch Park, Brittas
Take N81 S.W for 9 miles
from Dublin
(18) 5337 yards/**(not
Wed)/F

Stackstown G.C
(01) 942338
Kellystown Road,
Rathfarnham, Dublin 16
Take N81 through Terenure
to Rathfarnham
(18) 5952 yards/**/E

Sutton G.C
(01) 323013
Cush Point, Barrow Road,
Sutton, Dublin 13
Take coast road N.E from
Dublin towards Howth
(9) 5522 yards/***(not
Tues/Sat)/F

Co Kildare

Naas G.C
(045) 97509
Kardiffstown, Salins, Naas
Leave Dublin on the N7,
take R407 for Salins
(18) 6233 yards/***/D

Kildare Country Club ('K'
Club)
(01) 6273987
Straffan
(18) 7000 yards/***/A

Knockanally G.C
(045) 69322
Donadea, N. Kildare
3 miles past Kilcock on the
R407
(18) 6484 yards/***/E

Four Lakes G.C
(045) 66003
17 miles out of Dublin on
the N7
(18) ***/E

Curragh G.C
(045) 41238
Curragh
Take N7 to Kildare,
then R413 to Curragh
(18) 6565 yards/**
(am only, not Tues)/D

Cill Dara G.C
(045) 21433
Kildare Town
N. of Kildare on the R415
(9) 6196 yards/***/E

Bodenstown G.C

(045) 97096
Bodenstown, Sallins
N. of Naas on the R407
(18) 7031 yards/**/F
(18) **/E

Athy G.C
(0507) 31729
Geraldine, Athy
2 miles before Athy on N78
from Kilcullen
(9) 6158 yards/***(not
Sun)/F

Co Kilkenny

Callan G.C
(052) 25136
Geraldine, Callan, Co
Kilkenny
1 mile from town on the
N76
(9) 5844 yards/***/E

Castlecomer G.C
(056) 41139
Drungoole, Castlecomer
To th right of the town
on the N78
(9) 6985 yards/***/F

Kilkenny G.C
(056) 22125
Glendine, Kilkenny
2 miles N. of Kilkenny
on the N77
(18) 6374 yards/***/D

Mt Juliet G.C.
(056) 24725
Thomastown
5 miles from Thomastown
(18) 7100 yards/***/A

Co Laois

Abbeyleix G.C
(0502) 31450
Abbeyleix
Take N8 S. from Portlaoise
(9) 5680 yards/***/E

Heath G.C
(0502) 26533
The Heath, Portlaoise
On the N7 at the R419 turn-
off
(18) 6247 yards/**/F

Co Longford

County Longford G.C
(043) 46310
Dublin Road, Longford
E. of the town on the N4
(18) 5912 yards/***/F

Co Louth

Ardee G.C
(041) 53227
Town Parks, Ardee
On the N2, quarter mile N.
of town
(18) 5833 yards/**/E

County Louth G.C
(041) 22329
Baltray, Drogheda
On the N1 coastal road
(18) 6798 yards/***(by
arrangement)/F

Dundalk G.C
(042) 21731
Blackrock, Dundalk
Take the R172 from
Dundalk to Blackrock
(18) 6115 yards/***(not
Tues/Sun)/D

Greenore G.C
(042) 73212
Greenore, Dundalk
On the R73 from Dundalk
(18) 5614 yards/***/E

Co Meath

Black Bush G.C.
(01) 250021
Thomastown,
Dunshaughlin
1/2 mile E of Dunshaughlin
off N
(18) 7000 yards /***/F
(9) 2800/***/F

Headfort G.C
(046) 40146 Kells
(18) 6372 yards/**
(not Tues)/D

Laytown and Bettystown
G.C
(041) 27170
Bettystown, Drogheda
On the N1 coastal road
from Drogheda on the R150
(18) 6254 yards/**/D

Royal Tara G.C
(046) 25244
Bellinter, Navan
Take N3 N.W from Dublin
towards Navan
(18) 6300 yards/**(not
Tues/Wed)/D

Trim G.C
(046) 31463
Newtonmuynagh, Trim
S.W of the town
off the R160
(9) 6266 yards/**/E

Co Monaghan

Castleblayney G.C
(042) 40197
Castleblayney
Take N2 from Monaghan to
Castleblayney
(9)2678 yards/***/E

Clones G.C
(049) 52354
Hilton Park, Scotshouse,
Clones
S. on the N54 towards
Scotshouse
(9) 5570 yards/***/E

Nuremore G.C
(042) 61438
Carrickmacross
Take 2 from Monaghan to
Carrickmacross
(9) 6700 yards/***/E

Rossmore G.C
(047) 81316
Rossmore Park, Monaghan
S. of the city on the B189
(9) 5859 yards/**/E

Co Offaly

Birr G.C
(0509) 20082
Glenns, Birr
N. of Birr on the R439
(18) 6216 yards/***/E

Edenberry G.C
(0405) 31072
Boherberry, Edenberry
Off the R402 just before
town
(9) 5791 yards/***/E

Tullamore G.C
(0506) 21439
Brookfield, Tullamore
Outside of town on the
R421 Birr road
(18) 6314 yards/***/D

Co Tipperary

Cahir Park G.C
(052) 41474
Kilcommon, Cahir
S. of the town on the R668
(9) 6262 yards/***/E

Carrick On Suir G.C
(051) 40047
Garravoone, Carrick On
Suir
S. of the town off the R676
(9) 5948 yards/***(not
Sun)/E

Clonmel G.C
(052) 21138
Lyteanearla, Mountain
Road, Clonmel
S. of the town on the R678
(18) 6330 yards/**/D

Nenagh G.C
(067) 31476
Beechwood, Nenagh
4 miles S. of the town
off the R491
(18) 5483 yards/**
(not Thurs or Wed pm)/E

Roscrea G.C
(0505) 21130
Derry Vale, Dublin Road,
Roscrea
Take N7 from Dublin to
Roscrea
(9) 6059 yards/***/E

Templemore G.C
(0504) 31522
Manna, South Templemore
S. of the town off the N62
(9) 5442 yards/***/E

Thurles G.C
(0504) 21983
Turtulla, Thurles
S. of the town off the N62
(18) 6300 yards/**(not
Tues)/F

Tipperary G.C
(062) 51119
Rathanny, Tipperary
S. of the town off the R664
(9) 60774 yards/***/E

Co Waterford

Dungarvan G.C
(058) 41605
Ballinacourty, Dungarvan
Out on the point off the
R675 from town
(9) 5721 yards/**/E

Lismore G.C
(084) 54026
Lismore, Ballyin
Take N72 from Dungarvan
to Lismore
(9) 5600 yards/***/E

Tramore G.C
(051) 81247
Newtown Hill, Tramore
Through the town off the
R675
(18) 6660 yards/***(by
arrangement)/D

Waterford G.C
(051) 76748
Newrath, Waterford
S. of Kilkenny on the
N10/N9
(18) 6237 yards/***/D

Co Weastmeath

Athlone G.C
(0902) 92073
Hodson Bay, Athlone
N. of the town off the N61
(18) 6000 yards/**/F

Moate G.C
(0902) 81271
Moate 8 miles E. of
Athlone on the N6
(9) 5348 yards/***/F

Mullingar G.C
(044) 48366
Belvedere, Mullingar
3 miles S.W of town off the
N52
(18) 6370 yards/**/D

Co Wexford

Courtown G.C
(055) 25166
Kiltennel, Gorey
At Courtown on the
R742 E. of Gorey
(18) 6435 yards/***(not
Wed)/D

Enniscorthy G.C
(054) 33191
Knockmarshal, Enniscorthy
2 miles from town on the
New Ross Road
(9) 6368 yards/**/E

New Ross G.C
(051) 21433
Tinneanny, New Ross
W. of the town on the R704
(9) 6133 yards/***(not
Sun)/E

Rosslare G.C
(053) 32203
Rosslare
Out of Wexford on coast at
Rosslare Point
(18) 6485 yards/***/F/H

Co Wicklow

Arklow G.C
(0402) 32492
Abbeylands
On S. of town off the N11
(18) 5770 yards/**/E

Baltinglass GC
(0508) 81350
Baltinglass
W. of the town
off the R747
(9) 6070 yards***F

Blainroe G.C
(0404) 68168
Blainroe
3 miles from Wicklow on
the N11
(18) 6681 yards/***(by
arrangement)/D

Bray G.C
(01) 862484
Ravenswell Road, Bray
N. of the town off the N11
(9) 5230 yards/**/E

Delgany G.C
(01) 2874536
Delgany
Just off the R762 after Bray
(18) 6000 yards/***/C
European Club
(01) 2808459

Brittas Bay
(18) 7150 yards/**/F

Greystones G.C
(01) 876624
Greystones
Take coast road R761 fom
Bray to Greystones
(18) 5227 yards/(Mon and
Fri only)/D

Wicklow G.C
(0404) 67379
Dunbar Road, Wicklow
S. off Wicklow off the R750
(9) 5536 yards/*(intro
only)/F

Woodbrook G.C
(01) 2824799
Bray
S. of Dublin on the N11
(18) 6541 yards/**(not
Tues/Wed)/F

Woodenbridge G.C
(0402) 35202
Woodenbrige, Avoca
W. of the town off the
R752
(9) 6104 yards/***(not Sat)/F

The Golf Collection

Featured Hotels
in the British Isles

72
5+18
46
22
26 Inverness
60
Aberdeen 9
4+27
67
25 Perth
Dundee
53
71 32
10
Edinburgh 15
44
Glasgow 24
62
Newcastle Upon Tyne
52
56 20 23 31
not to scale 14 Carlisle
19 8
29 61+68
69 Belfast 70 33
78 42 2+65
Dublin Manchester York Hull
77 40 Leeds
59 Liverpool Sheffield
64
36
1+43 54
38
Norwich
51
66
11 Birmingham
47 35
76
Swansea 75 17
63
73 57 London 34
Cardiff Bristol 7
45 41
6 30
21 Southampton
Exeter 48 28 Portsmouth
74
Plymouth
49 58 13 16 55

1 Aghadoe Heights, Killarney, County Kerry.
Tel: (010 353 64) 31766

With its unique location and breathtaking panoramic views of the Lakes and Mountains, the Aghadoe Heights is recognised as one of Ireland's finest hotels. With 60 luxuriously furnished bedrooms, a superb leisure centre with indoor pool, plus the acclaimed Frederick's Rooftop Restaurant offering outstanding cuisine, the Aghadoe Heights provides the perfect base for playing Kerry's championship golf courses, exploring South West Ireland or just rest and relaxation.

2 Aldwark Manor Golf Hotel, Aldwark, York. Tel: (0347) 838146

This impressive Victorian Manor stands in over 100 acres of mature parkland complete with its own 18 hole golf course. The beautifully furnished, individually designed bedrooms, all have en suite facilities. Our Restaurant offers traditional food and fine wines. Aldwark Manor combines luxury living with an atmosphere of period charm and elegance.

3 Allt-Yr-Ynys, Walterstone, Herefordshire.
Tel: (0873) 890307

Built in 1550 and set in magnificent surroundings this elegant hotel has kept its historical appeal and yet offers the finest of modern comforts. All bedrooms are en suite and individually furnished. Leisure facilities are excellent and if you are a keen golfer the hotel is conveniently situated for Abergavenny, Monmouth, Chepstow and Hereford Golf courses.

4 Altamount House Hotel, Blairgowrie, Perthshire. Tel: (0250) 873512

Just as the discerning golfer will always include the Rosemount course in his plans when visiting Perthshire, any pursuit of excellence would be incomplete without experiencing the delights of the Altamount House Hotel at Blairgowrie.

5 Alton Burn Hotel, Nairn, Highland.
Tel: (0667) 53325

This imposing hotel stands in its own grounds overlooking the 17th Tee of Nairn Golf Club. The Alton Burn offers a wide range of recreational facilities whether or not guests wish to golf on one of the many excellent courses in the area. To get away from it all and enjoy good golf, food and company there is no better choice than the Alton Burn.

6 Anchorage Hotel, Instow, Nr Bideford, Devon. Tel: (0271) 860655/860475

The Anchorage at Instow specialises in "golfing breaks". Former international golfers Jon and Margaret Cann, cater for parties of up to 28 golfers with concessionary rates at Royal North Devon and Saunton amongst others. With cordon bleu cooking and a well stocked bar could any golfer ask for more?

7 Anugraha Hotel & Conference Centre, Englefield Green, Egham, Surrey. Tel: (0784) 434355

Nestling in 22 acres of glorious parkland on the edge of Windsor Great Park, this superb Jacobean style mansion offers fine hospitality and a relaxing atmosphere. The light and spacious Orchid Restaurant provides diners with first class cuisine. Golfers are particularly well provided for but the area also has a wealth of activities for the non - golfer.

8 Appleby Manor Hotel, Appleby-in-Westmorland, Cumbria.
Tel: (07683)51571

The delights of the hotel's leisure centre and pool, together with the Lake District's breathtaking beauty, are your recipe for a superb country holiday. Friendly staff, mouth-watering meals, log fires and comfortable bedrooms are the extra ingredients which make it perfect. Local active ingredients include golf, horse-riding, squash and fishing.

9 Ardoe House, Blairs, Aberdeen.
Tel: (0224) 867355

Ardoe House Hotel is a Scottish Baronial style mansion set in 17 acres of its own ground with commanding views across Royal Deeside. The hotel is a popular base for golfing parties with its proximity to many leading courses and golf packages, which include de luxe room, dinner and packed lunches, are available all year.

10 Balbirnie House, Markinch, Fife.
Tel: (0592) 610066

Near Keilre Castle and the Scottish Deer Centre, this 18th century former ancestral mansion of the Balfours of Balbirnie commands 416 acres of parkland and is flanked by Balbirnie golf course to which guests have access.

11 Bank House Hotel Golf and Country Club, Bransford, Worcester.
Tel: (0886) 833551

This luxurious hotel and leisure complex boasts its own 18 hole golf course set in 123 acres of attractively landscaped Worcestershire countryside. The golfing gourmet will not be disappointed by the cuisine of the Elgar restaurant, while a wide selection of real ales and excellent bar meals are to be had in the Exchange bar.

12 Black Heath House, Coleraine, Co Londonderry, Tel: (0265) 868433
The house which dates from 1791 is set in two acres of gardens and has a fascinating history. It also offers individually styled bedrooms and a fine restaurant which makes the most of freshly grown produce. Blackheath has special rates with local golf courses.

13 Bolt Head Hotel, Salcombe, Devon. Tel: (0548) 843751
This is a delightful hotel set on the north Devon coast. Dining here is a pure delight and staff take care to ensure that all tastes are catered for. There are excellent leisure facilities in the area including a good golf course within a few miles of the hotel and guests are really ensured an enjoyable holiday.

14 Burn How Garden House Hotel, Bowness-on-Windermere, Cumbria. Tel: (05394)46226
Burn How is situated in secluded, peaceful and beautiful gardens in the heart of Bowness only two minutes walk from Lake Windermere. The elegant restaurant specialises in English and French cuisine using only fresh produce. Nearby Windermere Golf Course, now in its second century, comprises 200 acres of undulating terrain often described as a 'mini' Gleneagles.

15 Channings, South Learmonth Gardens, Edinburgh. Tel: 031 315 2226
Just a short way from Edinburgh castle is this quiet, classical hotel. Channings is made up from five Edwardian townhouses and has a cosy, old fashioned club-like ambience. Golfers are within easy reach of many of the famous golf courses of Scotland.

16 Chedington Court, Chedington, Dorset. Tel: (0935) 891265
A traditional country house hotel set in a beautiful ten acre garden on the edge of of Thomas Hardy country. The renowned restaurant offers excellent French and English cuisine. The hotel has a nine hole golf course which measures 3425 yards and is one of the longest in the country.

17 Cheltenham Park Hotel, Cheltenham, Gloucestershire. Tel: (0242) 222021
The Cheltenham Park Hotel is a beautiful recently extended Regency Manor House with luxury bedrooms set in nine acres of landscape gardens. The Hotel's Lakeside Restaurant and Bar overlook both the trout lake and adjacent Lilleybrook Golf Course.

18 Claymore House Hotel, Seabank Road, Nairn, Inverness-shire. Tel: (0667) 53731
Situated only 300 yards from Nairn's Championship Golf Course this hotel has everything to offer the golfer. Since being completely refurbished the hotel offers the highest standards in luxury. The speciality of the hotel is tailored golf breaks and as there are 25 golf courses within one hour of the hotel it really is ideally placed.

19 Coopershill, Riverstown, Co Sligo, Tel: (010 353 71) 65108
This elegant Georgian manor house has been in the same family since 1774 and commands 500 acres. There are five 18 hole links courses within an hours drive of Coopershill including the county Sligo Golf Club at Rosses Point.

20 Corsemalzie House Hotel, Newton Stewart, Wigtownshire. Tel: (0988 886) 254
This secluded country mansion set in the heart of Wigtownshire allows guests to relax away from the rigours of city life. The surrounding area has much to offer, including a host of 18 hole golf courses. The hotel pays half your green fees on the 18 hole course at Glenluce.

21 Court Barn Country House Hotel, Holesworthy, Devon. Tel: (040927) 219
Set in five acres of beautiful grounds, amidst the delightful Devon countryside, this award winning Hotel and Restaurant is a place to remember. Enjoy the excellent Cordon Bleu cuisine in the antique furnished restaurant and take your pick from the Wine List of over 350 wines. The hotel has special arrangements at three local golf clubs.

22 Craigellachie Hotel, Craigellachie, Banffshire. Tel: (0340) 881204
At the confluence of the Fiddish and Spey rivers, in a beautiful Moray village, lies this elegant Victorian hotel, complete with blazing log fires and early morning Scottish

piper. For golfers there are a variety of courses nearby and golf club hire and private tuition by professionals can be arranged at selected clubs.

23 Crosby Lodge Hotel, Crosby-On-Eden, Cumbria. Tel: (0228) 573618

An elegant country mansion combining a tasteful collection of antiques with fine furniture in both private and public rooms. The restaurant serves delicious food and is open to non residents. For the golfer arrangements can easily be made on the nearby Riverside Course and on a variety of courses at Carlisle, Brampton, Penrith and Silloth.

24 Cross Keys Hotel, Kelso, Borders. Tel: (0573) 223303

Kelso is one of Scotland's marvellous border towns. The Cross Keys is one of the country's oldest walking inns and one of its most welcoming. This is an ideal point from which to explore the Borders and the hotel can arrange golf at nearby courses.

25 Culcreuch Castle, Fintry, Stirlingshire. Tel: (036 086) 228

This beautiful castle has been lovingly converted by its present owners into a comfortable, friendly country house hotel. The eight individually furnished bedrooms are en suite and have full modern facilities. There is a wide range of activities in the area and golfers are particularly well catered for with 40 courses within a 25 mile radius of the castle.

26 Culloden House Hotel, Inverness. Tel: (0463) 790461

Historically linked to Bonnie Prince Charlie, this impressive Georgian House commands 40 acres of garden, parkland and tranquil woodland. The resident proprietors extend a warm welcome to all their visitors and are only too happy to arrange golfing, fishing or shooting activities.

27 Dalmunzie House, Blairgowrie, Perthshire. Tel: (0250) 885224

Standing in its own 6000 acre estate in the Scottish Highlands the hotel can offer turreted bedrooms, antique furnishings and even the highest 9-hole golf course in Britain. Some of Scotland's finest mountains surround the hotel and the Glen Shee Ski Centre is only a few minutes drive away.

28 Donnington Valley Hotel & Golf Course,

Newbury, Berkshire. Tel: (0635) 551199

Set in the beautiful countryside of Royal Berkshire and surrounded by an 18 hole golf course, Donnington Valley Hotel is a unique venue, blending charm and elegance with the luxury and personal service expected from an individually designed, privately owned, four star hotel.

29 Downhill Hotel, Ballina, Co Mayo. Tel: (010 353 96) 21033

Adjacent to the famous salmon fishing river - the Moy, the luxurious Downhill Hotel offers fine cuisine and personal, friendly service. The grounds are beautiful and there are extensive leisure facilities. Guests may enjoy golf on one of the three championship courses close by, Enniscoe, Rosses Point and Westport.

30 Egerton Grey Country House Hotel, Porthkerry, South Glamorgan. Tel: (0446) 711666

This nineteenth century former rectory is Egon Ronay's 'definitive country house hotel for South Wales'. The interior is furnished with antiques, open fireplaces, original Victorian baths and brass work, with rooms boasting mahogany and oak panelling. With Royal Porthcawl and other fine golf courses just a short drive away, this is the ideal base for the golfing gourmet.

31 Farlam Hall Hotel, Brampton, Cumbria. Tel: (06977) 46234

Dating back to the 17th century, Farlam Hall is set in four acres of grounds with a lake and offers great comfort. It is ideally located for visiting Hadrian's Wall, Naworth Castle and Lanercost Priory. For the golfer there are 8 golf courses within 30 minutes of the hotel.

32 Fernie Castle, Letham, Fife. Tel: (033781) 381

Steeped in history, Fernie Castle is a small luxury hotel specialisng in the care of its guests and the quality of food offered. Located in the heart of the historic kingdom of Fife it is the ideal base for a golfing holiday with more than 30 championship courses within 25 miles of the hotel.

33 Feversham Arms Hotel, Helmsley, North Yorkshire. Tel: (0439) 70766

A luxuriously modernised, historic coaching inn set in over an acre of walled gardens, this hotel offers every comfort and an outstanding quality of cuisine. If you are contemplating a round of golf there are over twenty golf clubs within a radius of 35 miles, the nearest being Kirkby Moorside.

34 Fredrick's Hotel and Restaurant, Maidenhead, Berkshire.
Tel: (0628) 35934
Set in 25 acres of attractive gardens, this sumptuous hotel houses one of the finest restaurants in the South of England. With 37 luxuriously furnished bedrooms and award-winning cuisine Frederick's is renowned for providing comfort, good food and individual hospitality. Frederick's highly accessible location is ideal for golfing at Wentworth and Sunningdale.

35 Gliffaes Country House Hotel, Crickhowell, Powys. Tel: (0874) 730371
Dating from 1885, this distinctive hotel is set in 29 acres of private gardens offering stunning views of the surrounding National Park and River Usk. The hotel is elegantly furnished although the atmosphere is distinctly informal. The hotel is justly proud of its in house cooking and the resident proprietors carefully maintain country house standards of the old order.

36 Glin Castle, Great Limerick, Ireland.
Tel: (010 353 68) 31173
Glin Castle is a superb hotel built in the 18th century with entertaining in mind. The reception rooms are unique and the hotel even has a rare flying staircase. For golfing enthusiasts Ballybunion Golf Course is only a short drive away as are the courses of Killarney, Dooks, Tralee and Lahinch.

37 Hanbury Manor, Thundridge, Nr Ware, Hertfordshire. Tel: (0920) 487722
From beamed ceilings and oak panelling to fascinating tapestries this hotel is nothing less than impressive and is to be savoured. With its huge range of facilities Hanbury Manor caters for nothing less than the civilised aesthetic. Golfers can choose to play either the magnificent 18 hole golf course or the Downfield nine.

38 Hawkstone Park Hotel, Shrewsbury, Shropshire.
Tel: (0939) 200611
This renowned golfing hotel is set in a 300 acre estate and features a fine 18 hole golf course and a 9 hole course. The hotel itself

was built in 1790 and is steeped in history. It now provides a catalogue of sporting and leisure facilities. The restaurant offers traditional English cuisine and the whole ambience is one of taste and luxury.

39 Hintlesham Hall, Hintlesham, Suffolk.
Tel: (047387) 334
Hintlesham Hall, originally built in the 1570's with a stunning Georgian facade offers the best in country house elegance and charm. Gracious living, good food and wine, attentive service and tranquil relaxation greet every guest to the hotel. Golf enthusiasts will enjoy the beautiful 18 hole championship full length golf course.

40 Hunter's Hotel, Newrath Bridge, Rathnew, Co. Wicklow.
Tel: (0404) 40106
Hunter's Hotel is one of Ireland's oldest coaching inns, established for 200 years in the beautiful county of Wicklow. The hotel has been run by the same family for five generations and is justly famous for its high standards of accommodation, cuisine and service. Delightfully situated on the banks of the River Vartry, Hunter's is guaranteed not to disappoint sportsmen, tourists and businessmen alike.

41 Hutton Court, Hutton, Avon.
Tel: (0934) 814343
This is a hotel and restaurant in classic country house style that caters for every golfer's needs. The championship links of Burnham and Berrow are only twenty minutes away and golf there is available to reidents by special arrangement as it is at five other courses equally as close to the hotel.

42 Inn at Whitewell, Clitheroe, Lancashire.
Tel: (02008) 222
Originally built for the Keeper of the King's deer in the 14th century, the Inn at Whitewell still retains associations with field sports. Grouse and pheasant shooting can be arranged.The hotel serves classic English food with an emphasis on quality.

43 International Best Western Hotel, Killarney, Co. Kerry.
Tel: (010 353 64) 31816
Right in the heart of Killarney within minutes of the lakes. Ideally located for touring, entertainment and shopping. The hotel

has 88 rooms with bath/shower, television, radio, direct dial phone. There are three restaurants with entertainment nightly in season. Nearby are Killarney's two 18 hole championship golf courses. Good transport links. Bookable worldwide through Best Western Hotels.

44 Johnstounburn House, Humbie, East Lothian. Tel: (087533) 696
Located 15 miles from the finest East Lothian links courses (Muirfield, North Berwick, Dunbar), Johnstounburn offers the golfer comfort, fine food and drink in one of Scotland's heritage country houses, in the most peaceful and aesthetic setting at the foot of the Lammermuir Hills. Twenty bedrooms, each with private facilities.

45 Kittiwell House Hotel and Restaurant, Croyde, North Devon. Tel: (0271) 890247
This delightful thatched hotel dates from the 16th century and has retained much of its charm. The restaurant is distinctive with its massive stone fireplace and low beamed ceiling which give it such character. Golf can be arranged at concessionary rates and being only two miles from Saunton Golf Club and near to the Royal North Devon Club this is an ideal hotel for those who are following the fairways.

46 Knockomie Hotel, Forres, Morayshire. Tel: (0309) 673290
The hotel lies well off any main road and has fine views over this impressive area. The restaurant specialises in using local produce and there is an excellent selection of malt whiskies. The hotel is within easy reach of Forres, Moray and Nairn Golf Clubs.

47 Lake Country House, Llangammarch Wells, Powys. Tel: (05912) 202
Complete with open fireplaces and antiques, this riverside hotel set in 50 acres of beautiful lawns and woods offers spacious and luxurious accommodation and has a splendid restaurant which has won several commendations. For golfing enthusiasts there are four full size courses in close proximity. Builth Wells Course is only 10 minutes away and the hotel can organise concessionary tickets for guests.

48 Langtry Manor, East Cliff, Bournemouth, Dorset. Tel: (0202) 553887
Very occasionally you stumble upon a rare gem of an hotel where the building, food, service and history blend to form something quite exceptional, such as Langtry Manor Hotel in Bournemouth. There are about 20 golf courses in the vicinity of Bournemouth catering for all standards of player - Langtry Manor would be pleased to make arrangements for you to be able to play at most of them.

49 Lanteglos Country House Hotel, Camelford, Cornwall. Tel: (0840) 213551.
Long established as one of the major golfing centres in Cornwall.Situated in a secluded valley in a beautiful and unspoilt part of Cornwall and on the very edge of the Bowood Park Golf Club.The hotel provides quality accommodation,good food and friendly service in a relaxed enjoyable atmosphere.

50 Le Manoir aux Quat' Saisons, Great Milton, Oxfordshire. Tel: (0844) 27881
The history of this outstanding manor dates back 750 years. Set in 27 acres of beautiful landscaped gardens and woodland this is an internationally acclaimed hotel. Each one of the 19 elegant bedrooms has been individually designed and the bathrooms are equally luxurious. Le Manoir is widely acknowledged as Britain's finest restaurant and the superb cuisine is complemented by an extensive wine list.

51 Llangoed Hall, Llyswen, Brecon, Powys. Tel: (0874) 754525
A splendid house which was the first major commission of architect Sir Clough Williams-Ellis. Sir Bernard Ashley has bestowed similar love in its restoration and the bedrooms are simply marvellous. For the sportsman, three superb golf courses are within easy driving distance; all 18- hole with breathtaking scenery.

52 Lockerbie Manor Country Hotel, Lockerbie, Dumfries and Galloway Tel: (05762) 2610
Built in 1814 this luxurious country house hotel stands in 78 acres of park and woodland. The period furniture, Adam fireplaces and wood panelled dining room combine to create an atmosphere of history and hospitality. Golfers will love the courses in the area, offering challenges of varying degrees of difficulty.

53 Lomond Hills Hotel, Freuchie, Fife.
Tel: (0337) 57329
The Hotel is set in the heart of Fife in the charming village of Freuchie. Guests will enjoy the wealth of history in the area or may choose to play one of the 30 courses within easy reach of the hotel. Character and comfort combine to make a stay at the Lomond Hills extremely enjoyable.

54 Longueville House, Mallow, Co Cork.
Tel: (010 353 22) 47156
Resting in a 500 acre cattle and sheep farm this substantial Georgian hotel has a very relaxed and informal atmosphere, with a fine collection of antiques to decorate the interior. There is horseriding at nearby stables and golf at a dozen courses close by including Premier Championship Courses at Killarney, Ballybunion and Tralee.

55 Longueville Manor, St Saviour, Jersey.
Tel: (0534)25501
The 13th Century Manor stands in 15 acres at the foot of its own private wooded valley and is one of the most prestigious small hotels in Europe. Exquisitely furnished with fine antiques and fabrics, the manor is a haven of tranquillity in which to enjoy fine food and wine. Winner of Egon Ronay "Hotel of the Year" award.

56 Magherabuoy House Hotel, Portrush, Co. Antrim. Tel: (0265) 823507
Located in natural golfing country the famous fairways of the championship course of Royal Portrush are barely five minutes from the hotel. The house incorporates the period home of the former Minister of Home Affairs and has been carefully restored and extended, providing modern comforts in a majestic setting. Opulence is the key note.

57 Manor House, Castle Combe, Wiltshire.
Tel: (0249) 782206
The Manor House is idyllically set in 26 acres of grounds with a trout stream and terraced Italian garden. The hotel offers five star luxury in a relaxed atmosphere with excellent cuisine. Castle Combe Golf Club is only two minutes driving distance from the Manor House.

58 Manor House Hotel and Golf Course, Moretonhampstead, Devon.
Tel:(0647) 40355
An hotel of grand tradition, the Manor revels in its oak panelled lounges, open fire-

places and wide sweeping staircases. The superb cuisine and impeccable service combine with the challenging, par 69, 18 hole championship golf course - reputed to be one of England's finest inland courses, to give you a break to remember.

59 Marlfield House, Gorey, Co Wexford.
Tel: (010 353 55) 21124
A fine 18th century mansion set in 35 acres of woodlands and gardens and only 80 kilometres from Dublin. Accommodation is in 19 superb rooms all decorated using period furniture. The award winning restaurant serves modern French cuisine with a classical base - making use of the vegetables, herbs and fruits that are grown in the kitchen garden.

60 Meldrum House Hotel,
Old Meldrum,Grampian.Tel:(0651)872294.
Set in several hundred acres of fields and gardens, and beside a small lake, Meldrum is the ideal place for a holiday. The hotel is internationally known for its cuisine and is conveniently situated for visits to many of the top-class golf courses in the surrounding areas. Guests are made to feel thoroughly at home in the hotel's relaxed and friendly atmosphere.

61 Michael's Nook, Grasmere, Cumbria.
Tel: (05394) 35496
A gracious stone built lakeland house overlooking the Grasmere Valley. This hotel is beautifully furnished with antiques and provides memorable high quality cuisine. The hotel enjoys a close proximity to some of the excellent northern links courses and also ofers special arrangements with Keswick Golf Club.

62 Montgreenan Mansion House Hotel, Kilwinning, Strathclyde.
Tel: (0294) 57733/4
Magnificent Georgian Mansion set in 50 acres of secluded parklands. Offering 21 beautifully appointed bedrooms, award winning cuisine and high standards of personal service and comfort. Situated in Ayrshire's golf coast, Montgtreenan boasts over 30 courses within 45 minutes as well as its own 5 hole practise course.

63 Moore Place, Apsley Guise, Woburn, Bedfordshire. Tel: (0908) 282000
An elegant Georgian mansion with a locally acclaimed restaurant, Moore Place offers mainly facilities and is an ideal base for vis-

iting Woburn Abbey, Whipsnade Zoo and Dunstable Downs. Woburn Golf Course is also nearby.

64 Mount Juliet, Thomastown, Co Kilkenny, Tel: (010 353 56) 24455
One of Ireland's premier hotels and sporting estates set in 1500 acres of unspoiled parkland in the south east of Ireland. The Jack Nichlaus designed golf course was home to the Carrolls Irish Open in 1993 and 1994 and ranks as one of the top parkland courses in Europe.

65 Mount Royale Hotel, York, North Yorkshire. Tel: (0904) 628856
The elegant combination of two beautifully restored William IV houses with an acre of old English gardens has created this gracious hotel only minutes away from the historic city of York.

66 Moxhull Hall, Holly Lane, Wishaw, Warwickshire. Tel: 021 329 2056
Moxhull Hall is situated on a hill adjacent to the Old Manor, which is now better known as the Belfry. This fine country hall with beautiful grounds and splendid interior offers excellent cuisine and access to the many immediate attractions of the area and is just seven miles from the centre of Birmingham.

67 Murrayshall Country House Hotel and Golf Course, Scone, Perthshire. Tel: (0738) 51171
Recently refurbished to give the atmosphere and style of a Country House Hotel and set in 300 acres of parkland this is an attractive venue whatever brings guests to this area of Scotland. The Old Masters Restaurant offers a wide variety of dishes with the emphasis on wholesome fayre. There is much to interest the golfer with an excellent course and membership is available.

68 Nanny Brow Country house Hotel, Ambleside, Cumbria. Tel: (05394) 32036
The comfort and contentment of gracious country life at the Nanny Brow contrasts with challenging golf at Windermere and other courses in the locality. Michael and Carol Fletcher take the strain out of organisation and provide elegance, haute cuisine, modern comforts and spectacular surroundings for their discerning guests.

69 Newport House, Newport, Co Mayo.
Tel:(010 353 98) 41222
This is a superb ivy clad, bow fronted Georgian Mansion encircled by mountains, lakes and streams. The hotel is famed for its hospitality and there is a rare feeling here of continuity and maturity. The discerning golfer has the pleasure of the 18 hole championship course at Westport as well as the more relaxed nine hole course near Mulraney.

70 Nuremore Hotel, Carrickmacross, Co Monaghan Tel: (010 353 42) 61438
Originally a Victorian country house, the Nuremore has been skilfully converted and extended into a magnificent luxury hotel, beautifully situated within 200 acres of woods and parkland. Guests are offered an unrivalled range of sports and leisure facilities. For instance in 1992 the Nuremore was the venue for the PGA Ulster Open professional championship.

71 Old Manor Hotel, Lundin Links, Fife. Tel: (0333) 320368
Within a short distance of Lundin Links are some of the finest in the world at St. Andrews, Elie, Crail, Scotscraig and Ladybank. The Old Manor overlooks the two adjacent championship courses at Leven and Lundin Links, both qualifiers for the Open. Carnoustie, Gleneagles and Rosemount are within easy travelling distance. The Clark family, all keen golfers with a wealth of knowledge of the game, are delighted to assist in arranging tee times and golf itineraries to suit all handicaps.

72 Ord House Hotel, Muir of Ord, Ross-shire. Tel:(0463) 870 492
Ord House is primarily a country house which offers all the comforts and amenities of a hotel. There are 12 individually designed en suite bedrooms and one even has a four poster bed. Ideally situated for the sportsman to enjoy fishing or golf, the hotel something to offer for everyone.

73 Penally Abbey, Penally, Pembrokeshire. Tel: (0834) 3033
Penally Abbey is one of Pembrokeshire's loveliest country houses. Ideally situated to enjoy both splendid views and the area's many attractions, not the least of which is the golf at adjacent Tenby Golf Club. With mouthwatering food and an excellent cellar, the Abbey is a haven of comfort, excellence and cheerful ambience.

74 Port Gaverne Hotel, Nr Port Isaac, North Cornwall. Tel: (0208) 880244

The proprietors of this pretty hotel on the spectacular North Cornwall coast believe in offering pleasant comfortable accommodation and good food, prepared from the best ingredients. The hotel also owns and runs Green Door Cottages which offer self catering accommodation. For golfers, rounds can be arranged at any of the 26 courses within the Royal Duchy.

75 Priory Hotel, Bath, Avon. Tel: (0225) 331922

This well run former private residence has retained many of the early 19th century gentleman's necessities - croquet lawn, orangery, lovely furniture. There is also a wonderful and widely acclaimed restaurant featuring local produce. The city of Bath offers a multitude of interesting attractions and there are numerous golf courses within easy distance.

76 Puckrup Hall Hotel, Tewkesbury, Gloucestershire, Tel: (0684) 296200

Just west of the hotel, the River Severn makes its way towards the beautiful Tewkesbury Abbey. Not far from Shakespeare country this imposing country house commands 114 acres of idyllic parkland. The emphasis at Puckrup Hall is on a relaxing and luxurious stay.

77 Rathsallagh House, Dunlavin, Co Wicklow, Ireland Tel: (010 353 45) 53112

This large comfortable farmhouse is situated in 500 acres of peaceful parkland, surrounded by some of the most beautiful countryside of eastern Ireland. The atmosphere is happy and relaxed in this hotel with its huge variety of diversions; choose from tennis, golf, driving range, practice holes, putting, archery or take a dip in the indoor swimming pool.

78 Rock Glen Hotel, Clifden, County Galway, Ireland Tel: (010 353 95) 21035

A converted shooting lodge first built in 1815, the Rock Glen is now a 29 bedroomed, cosy, first class, Grade A hotel, nestling in the heart of Connemara. Family run, this hotel is renowned for its exceptional cuisine and traditional hospitality. Connemara's 18 hole championship course is just a 15 minute drive from the hotel.

79 Rufflets Country House Hotel, St Andrews, Fife Tel: (0334) 72594

An outstanding country house set in 10 acres of award winning gardens. There are 25 tastefully decorated bedrooms, attractive public rooms and a restaurant renowned for good food, using fresh local produce. St Andrews offers 5 golf courses - 16 other courses are within 30 minutes drive.

80 Selsdon Park, Sanderstead, Surrey Tel: (081) 657 8811

Set high in the rolling hills of the Surrey countryside, Selsdon Park combines the ancient virtues of hospitality and courtesy with the modern attributes of efficiency and friendliness. An outstanding asset to Selsdon Park is the 18 hole championship golf course laid out in 1929 by British Open Champion, J H Taylor.

81 Slieve Russell Hotel, Golf and Country Club, Ballyconnell, Co Cavan Tel: (010 353 49) 26444

The Slieve Russell Hotel, Golf and Country Club opened its doors on 1 August 1990. The hotel stands in 300 acres of parkland which encompasses gardens and two natural lakes. Opened in 1992, the 18 hole championship standard golf course blends well with the typical Cavan drumlin and valley landscape.

82 Smuggler's Inn, Anstruther, Fife. Tel: (0333) 310506

With 17 courses within a 15 mile radius including the venerable Royal and Ancient at St Andrews, the no less historic Smuggler's Inn at Anstruther is an ideal base for a golfing break. A traditional warm welcome, and fine food and drink await all those who pass through its doors.

83 Sodbury House Hotel, Old Sodbury. Tel: (0454) 312847

This 18th century former farmhouse is set in six acres of attractive grounds. Only 12 miles south of Bath and on the edge of the Cotswolds it is an ideal base for exploring the West Country. The hotel has been tastefully refurbished to retain its original character and all 14 bedrooms are well-appointed and stylishly furnished.

84 South Lodge, Lower Beeding, Hampshire. Tel: (0403) 891711

An elegant country house with one of the finest Victorian rock gardens in England. The light and spacious bedrooms have fine views over the South Downs. The hotel is only a short drive from the challenging 18 hole Mannings Heath Golf Club, where hotel guests enjoy special privileges.

85 St Andrews Golf Hotel, St Andrews Fife. Tel: (0334) 72611
A tastefully modernised Victorian House, situated on the cliffs above St Andrews Bay, the Hotel's central feature is the candlelit, oak panelled restaurant with magnificent sea views. Golf, of course, is the speciality of the hotel offering special packages using any of the thirty or so courses within 45 minutes of St Andrews.

86 St David's Park Hotel and Northrop Country Park Golf Club, Ewloe, Clwyd. Tel: (0244) 520800 and (0352) 840440
St David's Park Hotel is operationally linked to Northrop Country Park Golf Club and the hotel provides a perfect combination of superb modern facilities and traditional comfort. The hotel is designed in a Georgian style and offers 121 bedrooms all luxuriously furnished. A full range of golf and leisure related packages are available through the hotel and transport to the Club can be arranged.

87 St Mellion Golf and Country Club, Saltash, Cornwall Tel: (0579) 50101
Just ten miles from Plymouth, St Mellion has everything to make the guest's stay enjoyable and comfortable. A stunning variety of sporting facilities is offered. The bedrooms are attractively furnished; the restaurant superb. And it is one of the few places in Britain where one might bump into Jack Nicklaus.

88 St Pierre Hotel, Chepstow, Gwent Tel: (0291) 627402
A 14th century mansion standing in 400 acres, the St Pierre Hotel is a fine place to unwind. There are two golf courses, a lake and a leisure centre; three restaurants and a poolside bar. With a conference area and thirty executive bedrooms there are also excellent facilities for business delegations.

89 St Tudno Hotel, Llandudno, Gwynedd. Tel: (0492) 874411
Recent winner of the Johansens Guide 'Hotel of the Year' award for excellence. This delightful 21 bedroom hotel situated on Llandudno's seafront has to be experienced, having a style and a splendour all of its own. Two AA Rosettes for food. Indoor

heated swimming pool. Close to three championship courses.

90 Stanneylands, Wilmslow, Cheshire Tel: (0625) 525225
A handsome country house set in several acres of gardens, Stanneylands offers quiet luxury in the heart of the rolling Cheshire countryside. There are two dining rooms, seating up to 100 guests between them, and the cuisine is of an extremely high standard. Once the home of a Mancunian businessman, Stanneylands continues to attract today's executive.

91 Stocks Country House Hotel, Aldbury, Hertfordshire Tel: (044285) 341
Stocks, an elegant country house hotel in the heart of the Chilterns, dates back to 1176. Not only a peaceful house for unwinding and enjoying the delightful atmosphere and excellent cuisine, Stocks offers sporting and leisure facilities second to none, with an 18 hole golf course due to open in Spring 1994.

92 Stotfield Hotel, Lossiemouth, Moray. Tel: (0343) 812011
The Stotfield is situated overlooking the superb championship golf course at Moray Golf Club. It has the comfortable and friendly atmosphere of a family-run hotel. A high standard of service and cuisine is offered in both the Firth Bar and the main dining room. More specialised cuisine is served in the sun lounge, overlooking the sparkling water of the Moray Firth.

93 Sunlaws House Hotel, Kelso, Roxburghshire. Tel: (0573) 5331
Owned by the Duke of Roxburgh and resting in 200 acres of beautiful gardens beside the Teviot, this hotel boasts a fine library bar with open log fire and leather bound tomes. The 22 bedrooms have all been furnished with care and include every modern comfort.

94 Telford Hotel, Golf & Country Club, Sutton Hill, Shropshire. Tel: (0952) 585642
Set in the beautiful Shropshire countryside, not far from the famous Ironbridge - this hotel offers many and varied facilities. From the luxurious en suite bedrooms to delicious food served in imaginative surroundings, to the many sports activities, keep fit, ballooning, archery etc. Paramount amongst these is the nine hole golf course and floodlit all weather driving range.

95 The Cally Palace Hotel, Gatehouse of Fleet, Dumfries and Galloway. Tel: (0557) 814341

This impressive establishment offers the very best of service in a totally secluded location. The hotel grounds extend more than 100 acres and include a private fishing/boating loch. The splendid restaurant is renowned for the excellence of its cuisine. To be ready for Spring 1994 is an exclusive 18 hole golf course.

96 The Castle Hotel, Huntly, Aberdeenshire. Tel: (0466) 792696

This magnificent hotel stands in its own grounds above the ruins of Huntly Castle on the banks of the River Deveron. A family run hotel, there is comfortable accommodation and good food. Conveniently situated for several golf courses, the hotel is ideal for a golfing holiday and there are plenty of other activities for the non player.

97 The Crown at Whitebrook, Nr Monmouth, Gwent. Tel: (0600) 860254

Remotely situated one mile from the River Wye on the edge of the Tintern Forest this is the ideal place to get away from it all. The bedrooms are comfortable and are all en suite. The chef specialises in creating original dishes from fresh local ingredients and to compliment these there are fine wines from the interesting cellar.

98 The Dowans Hotel, Aberlour, Banffshire. Tel: (0340) 871488

Overlooking the Spey in beautiful countryside the Dowans Hotel has recently been refurbished. Meal times are flexible to suit the needs of sportsmen and the hotel is happy to arrange fishing, shooting or stalking by prior arrangement. There are 15 golf courses within a half hours drive of the hotel, so there really is something for everyone here.

99 The Glenfarg Hotel, Glenfarg, Perthshire. Tel: (0577) 830241

Situated amidst some of Perthshire's finest scenery, yet only 30 miles north of Edinburgh this elegant two star hotel enjoys a well-earned reputation for sporting holidays, including an array of golfing packages. The period restaurant offers an excellent selection of dishes, prepared by the hotel's award winning chef or, if you prefer a more informal atmosphere, you can choose from a delicious range of home-cooked bar meals.

100 The Lands of Loyal Hotel, Alyth, Perthshire. Tel (08283)3151.

An impressive Victorian mansion overlooking the Vale of Strathmore and set in ten acres of tiered and rambling gardens. An ideal base for the ambitious golfer with thirty courses all within an hour's drive of the hotel. With a highly acclaimed restaurant, the Lands of Loyal provides a complete golfing package.

101 The Links Hotel, Brora, Sutherland. Tel: (0408) 621225

The Links Hotel has a magnificent situation overlooking the 18 hole links course at Brora. All bedrooms have a sea view and the Seaforth Restaurant offers one of the finest views in the North of Scotland. Golfers are spoiled for choice with several courses within easy travelling distance.

102 The Thatched Cottage Country Hotel and Restaurant, nr Lifton, West Devon. Tel: (0566) 784224

Set in the middle of the West Country, surrounded by Bodmin Moor, Exmoor and Dartmoor this delightful hotel nestles in two and a half acres of landscaped cottage gardens. For the keen golfer there is the challenge of approximately 50 courses in Devon and Cornwall, all within easy reach of the Thatched Cottage.

103 The Rescobie Hotel and Restaurant, Leslie, Fife Tel: (0592) 742143

A 1920's country house set in two acres of grounds on the edge of the old village of Leslie, the gardens contain a herb garden and a wild flower meadow. Perfectly positioned for golfers, the owners endeavour to preserve the atmosphere of a traditional country house.

104 The Roman Camp, Callander, Perthshire. Tel: (0877) 30003

Standing on the banks of the River Tieth amongst twenty acres of secluded gardens, the house was originally built as a hunting lodge in 1625. At the Roman Camp you are within easy reach of many championship and picturesque golf courses and the hotel can arrange and book tee times at the local course.

105 The Royal Marine Hotel, Brora, Sutherland. Tel: (0408) 621252

This charming country house hotel has undergone major refurbishment recently but great trouble has been taken to maintain the character of the original building. The hotel offers golfing breaks on the Brora links course and there are three other championship courses within 30 minutes of the hotel.

106 Trearddur Bay Hotel, Holyhead, Anglesey. Tel: (0407) 860 301
Situated on the Isle of Anglesey the hotel is of distinctive character with the 31 bedrooms helping to create a lasting impression due to their panoramic views. Seafood is a menu speciality in the restaurant although all tastes and appetites are catered for. Separate conference facilities are available and guests may choose to relax by the indoor heated pool.

107 Turnberry Hotel, Turnberry, Strathclyde. Tel: (0655) 31000
This world famous resort has been extensively restored and offers luxurious accommodation for the most discerning individual. Its two championship links golf courses are for priority use by hotel guests and the Ailsa Course is the venue for the 1994 British Open Championship. The Spa opened in 1991 and is unrivalled in Britain. A new Clubhouse opened in June 1993. Choice of 3 restaurants and five bars.

108 Ufford Park Hotel, Woodbridge, Suffolk.
Tel: (0394) 383555
With a setting amidst Suffolk's beautiful countryside Ufford Park provides a relaxing haven for the business visitor and the weekend guest alike. There are first class facilities including an 18 hole golf course, the Cedar Restaurant and the leisure club. Good value breaks are offered as well as facilities for a board meeting or conference.

109 Waterford Castle, The Island Ballinakill, Co Waterford, Tel: (010 353 51) 78203
Set on a private 310 acre island and reached by ferry, this 18th century castle is beautifully tranquil and impressively decorated inside with stone walls, old panelling and a gorgeous ribbon plastered ceiling. The Castle also boasts its own leisure club and 18 hole championship golf course.

110 Waterville House and Golf Links, Waterville, Co Kerry, Ireland.
Tel: (010 353 667) 4102
Built in the 18th century, Waterville House presides serenely on the shores of Ballinskelligs Bay. All 10 bedrooms have wonderful views and in addition to warm

hospitality and fine cuisine guests can enjoy a heated pool, sauna, steam room, snooker and billiard room and of course, for golfers, the world class Waterville Links.

111 Westcliff Hotel, Sidmouth, Devon. Tel: (0395) 513252
Surrounded by superb golfing country and with the additional attractions of Devon's lanes and moors nearby, The Westcliff Hotel offers its guests an ideal base for exploring this beautiful part of Britain. There are excellent leisure facilities and the 40 bedrooms are all fitted to a very high standard.

112 Westerwood Hotel Golf and Country Club, Cumbernauld, Glasgow.
Tel: (0236) 457171
Set in excellent golfing country, Westerwood's course offers an exciting challenge to golfers. The hotel itself has 47 bedrooms comprising of standard and executive rooms, as well as suites. Dining at Westerwood can be either in the Old Masters Restaurant or more informally in the Club House overlooking the course.

113 Whitechapel Manor, South Moulton, North Devon. Tel: (0769) 573377
In the foothills of Exmoor lies Devon's only Michelin starred hotel restaurant - a tribute to the superior cooking and local Devon produce. Here you will find a part of English heritage encapsulated by this old Elizabethan Manor House. For golf enthusiasts there is a choice of eight courses within 40 minutes.

114 Wordsworth Hotel, Grasmere, Cumbria. Tel: (09665) 592
In the heart of Lakeland, this first class, four star hotel has a reputation as one of the areas finest. It offers comfortable bedrooms and many leisure facilities, together with superb cuisine. For the golfer, the hotel can arrange free rounds from Monday to Friday at Keswick Golf Club.